ACCESSION AND MIGRATION

Studies in Migration and Diaspora

Series Editor:
Anne J. Kershen, University of London, UK

Studies in Migration and Diaspora is a series designed to showcase the interdisciplinary and multidisciplinary nature of research in this important field. Volumes in the series cover local, national and global issues and engage with both historical and contemporary events. The books will appeal to scholars, students and all those engaged in the study of migration and diaspora. Amongst the topics covered are minority ethnic relations, transnational movements and the cultural, social and political implications of moving from 'over there' to 'over here'.

Also in the series:

Gendering Migration: Masculinity, Femininity and Ethnicity in Post-War Britain
Edited by Louise Ryan and Wendy Webster
ISBN 978-0-7546-7178-7

Contemporary British Identity: English Language, Migrants and Public Discourse
Christina Julios
ISBN 978-0-7546-7158-9

Migration and Domestic Work: A European Perspective on a Global Theme
Edited by Helma Lutz
ISBN 978-0-7546-4790-4

Negotiating Boundaries in the City
Joanna Herbert
ISBN 978-0-7546-4677-8

The Cultures of Economic Migration: International Perspectives
Edited by Suman Gupta and Tope Omoniyi
ISBN 978-0-7546-7070-4

Writing Diaspora: South Asian Women, Culture and Ethnicity
Yasmin Hussain
ISBN 978-0-7546-4113-1

Accession and Migration
Changing Policy, Society, and Culture in an Enlarged Europe

Edited by

JOHN EADE
Roehampton University, UK

and

YORDANKA VALKANOVA
Canterbury Christ Church University, UK

ASHGATE

Published by
Ashgate Publishing Limited
Wey Court East
Union Road
Farnham
Surrey GU9 7PT
England

Ashgate Publishing Company
Suite 420
101 Cherry Street
Burlington, VT 05401-4405
USA

www.ashgate.com

British Library Cataloguing in Publication Data
Accession and migration : changing policy, society, and culture in an enlarged Europe. -- (Studies in migration and diaspora)
1. Immigrants--Great Britain--Social conditions--21st century. 2. Bulgarians--Great Britain--Social conditions--21st century. 3. Immigrants--Bulgaria--Social conditions--21st century. 4. British--Bulgaria--Social conditions--21st century. 5. Great Britain--Emigration and immigration--Social aspects--21st century. 6. Bulgaria--Emigration and immigration--Social aspects--21st century. 7. Mass media and immigrants.
I. Series II. Eade, John, 1946- III. Valkanova, Yordanka.
304.8'410499-dc22

Library of Congress Cataloging-in-Publication Data
Accession and migration : changing policy, society, and culture in an enlarged Europe / [edited] by John Eade and Yordanka Valkanova.
p. cm. -- (Studies in migration and diaspora)
Includes index.
ISBN 978-0-7546-7503-7
1. European Union countries--Emigration and immigration--Social aspects. 2. European Union countries--Emigration and immigration--Economic aspects. I. Eade, John, 1946- II. Valkanova, Yordanka.
JV7590.A25 2009
304.8'4--dc22

2009008827

ISBN 978-0-7546-7503-7

Mixed Sources
Product group from well-managed forests and other controlled sources
www.fsc.org Cert no. SGS-COC-2482
© 1996 Forest Stewardship Council
FSC

Printed and bound in Great Britain by
TJ International Ltd, Padstow, Cornwall

Contents

SECTION 3: GOING WEST: THE BULGARIANS AND OTHER 'NEW' EUROPEANS IN BRITAIN

List of Figures and Tables

Figures

Tables

List of Contributors

Irina Chongarova is Associate Professor in Russian Cultural Studies at the University of Plovdiv, Bulgaria. She is also a Visiting Research Fellow at CRONEM (Centre for Research on Nationalism, Ethnicity and Multiculturalism at the University of Surrey and Roehampton University. Her latest research and publications focus on Russian and British immigration to Bulgaria, the identity of children of mixed marriages and their multilingual and intercultural potential.

Laurence Cooley is an ESRC-funded PhD student in the Department of Political Science and International Studies at the University of Birmingham, where his research focuses on EU policy-making towards ethnic conflicts. His research interests include ethnic conflict resolution, EU enlargement and migration. He previously worked as a research assistant on a number of projects for the Migration, Equalities and Citizenship team at the Institute for Public Policy Research.

John Eade is Professor of Sociology and Anthropology at Roehampton University, London, and Executive Director of CRONEM (Centre for Research on Nationalism, Ethnicity and Multiculturalism) at the University of Surrey and Roehampton University. His research has focussed on urban ethnicity, identity politics, globalisation and the global city. His publications include *Placing London* (2000) and *The Politics of Community* (1989), the single edited *Living the Global City* (1997) and the co-edited *Transnational Ties* (2008), *Global Ethics and Civil Society* (2005) *Reframing Pilgrimage* (2004), *Understanding the City* (2002), *Contesting the Sacred* (2000/1991) and *Divided Europeans* (1999).

Michal P. Garapich is Research Fellow at the Centre for Reresearch on Nationalism, Ethnicity and Multiculturalism Migration at Roehampton University and University of Surrey. He has undertaken various research projects for BBC Newsnight, Greenwich Council and is currently conducting a detailed study on Polish, Slovak and Hungarian migrants living and working in Hammersmith and Fulham borough in West London. He is also writing, with John Eade, a monograph on recent migrations from Poland to the UK.

Zhivko Ivanov is Associate Professor in the Departments of Comparative Literature; Dean of Faculty of Languages and Literature, University of Plovdiv 'Paisii Hilendarski', Bulgaria. He is the author and co-author of eight books and monographs and more than 80 peer-reviewed articles describing issues in the areas of Bulgarian, Slavic and Balkan Literary history and cultures.

Deema Kaneff was a Senior Research Fellow at the Max Planck Institute for Social Anthropology, Halle, Germany, before taking up the position of Reader in European Studies at the Centre for Russian and East European Studies, European Research Institute, University of Birmingham, England. She has edited several volumes and is the author of numerous articles as well as of the book *Who Owns the Past? The Politics of Time in a 'Model' Bulgarian Village* (Berghahn, 2004). Her current research interests include: property relations and emerging inequalities in the context of neoliberal reforms.

Daryana Kotzeva is a Head of Social and Labour Affairs Office at the Embassy of Bulgaria in London since 2007. Her main fields of research are management of migration; links between labour market and migration; integration policies for migrants; diaspora studies and human rights approaches to migration. Between 2003–2006 she undertook doctoral research on interrelation between national health policy of Bulgaria and international and EU legal framework, receiving the Doctor of Juridical Science Degree from the University of Madison (USA).

Eugenia Markova is Research Fellow at the Working Lives Research Institute of the London Metropolitan University. Previously, she worked at the Department of Economics, University of Athens, the Sussex Centre for Migration Research at the University of Sussex, before becoming a Senior Research Fellow at the Hellenic Observatory at the London School of Economics, studying Bulgarian and Romanian migration to Greece. She has published extensively in the area of economic and social effects of migration.

Andreas Pribersky is Associate Professor at the Institute for Political Science, Vienna University (since 2003), Marshall Plan Chair for Comparative Politics at the University of New Orleans (2007/8) and Visiting Professor at the Institut d'Études Politiques, Lyon (2006). From 1990 to 2003 he was Senior Research Fellow at the Austrian Institute for East and Southeast European Studies. Recent publications include with P. Bernhardt, K. Liebhart and L. Hadj-Abdou (2009), *Europäische Bildpolitiken. Politische Bildanalyse am Beispiel der EU-Politik* (UTB wuv, in print) and 'Europe as a symbol in political image constructions' in *Semiotica* 159–1/4 (2006).

Dhananjayan Sriskandarajah is currently Director of the Royal Commonwealth Society. Prior to joining the RCS in January 2009, he spent five yeas at the Institute for Public Policy Research (IPPR) where he was head of migration research and, latterly, Deputy Director. His interests include the economic impacts of immigration, the relationship between migration and economic development, identity and multiculturalism, and the political economy of ethnic conflict. He holds an MPhil and DPhil from the University of Oxford, where he was a Rhodes Scholar.

Yordanka Valkanova is Senior Lecturer in Childhood Studies at Canterbury Christ Church University. Previously, she was a Lecturer at Roehampton University and an Assistant Professor at Plovdiv University. She is a TLRP/ESRC Meeting of Minds Fellow (2006–2008). Her main research interests and publications, which cover cognitive development in children, intercultural education and history of education have largely focused on the exploration of learning in a variety of settings.

Acknowledgements

The contributions to this book have emerged from a collaboration between British and Bulgarian researchers funded by the British Academy between 2006 and 2007. A key role was played by Prof. Suman Gupta from the Open University, UK. He inspired the research application and the workshop which was held at the University of Plovdiv in October 2006, as well as helped to shape this volume. We are also grateful for the welcome, which we received at the Bulgarian Embassy in London where we held a one day seminar on the changing relationship between Britain and Bulgaria.

CRONEM (Centre for Research on Nationalism, Ethnicity and Nationalism) helped to keep up the momentum after the completion of the British Academy project (thanks to Prof. Chris Flood and Mirela Dumic especially) and an exchange of visits between CRONEM, represented by John Eade, and CERMES (Centre for European Refugees, Migration and Ethnic Studies), New Bulgarian University, Sofia, represented by Prof. Anna Krasteva. The cover picture was provided courtesy of Karen Fox at the Book Cave, www.bulgarianbuddies.com. We are also grateful to Dr Kathy Burrell (De Montfort University) and Anna Krasteva for their generous endorsements of the volume.

John Eade
CRONEM, Roehampton University and University of Surrey

Yordanka Valkanova
Canterbury Christ Church University

Series Editor's Preface

Accession and Migration: Changing Policy, Society and Culture in an Enlarged Europe

The accession of the A8 countries to the European Union in 2004, and the subsequent addition of Bulgaria and Romania in 2007, changed the migrant landscape of Britain. The nation had been a beacon for economic migrants for centuries; the traditional pattern of settlement having been one of clustering, of new arrivals settling in major industrial towns and cities, creating the nucleus of minority communities or joining those already formed. However, clustering has not been a characteristic of the twenty-first century incomers from Eastern Europe. They have settled the length and breadth of the United Kingdom, rarely creating the large-scale visible concentration that was a feature of earlier immigration. For students of migration, the accession and its implications was the stimulus for studies of migration to focus more closely on the movements from Eastern Europe. As the majority of new entrants were from Poland, it is not surprising that Polish migratory patterns were amongst the first to be studied. However, it is the accession of Bulgaria that is under the spotlight in this volume. As one of the two most recent Eastern European arrivals to the European Union it offers the opportunity both to compare and contrast this latest phase in migration across a continent with a near-neighbour's – Poland – earlier experience.

Though numerically the inflow to Britain has been much smaller than that from Poland, as this volume shows, Bulgaria presents an important new template of European migration. Significantly, the movement has been two-way. Economic conditions in Britain – the spiralling cost of property and the onset of the recession – encouraged a number of British citizens to leave their homeland for a country where they could afford to buy a property, enjoy the benefits of a warm climate and become part of a tight knit and supportive community. The cutting edge contemporary research that has explored this phenomenon provides the reader with an opportunity to gain an insight into the processes of settlement and integration experienced by 'Brits' overseas. The voices of the British migrants, for the most part, send positive messages back home. These can be compared and contrasted with the Bulgarian immigrant experience. Through the use of a triangulated locational approach which enables an in-depth analysis of behaviour and expectations in three contrasting boroughs, two in London and one on the south coast, we learn how

Bulgarians, together with other Eastern European migrants, have adapted to life in Britain. Further empirical research, this time engaging with Bulgarian school children and their parents, highlights the influential role parents play in their children's experience of, and performance at, school. The editors' decision to close the volume with the results of a survey of Polish migrants in a London borough makes it clear that, irrespective of country of departure, in undertaking the processes of settlement and integration, migrants' concerns are no different from those of their indigenous counterparts – job security, crime, health, housing and education.

In producing an up-to-the minute volume of research and analysis on a subject which is a constant in the minds of academics, policy makers and the public, the editors have brought together a truly transnational group of contributors whose depth of knowledge of Eastern European migration embraces both the academic and the personal, eight of the contributors being Eastern European. The British contributors represent both ends of the academic scale; a student in the final stages of his PhD and Professor John Eade, a leading, internationally renowned, specialist in migration studies. The result is a book which demands its place in the library of migration, yet which, at the same time, is setting the agenda for future works which acknowledge new patterns and flows of migration in Europe.

Anne J. Kershen
Queen Mary University of London
Spring 2009

Chapter 1
Introduction

John Eade and Yordanka Valkanova

Migration Flows in an Expanding European Union

The expansion of the European Union in May 2004 through the entry of ten countries from central and eastern Europe has generated considerable interest in the British media. While the influx of Polish migrants attracted particular attention, a further twist in media representations about immigration from the 'new' European Member States immigrants' was given by the next stage of EU expansion when Bulgaria and Romania joined in January 2007. Given the history of media suspicion, if not downright hostility towards 'immigrants', media stories concerning this expansion have focused on the consequences of this expansion for immigration and the development of Britain's multicultural diversity. Far less attention has been paid to the other side of the coin – British migration eastwards to these new Member States.

Within a very short period a considerable volume of research into this new transnational migration has been generated by universities, think tanks, consultancy firms and government agencies. Funding has been available for studies of the impact of this migration on the British labour market and the implications for public policy (see, for example, Boeri and Brücker 2000; Dustmann et al. 2005; Salt 2005; Dench et al. 2006; Drew and Sriskandarajah 2006; Drinkwater et al. 2006, Ernst and Young 2006; Gilpin et al. 2006; Ruhs 2006; Markova and Black 2007; Pollard et al. 2008).

The social and cultural aspects of migration across the expanding EU have attracted far less attention and British research has, not surprisingly given funding priorities, focused on the lives of 'new' European migrants in Britain rather than on those migrating eastwards (see, for example, Eade et al. 2006; Spencer et al. 2007; Markova and Black 2007; Vertovec 2007; Pillai 2007; Ryan 2008; Burrell 2008). However, the substantial flow of British citizens to France, Spain and Italy, in particular, during the last 40 years and the relationship between tourists and locals in particular has attracted some research interest (see, for example, Abram 1997; Sheller and Urry 2004; Sriskandarajah and Drew 2006). As British migration starts to flow south-east to one of the newest EU Member States – Bulgaria – so pioneering research has begun on the economic, social and cultural aspects of this movement within Bulgaria (see Kaneff 2006, 2009).

The Wider Context

There is now an extensive literature on transnational migration, which reflects academic awareness of the rapid growth of global flows of people, goods, information and images which move between and across nation-state boundaries (see, for example, Glick Schiller et al. 1994; Cohen 1997; Portes et al. 1999; Vertovec and Cohen 1999; Levitt 2001; Castles and Miller 2003; Vertovec 2002, 2004; Smith and Favell 2006). Empirical research has been accompanied by the generation of new concepts to analyse the new social and cultural formations created through these global flows – diasporic community, cultural hybridity, new ethnicities, transnationalism, glocalisation and globalism, for example (see Hall 1991; Robertson 1992; Albrow 1996; Appadurai 1996; Bhabha 1996; Smith and Guarnizo 1998; Glick Schiller 2005; Portes and DeWind 2007).

These migrants include relatively wealthy tourists as well as poorer and more vulnerable labour migrants, refugees and asylum seekers. Those who chose not to return to their countries of origin have made a major contribution to the multicultural diversity of the countries they have settled in, even if the concept of multiculturalism has been under political attack in various Western European countries in the aftermath of terrorist violence and the murders of high profile critics of Muslim beliefs and practices.

The academic focus in Britain has been on the migration and settlement of 'black and Asian' groups from the former empire. However, the arrival of refugees and asylum seekers during the 1990s has encouraged an ethnic 'superdiversity' which overlays the colonial heritage through the settlement of people which had no connection with the British Empire (see Vertovec 2007). As we have already noted, further diversity was created through EU expansion in 2004 and the arrival in Britain of over a half a million of workers from Poland and the other accession countries. Many of these stayed for a short time before returning or were undecided about their intentions (see Eade et al. 2006). The entry of Bulgaria and Romania into the EU added a further twist to this tale of coming and going, sojourning and staying.

This Volume

The volume has emerged from a British Academy-funded collaborative project between the Centre for Research in Nationality, Ethnicity and Migration (CRONEM) at Surrey and Roehampton universities, the Faculty of Humanities, Paissij Hilendarski University of Plovdiv, Bulgaria and the Globalization, Identity Politics and Social Conflict (GIPSC) Project at the Open University, UK. The project entailed a series of meetings and workshops over 2006 and 2007 in which discussions in this area were structured around specific themes. The general structure and chapters of the proposed volume were informed by and developed through these discussions.

Through a careful, grounded academic analysis of the social and cultural processes bound up with migration, the volume seeks to put into perspective the media hype about the dire consequences of immigration from these new accession countries. It pursues this aim by bringing together researchers from different disciplines in the humanities and social sciences to explore:

- the social and cultural changes taking place within Bulgaria and involving the relationship between Bulgarian locals and British migrants;
- the engagement by Bulgarian migrants in Britain with other migrants and British locals;
- the representations of people and places through media and other forms of communication linked to flows of information and people between Bulgaria and Britain;
- comparison with other migration flows into Britain from the new accession countries, especially Poland;
- political developments within Britain, Bulgaria and other EU Member States in response to these migration flows and to the possibilities of new alliances across national borders.

The volume is divided into three sections. In the first section we examine the social, economic and cultural processes bound up with policy making at the national and cross-national level. In Chapter 2, Andreas Pribersky explores the relationship between Europeanisation and national identity.[1] He argues that although at the negotiation and policy level, the EU accession process may simply appear to involve the transformation of a political system according to the *Acquis Communautaire*. However, EU enlargement from the 1990s shows that the frame of references involved go further than the legal and policy transformation process and raise a series of questions concerning the cultural frames of the national and/or the European identity of the new member states.

He examines some characteristics of this public political debate – namely, the ways in which particular nations are symbolically repositioned in the recent EUropean political design. By focussing on Austria, Bulgaria, Hungary and Slovakia, he reveals the ambiguities surrounding this process of symbolic repositioning, which include a sense of belonging to the 'New Europe' as well as fears about the loss of national (or regional) identities. Through this comparison we are able to understand more clearly the frame of references shaping the political positions, which have been developed by these new

1 The following description of the chapters is primarily based on the outlines provided by the contributors.

Member States both with regard to European policy making processes and their relations with their neighbours.

In Chapter 3 the implications of EU membership for national political institutions and elites is explored by Daryana Kotzeva in the context of Bulgaria. As an EU Member State from 2007, the country was expected to develop its migration policy in full accordance with the law and practice of the EU. At the same time it had to consider its interests in developing and retaining its labour force. Recent initiatives of the Bulgarian government, more specifically the Ministry of Labour and Social Policy, prove the commitment to set up open forums to discuss the issues of migration and integration of migrants. An important tool in the management of migration is statistical data -- Bulgaria keeps statistics about labour resources in the country, identifies trends, and updates the measures related with them.

The situation in Bulgaria since accession to the EU needs to be analysed carefully so that new trends can be outlined. The state of the labour market has to be studied with a view to meeting the needs of employers in sectors where a shortage of Bulgarian workers has emerged. Daryana Kotzeva draws on the currently available data, which are informing the Bulgarian government's policies on migration, and makes a move in the direction of the much needed analysis and study of Bulgaria's post-accession situation with regard to migration.

In Chapter 4, the focus shifts to British government policies towards immigration as the EU expanded. Laurence Cooley and Dhananjayan Sriskandarajah describe the pressure on the government during 2004 to restrict the right of free movement of workers from new EU member states. In the event, the Government stood firm and allowed free movement with a registration scheme for newcomers. The decision was motivated by a range of factors, including a strong domestic labour market, the desire to 'regularise' many accession nationals already living without documentation in the UK, and because expert predictions were of relatively small flows.

Two years later, the UK reversed its decision and announced a restrictive approach towards Romanians and Bulgarians wishing to work in the UK after they joined the EU on 1 January 2007. This policy volte-face has clearly been influenced by, yet is counter to, some of the experiences of the previous round of accession. Since May 2004, Central and Eastern European workers have arrived on an unprecedented scale and have been disproportionately employed in certain sectors, causing much anxiety amongst the media and the public. However, the evidence suggests the overall experience of these flows has been economically beneficial and fears of new arrivals placing excess pressure on the UK's welfare state have not materialised.

The authors move on to review the empirical evidence concerning the impact of migration from the new member states on the British labour market and tracks the extent to which the decision over granting free movement to Bulgarians and Romanians was based on the actual experience of previous accession or on wider discourses and concerns about immigration prevailing within the UK.

Finally, the chapter considers the consequences of operating 'closed' labour markets, focusing on the potential for irregular working of EU citizens, who can travel visa-free to the UK but who are not permitted to work.

In the second section the focus shifts to Bulgaria. Chapter 5 by Deema Kaneff examines the influx of British migrants as a transnational process. She notes that while much has been written academically and in the media about the 'problem' of east European migration to the west, far less attention has been given to the reverse process: westerners moving to eastern Europe. Yet this movement appears to be an equally significant part of the EU accession story. Adopting a long term perspective, she analyses population flows in the rural central northern region of Bulgaria. Contemporary British migration to the region is understood in terms of earlier internal urban-rural migration that was driven by the implementation of socialist state industrialisation policies. Such policies left rural communities emptied of inhabitants and houses empty, and it is these that are being bought by British moving to rural Bulgaria.

Restructuring the political economy encourages migration flows. A detailed look into the sorts of people involved in permanent migration to Bulgaria from Britain indicates that it is those, who have experienced the greatest negative effects of neoliberal reforms – often members of the middle class – who are now buying in rural Bulgaria. Neoliberal reforms are also a catalyst for Bulgarians selling their properties to foreigners. Decentralisation, privatisation and deregulation of markets after 1989 has resulted in the withdrawal of state resources that has either eliminated or dramatically reduced services, such as the closure of medical facilities. Individuals can no longer rely on state services and benefits – a problem that is particularly dire in the rural areas where the vast majority of the population are pensioners. The latter find themselves heavily in debt and struggling to survive in a market oriented economy.

British migrants moving to rural Bulgaria are welcomed, therefore, not only because they provide a possible means of alleviation from debt for individual Bulgarian house sellers, but also because, through conducting renovations and house improvements, they offer local hope for a reversal in the decline of the community. Here at last are 'wealthy' foreigners, whose presence and new connections add prestige to the rural region. Selling houses to foreigners is the latest local strategy that attempts to reverse both village and individual fortunes.

Analysis of British property buyers in Bulgaria (at least in the rural area which is the focus of this chapter) reinforces research findings from elsewhere that migration is triggered by economic insecurity and/or crisis. What this case study adds to this picture is that such findings are equally relevant for migrants from relatively more wealthy countries, who are similarly experiencing a decline in their living standards. Indeed, an increasing proportion of the European population is experiencing economic insecurity and this is resulting in new population exchanges across the continent, as well as new forms of transnational economic integration and exclusion.

The relationship between local Bulgarians and British newcomers is explored further in Chapter 6 through an analysis of newspaper coverage. Irina Chongarova begins by discussing the images of the British in *Standart*, a national daily newspaper with the third largest circulation in the country. She supplements her analysis by also referring to two regional newspapers from areas where significant British settlements have developed. Data covering the period between 2001 and 2006) reveal discursive patterns and one of these patterns, associated with the idea of Bulgarian and British people being 'neighbours'. The chapter then delves into part played by these Bulgarian newspapers in the process of mutual learning and discovering or failing to discover a common language.

Looking at the images of the British in the Bulgarian newspapers through the lens of the theory of social representations, the study shows how the mass media provides the major source of these representations, and both cultivates and reflects them. British migration is seen as highlighting the positive aspects of Bulgaria's recent migration story. Unlike others approaching Bulgaria (from the neighbouring countries as well as from Ukraine, Moldova, the newcomers from Asian and African countries), British enjoy media comfort. The stories analysed in the chapter show how the media can promote a welcoming environment. Between 2001 and 2006 the Bulgarian newspapers encouraged a sense of neighbourliness between Bulgarians and the newcomers from the West. They show how media can contribute to constructing civic and cultural concepts of Europe including the widely discussed concept of European citizenship.

The final chapter in the second section continues the exploration of how British and locals relate to one another. Zhivko Ivanov focuses here on the domestication of the Other within typically Balkan and Bulgarian post-communist realities. He wants to examine how post-patriarchal, conservative distrust of foreigners reacts to the British presence, how the British are involved in changing life in a Bulgarian province, which has experienced considerable decline, and how the British relate to local customs.

More than 30,000 British have come to possess properties in Bulgaria between 1997 and 2007 and Zhivko Ivanov seeks to describe the experiences of the 'ex-pats', holiday-makers and home owners, who have fallen in love with (or not) Bulgaria and the problems and situations they have encountered in the process of social and cultural adaptation. He draws on data collected in South Bulgaria, Plovdiv and Stara Zagora region, i.e. far from the hotspots along the Black Sea coast or in the popular ski centres in the mountains. He concludes by looking forward to the next influx anticipated from outside Europe and the cultural contribution which British settlers could make to promoting cooperation with these even newer and even more culturally different immigrants.

In the third section the focus switches to Britain. Chapter 8 is concerned with the experiences of the Bulgarian immigrants living in the two London boroughs of Harrow and Hackney, and the City of Brighton and Hove. Eugenia Markova draws on a survey which includes those from Albania, Russia, Serbia and Ukraine as well as Bulgaria. She examines their employment, education and housing as well as their broader interactions within local communities, with particular emphasis on the issue of community cohesion.

While there are differences in the socio-economic position of Bulgarians in Brighton and Hove compared with the two London boroughs, in general they are adapting well to life in Britain. They are not wealthy but a high proportion are employed, even if half of them have found only low paid jobs and have limited prospects of occupational mobility. Furthermore, most are relatively well-educated (52 per cent arrived with a university degree) and although they reported low levels of English language competence at the time of their arrival, their English had improved remarkably over time.

As for their sense of belonging, like other migrants they felt attached to both the UK and Bulgaria. Identification with locality was clearly shaped by housing status, length of stay in the UK, plans to remain in the UK and the arrival of children. The chapter concludes by considering the implications of the study for government policy concerning other migrants from eastern Europe as the EU continues to expand. Rather than focussing on community leadership as the way to strengthen social cohesion in a multicultural society, Eugenia Markova suggests that government should also engage employers and schools, since these play a more important role in the lives of these east European newcomers.

In the second chapter of this last section, Yordanka Valkanova explores the educational experiences of Bulgarian children in Britain. She draws on a study of Bulgarian children in London which was designed to identify key issues in the learning experiences of recently arrived children of Eastern European and a grounded conceptualisation of their educational needs. The general aim of the study was to inform policy towards creating educational opportunities, which suits the specific needs of these newcomers.

The study sought to identify what the learning experiences of the Bulgarian children during the transition from their home countries to the UK are. It considered their prior learning experiences in their home country as well. In addition, the study sought to examine parents' understandings of the philosophy of schooling in Britain in relation to the needs of their children and the way they seek to attain them.

The research methodology, which was informed by cultural-historical activity theory, revealed the ways in which the experiences of the young people were mediated through the economic, social and cultural dynamics associated with the transition process. The study reported findings from in-depth interviews with 12 children and their parents. The results would appear to suggest that children's experiences were shaped by their parents' strategies. Their parents' lack of confidence, increased anxiety and misunderstandings about British schooling appear to be key influences on children's successful adjustments to the new learning environment. As for the school environment, both children and parents found that practices designed to support children's adjustment to the life in the new country do not consider the families' particular needs in terms of their parents' language fluency and their ability to access information which was necessary for the children's education.

The final chapter seeks to place Bulgarian migration in the broader context of the massive influx of predominantly Polish workers after May 2004. London again provides the context but this time the focus is on the west London borough of Hammersmith and Fulham. The borough reminds us that east European migration did not begin with EU Accession; the Polish community there has a much longer history since it was created after the end of the Second World War by members of the Polish armed forces and displaced persons who chose not to return to their homeland.

Drawing on a survey and focus group interviews, John Eade and Michal Garapich outline the socio-economic position of the more recent migrants – not just Poles, since those from Lithuania, Slovakia and Hungary were also contacted. They show the crucial role played by social networks in helping these newcomers to access jobs, housing, welfare rights and education, for example. Like the Bulgarians in Hackney, Harrow and Brighton & Hove, most of these newcomers are surviving quite well and helping the growth of a lively ethnic niche of business enterprises and community organisations.

At the same time, there is a darker side occupied by those who are the 'losers' and whose plight is exacerbated by the decline of the welfare state. The lack of state support, which has also encouraged the emigration of indigenous British people to Continental Europe and, most recently, to Bulgaria is offset by help from community organizations. However, even a group like Barka which helps people to return to Poland and receive support there, can only do so much – the borough council and central government also need to play a part.

So the volume ends on a sombre note. As the economic downturn strengthens, revealing once again the intimate relationship between local and global processes, conditions in Britain and the rest of the EU for poor migrants will get tougher. The weaknesses of the neoliberal, free market have been dramatically exposed and governments have been forced to intervene to shore up certain sectors of the economy, particularly the banking sector. This turbulence may encourage politicians to look for scapegoats and 'immigrants' will be an obvious target.

It remains to be seen how those from countries, which entered the EU, after 2004, will fare. The evidence collected here indicates that the British in Bulgaria and the 'new' Europeans in Britain have fared well, either in terms of the reception accorded to the British in Bulgaria or the ability of Bulgarians and others to enter the labour market and educational system in Britain. The darker side of the migration picture reminds us that this is not true for everyone and its shadow may cover more newcomers in the near future.

SECTION 1
Policies Towards Migration: Social, Economic and Cultural Dynamics

Chapter 2
Cultural Patterns of the EU: 'Eastern Enlargement' – Between Post-Socialism and the 'Longue Durée' of History?

Andreas Pribersky

From Political Cultures …

With the recent enlargement of the European Union (2004/07), the informal term 'Eastern enlargement' has been widely employed – in the media as well as in political science (see, for example, Ágh 2006). This development reflects not only the regional dimension of recent EU extension but also the history of state socialism, which most of the new members share.

It is this shared history, which introduced the notion of (political) culture from the very beginning as a key concept for analysing the transformation process in Central Eastern Europe and the post-Yugoslavian region and attempting to answer questions about the sustainability of regime change and democratisation. Given the complexity of this key structural change, which included the political as well as the economic sphere in one transformation process, the question mark about the stability of democratisation in East Central Europe (CEE) after 1989 led to questions about how confident those living in post-socialist countries were about the new, democratic political order and its institutions and representations. Furthermore, the dangers of authoritarian and/or nationalistic tendencies, given the histories of countries in the CEE region, were (and still are) considered to be an imminent threat to their relatively recent democratisation (see Beyme 1994).

The so-called 'political criteria' for EU membership, defined in the Maastricht treaty, became, therefore, part of the EU enlargement process for the first time. This encouraged a political evaluation of the democratic stability of the emerging member states, with an important focus on their political cultures. The influence of a change in government after the Slovakian parliamentary elections of 1998, which saw a shift from a right-wing populist to a liberal-conservative government, including the Hungarian minority party, on Slovakia's entry into the EU is an exemplary case, since it highlighted a number of democratic principles, ranging from the development and functioning of the institutional and legal system to its appliance in policies towards minorities, especially the living conditions of the Roma population.

For the evaluation of these criteria, political culture serves as an important frame of reference and therefore was included as a key issue in the annual Eurobarometer poll, for example.

An attempt to summarize these analyses of the so-called New Members of the EU under the (somewhat modified) traditional terms of political culture research, which were developed after the Second World War with a focus on post-fascist democratisation in Europe (see Almond and Verba 1963), shows ambiguous and contradictory results. The following brief typology of some key tendencies developed on the basis of the research results retains three main positions, which can be identified as central arguments in the discussion of CEE political cultures:

a. the 'stable democracies' thesis, which projects a trend towards an 'integration' of the political cultures within the EU drawing on comparative opinion research; research results (see, for example, Plasser, Ulram and Waldrauch 1998; Rose 2008) show the 'New Democracies' as within the European average on confidence in political institutions and parties, with significant differences mainly concerning their ranking. There is, for example, a greater trust in EU, rather than national, political institutions and actors. The confidence shown in democratic values by the majority of people in the New Democracies is seen as a strong basis for further democratisation and European integration;
b. the 'widening social gap' thesis (e.g. Offe 1994; Rose 2008) drew attention to the potential instability arising from growing economic differences between the 'winners' and 'losers' of economic transformation, with the immanent threat of political instability because of the growing number of losers and their lack of prospects. Declining living standards among an important part of CEE populations since 1989 is seen as encouraging a nostalgic image of socialism and the potential for growing distrust in the democratic system and authoritarian and/or nationalistic developments;[1]
c. the 'post-socialism' thesis (e.g. Bönker et al. 2004), which views the experiences of socialism as a cultural legacy with an inherent trend towards a deformation of both economic and political transformation; post-socialist attitudes and expectations among the elite towards the mass of people are described as 'undermining' capitalist as well as democratic institutional structures, thereby inhibiting the development of democratic political and capitalist economic cultures. The post-socialist attitude can be considered as similar in certain ways to the 'social gap' thesis, since the latter attempts also to focus on elite behaviour as well as on the economic losers of transformation. The

1 As the political expectations of the economic 'losers' are not (regularly) included in political culture research, their direct impact on political opinions remain unclear.

terminology of post-socialism serves especially for the characterisation of 'failed' democracies in the former Soviet Union region, data for this trend being provided from corruption and similar indicators (Rose 2008).

For each of these trends a series of examples can be and has been given. Looking back at what is now almost 20 years the fundamental democratic and institutional stability in the CEE region, especially among the EU 'new members', can hardly be denied. At the same time the parties, which organise and represent the losers during this period of economic (and political) transition and/or those fearing that they might become losers and which exercise a considerable political influence, constitute a political spectrum ranging from the Czech Communists or the German PDS to the Polish Samobrona (Self Defence) and the Bulgarian Ataca. They all represent more or less explicit xenophobic and/or anti-democratic tendencies, which are sometimes combined with a 'nostalgia for socialism'. Last but not least, the problems of legal reform and corruption have also been documented in the (post-)enlargement reports of the EU Commission and are especially present in the evaluation of the 2007 enlargement with Bulgaria and Romania. Corruption and the low performance of their legal systems also regularly serve as an indicator for the argument of the 'unfinished democratisation' in post-soviet states such as Moldova or the Ukraine.

Yet a very different perspective on the results of political culture analyses and of their projection as future trends is also evident. Political culture analyses of the CEE do not provide a coherent picture of the region's political developments, even in retrospect. Moreover, from a comparative reading they look as if they describe different aspects of political culture, not only concerning their 'material' basis for interpretation, but also in their definition of culture: as a set of opinions, a result of economic living standards or a background attitude for political behaviour.

If one follows the assumption that these results, nevertheless, can be attributed a certain explanatory value for the respective context they are referring to, the question about the interrelation of these contexts and their representation in the political field as a whole arises – or, at least, the request for a redefinition of political culture.

… to Cultural Patterns of Politics?

This question appears to be closely linked to the definition of culture(s) in a broader sense or to such a definition that could possibly bring together the different fields of its analysed political representation.

The terminology of cultural patterns seems more appropriate for the description of this variety of influences, life styles and/or representations, which may operate at different levels of the political field. Whereas the concept of (political) culture often seems inflexible in its attempt to define the basic and seemingly unchangeable characteristics on which political actors and or communities seem to rely, as can frequently be witnessed in debates about *the* Islam, cultural patterns enable us to explore the diversity of heterogeneous and often contradictory elements, which stimulate political processes.

During a one year stay in Vienna, the eminent anthropologist Clifford Geertz developed an alternative approach to the cultural analysis of the political consequences of the 1989 revolutions in Europe (Geertz 1996). According to him, the breakdown of the 'Iron Curtain' and the end of a bipolar image of global politics led to the disappearance of *the* unifying narrative for political differences. He proposed to replace this narrative with the image(s) of a fragmented world as the main structure for representing global politics, with each field of political relations demanding its own model of description. He therefore argues for a case-by-case approach in the analysis of the cultural frames on which politics relies or refers to.

In his earlier anthropological work, Geertz (1973) had already contributed to the methodology of a case-by-case analysis of cultural representations through the development of analytical concepts, which allowed for the comprehension of different forms of cultural expressions. Through such terms as 'symbolic action', 'patterned conduct' or 'frame of mind and, of course, their mixed appearances in everyday life, the multitude of phenomena addressed in the study of (political) culture seems to get a more distinctive definition than with the pretension connected to each of these expressions to represent *the* political culture. Moreover, with the concept of 'cultural patterns', the research interest invested in political culture(s), which aims at potential rules or repetitive habits of political behaviour with some future impact, seems more adequately articulated and allows a distinct representation of the respective field where these rules or habits are represented.

Cultural Patterns of Political Change in the Aftermath of 1989

Consequently, Geertz (1996) attempted to offer an alternative perspective under the concept of culture, which could contribute to the new models of a partitioned world, where 'cultural' blocs such as Islam or *the* West seem to have replaced the ideological divide of the Cold War. He argues that political transformation processes require a transformation in analytical approach, leading to a case-by-case study of the elements undergoing change as well as the reappearance and/or the continuity of traditions. The concept of cultural patterns allows him to follow the different scenarios of the collapsing socialist states, such as the CEE countries in the former Soviet Bloc or the post-Yugoslavian states, as they pursued their respective paths of development (see Geertz 1996).

On this methodological basis, strata or regularities of political text and imagery at various levels around what appear to be the key questions of transformation, which involve the actors in the political field, offer a way of understanding a variety of case studies, which seems much broader than the 'agenda' provided in political culture research. In the following, the characteristics of one exemplary case will be summarized in order to provide some insight into the cultural patterns referred to in 'post-transition' politics, which are not represented in political science, even though they seem to address at least some of the topics considered in the main trends of political culture research outlined above. The example is based on the results of a project on 'Cultural Patterns of European Enlargement',[2] which focused on a small, but representative, selection of topics that appeared in the discussion about the EU enlargement with and within several 'new' Member States between the enlargement rounds of 1995 and 2007. The choice of memory politics as one of these topics for the following example is due to the observation that the (re) construction of traditions as a basis for political argumentation can be regarded as a common structure for different aspects of political transformation, from the constitution of the legal and institutional system to single policy fields.

The Example of Memory Politics

Memory politics seems identifiable as one frame of reference for the political discourse about and the representation of the EU enlargement process with several countries,[3] which can be reconstructed under the concept of collective memory (Halbwachs 1992). Through numerous references to the topics summarized under this concept, the change of political systems in CEE of '1989' appears as a political challenge that seems to impose:

- the necessity to rearrange and rewrite/ or construct (in the case of new emerging nation states like Slovenia) a *national history* (with the focus on a very 'material' foundation involving a change or designing of national symbols, the abolition and/or replacing of monuments, the alteration of street names, etc.);
- the 'historicity' (*Historisierung*) of '1989' itself and its precursors under the socialist state (oppositional movements and dissidents) and

2 CULTPAT – Cultural Patterns of European Enlargement (2004–2007) – was a project funded by Framework Programme 5 of the European Commission under the direction of Silvia Mihalikova. The author participated in the project as leader of the Austrian national project team.

3 For the relevance of memory politics in the CEE region contemporary political debate see also the special issue on this topic in Eurozine 2006 (www.eurozine.com).

before through the amalgamation of a renewed history with a renewed historiography (Gyáni 2005);
- the reference of this effort to a broader European perspective under the emblem of the 'European destiny' of the respective national history – as expressed, for example, in the 'Return to Europe' slogans of several official campaigns for the referenda on EU membership.

The political, as well as the analytical focus, on symbols and/or 'images' for the public representation of this aspect of system change is based on the assumption that symbols, visual images and rituals function on the one hand as *public markers* of (memorial) communities – thereby having an extended reach compared to (the related) political discourse – and, on the other hand, as 'requisites' for the construction of the stage of the (public) 'political spectacle' (Edelman 1988).

On this 'stage' the rearrangement of historical symbols and narratives referred to in political ritual and discourse seems even today – almost 20 years after the system change – to constitute an ongoing 'battleground' in the new geopolitical order of Europe. A closer look at actual European politics shows a series of recent events, which seem to stress the importance of the political use of memory patterns with regard to different cultural backgrounds for political representation. Violent protests against the social-liberal government coalition in Hungary in 2006 and 2007 – though focusing on the demand for the resignation of the prime minister – did not accidentally break out around the commemoration of the Hungarian Revolution against the Communist state of 1956. The protests were part of a public dispute about who has the right to represent this founding tradition of the current democratic state and therefore who has political legitimacy. Again, the debates about and violent street rioting around the removal of the Memorial for the Red Army in Tallinn, the capital of Estonia, were not only part and/or a result of ongoing conflicts with the Russian minority, but showed at the same time the importance which this minority – and the government authorities – give to the representation of Soviet history as part of the national memory represented in the Estonian public space.

Memory – as pointed out in the examples above – must be considered as one of these imaginary perspectives that play a key role in the current attempts to redefine the European political space and its relationship to the different nation states as well as to the EU itself. These attempts go far beyond the period of socialism or what could be summarized under the post-socialist attitudes mentioned above. For example, when the acting president of Poland, Lech Kaczynski, closed his 2005 presidential election campaign in the National Museum in Warsaw in front of a nineteenth-century painting of the medieval Battle of Grünewald – where Polish nobility defeated the German Knight Order – he chose this representation of Polish history as a frame for contemporary Polish politics, its implications and boundaries, especially with other – national – political memories such as the German one. This and similar historical references frame the self-representation of the Polish national-conservative political camp and inspire contemporary Polish politics with the image of the struggle for establishing Poland's national identity between the East and the West. The 'West' includes in this representation the EU Poland recently joined, and is politically present through a series of political differences between Warsaw and 'Brussels', which emerged during the membership negotiations.

Memory politics appears to be accorded an increased importance especially by the Central European right wing parties and/or movements, even across the former Iron Curtain. In Austria the reopening of the question of a (financial) compensation for the German minority, forced to leave Czechoslovakia after 1945 by the so-called Beneš decrees, was put on the political agenda by the national-conservative coalition during 2000 and caught the attention of the 'national-liberal' FiDeSz government coalition in Hungary, which represented the similarly affected Hungarian minority in Slovakia. Furthermore, the recent plan to open a documentation centre in Berlin about the post-1945 European 'expulsions' and mass migrations, with a focus on the German populations, played an important role in the difficulties, which developed in Polish-German bilateral relations. During the 1990s the Italian government under Prime Minister Berlusconi opposed Slovenian membership of the EU because of historic territorial and similar expulsion questions concerning the Triestine border and the Istrian peninsula. Under the current Berlusconi government, there is a high probability that the EU membership of Croatia will encounter some Italian *and* Slovenian opposition on precisely the same topics.[4] These are just some of the recent examples, which can be provided from the realm of symbolic politics in the CE region and which illustrate the use of memory in EU politics.

The analytical approach to these memory patterns neither intends to contribute to the current and widespread critique of a 'misuse' of history for political purposes – as the 'post-socialist' perspective on political cultures would suggest – nor to an analysis of Polish versus German or to the antagonisms between other national identities; the focus on such case studies is on the reconstruction of the cultural – in this case memory patterns and the political importance they are accorded. The interest, indicated already in the term of memory itself, therefore does not lie in a contribution to the ongoing historical debates and a 'finding of the truth in history' – although such positions are necessarily (re)presented as part of the ongoing debates – but on a reconstruction of the space and the influence these debates occupy in or exercise on the representations of political differences and debates.

4 Slovenia recently blocked the enlargement negotiations with Croatia on the topic of their unresolved border questions.

In the context addressed here, the above mentioned examples should stand as a *Pars pro Toto* for an increasing importance given to those questions in Central Europe, especially by the CE right wing governments and political parties, thereby enhancing an increasing importance of memory-politics as a frame of reference for European politics as a whole: the public success of such attempts to frame (national) political discourse(s) can be seen as a crucial point for the consent with and the support of nationalistic tendencies. The potential for non- or anti-democratic trends seems therefore not only dependent on personal attitudes towards the political system – as related to in political culture research – but at least as well on the possibility of 'anchoring' these attitudes in the public political debate or in an actual political agenda.

The example of memory politics as an important part of the use of cultural patterns for the symbolic representation of contemporary politics in Central (Eastern) Europe has been reconstructed here with the intention to argue against a restrictive apprehension of political culture(s) in several points:

- in the field of memory politics, culture appears in a combination or 'mix' of different levels of expression, ranging from material manifestations to opinions, which on the 'stage' of politics often seem inseparable;
- these framing concepts are not only and always part of the competition in the field of politics, but attempt to define a common battleground or to express a 'common sense' basis for political debate that sets its boundaries of potential references;
- memory patterns, as other cultural patterns appear to be open for different, or even contradictory interpretations: as part and symbol of the democratisation processes, or directed against them.

The last point particularly accentuates the different approaches to political culture. Whereas the tradition of political culture research is based on the assumption of an unequivocal sense of cultural expressions, the example of memory seems to underline their ambiguous character and multidimensional meaning.

An 'Alternative Landscape' of Europe as a Consequence of EU Enlargement?

This multidimensional meaning also appears with regard to a series of countries where this memory debate can be reconstructed as an issue arising around the enlargement process in several features, one of them being the role in and the importance for contemporary European politics. In the case of Austria, the historical role of the country as a centre of the Habsburg monarchy has been evoked in official documents, as well as in public representations concerning EU accession (1995) in the sense of a renewal of the country's intermediary role between East and West. With the 2004/07 enlargement, this position – that remodelled Austria's role between the blocs during the Cold War period – not only quickly disappeared again, but the images of the self-(re)presentation of most of the new Central European EU members (Czech Republic, Hungary, Poland, Slovakia and Slovenia) turned out to be based on similar projections of a specific position in the new European geopolitical surroundings.

The unique role, which each of these countries claims for the relations between the EU and an Eastern European region, nowadays again situated outside its new border, is represented in similar terms and images, which range from historical experience to a specific mentality developed as a result of this experience. Following the political use of this image, it seems that precisely this same supposed difference of mentalities provides a basis both for calls for national seclusion and an international role. Returning to the example of Polish politics, the European role of Poland in negotiating recent government crisis in the neighbouring Ukraine fits perfectly the rhetoric about defending traditional national interests as well as the image of a new role for the country through an involvement in the further development of European democracy.

The above examples suggest an alternative perspective on contemporary politics in CEE, which can also be taken as an indicator for a changing European political landscape, where the strata of political discourse and agenda setting seem no longer to be confined within the boundaries of the recent history of European divide, but – still not? – melting in an average European (political) culture. On the contrary, the (re)appearance of supra-national European regions, such as the Central European or a Northern region, might just as easily shape important aspects of European politics. The common interest in a somewhat more open border with the Ukraine, which actually unites Poland, Slovakia and Hungary in their attempts to modify the application of the Schengen agreement for these cross-border relations, could be identified as one of these regional issues. This issue could allow a flow of migration into the EU that goes back to initial period of the aftermath of system change – an indeed uncommon and specific approach with regard to the restrictive direction the ongoing efforts towards a common EU migration policy actually take.

The observed signs of a resurgence of what could be summarized as Central European regional patterns of politics across the former Iron Curtain does not only result from the analysis of one field – it appears in various fields of the political discourse about Enlargement. Another example[5] could be reconstructed by following the debate concerning agricultural or rural land ownership in several Central European 'new' member states (including Austria). This debate showed similar references to endangered national

5 A comparative study of the debates about the legal regulations for agricultural or rural landownership after EU accession was also included in the CULTPAT project this chapter is referring to.

identities and traditional images of the respective rural world as an argument for a (temporary) restriction of the access for other EU citizens.

On the other hand, the same processes that look to be shaping the political agenda of a Central European region since the 2004 Enlargement have gained attention as a potential horizon for the development and representation of regional political interests within the EU (Ágh 2006). Here the so-called Visegrad group, which involves low scale, institutionalised cooperation between Czech Republic, Slovakia, Poland, Hungary and Slovenia, is considered by some analysts as a first step.

A closer look at these regional cultural patterns – as one case of post-transformation European developments – relates them to the ambiguous symbolic relationships with the EU these countries are expressing as well in political campaigns. We can already see this, for example, in the campaigns for the enlargement referenda, where the official campaigning materials showed an indistinguishable image of the respective national with *the* EUropean identity (Bernhardt et al. 2009).

It appears as if this ambiguity about the region's role in the new European contexts, which has still a prominent presence in the Central European political representations nearly 20 years after the system change and after several EU enlargement(s), could be reconstructed as a 'common denominator' for the regional political culture(s). An ambiguity, that seems to be based on the 'empty place' remaining for the representation of the region's history in a common narrative, a national and/or European memory. An ambiguity, which, of course, does not allow for a projection of future developments, but eventually for a reconstruction of past ones.

Chapter 3
The Contemporary Development of the Bulgarian Policy towards Migration, 2006–2007[1]

Daryana Kotzeva

Bulgaria was expected as an EU Member State from 2007 to develop its migration policy in full accordance with the law and the practice of the EU. At the same time Bulgaria was encouraged to maintain and develop its human capital. In this chapter the focus will be on the challenges which Bulgaria has had to confront during the early accession period immediately after 2007. The main objective of the policy makers has been to strike the right balance between the desire among Bulgarian nationals to find professional fulfilment in other EU Member States (which is their basic Community right) and achieving attractiveness and a living standard, which will keep them in Bulgaria – an aim which is especially relevant to highly qualified Bulgarian specialists.

I will argue in this chapter that migration policy has to be based on reliable and accurate data. The effectiveness of any migration strategy has to be underpinned by preliminary comprehensive quantitative analysis. Furthermore, exchange of information between the international partners is crucial to implementing a global or regional approach in policy-making. Consequently, the Bulgarian government conducted in August 2006 a study called 'Emigration attitudes among adult population in Bulgaria' with the aim of collecting evidence about the population's attitudes towards emigration. This research also facilitated the debate among the EU member states about whether to apply transitional measures for Bulgarian citizens with respect to their access to the labour market.[2] The survey was carried out by BBSS Gallup

---

1 Data and representations of emigration attitudes among the adult population in Bulgaria are gratefully reproduced from a study commissioned by the Bulgarian Ministry of Labour and Social Policy and carried out by Gallup International in August 2006.

2 According to the Accession Treaty of Bulgaria each member state had to declare its position regarding the application of the transitional measures for the free movement of workers, envisaged in Annex VI of the Accession Treaty of Bulgaria and Romania, *Official Journal of the European Union* L 157/11; 21 June 2005.

International.[3] As we shall see, the results clearly show that the number of people willing to work abroad for a long time has fallen by a half. The major trend is for Bulgarian citizens preferring to go abroad for only a short term.

Around 36,000 people declared an intention to work, live and study in the EU in the next five or more years. Where do the Bulgarians want to work? The most popular destination is Spain, followed by Germany, the USA, Greece and Great Britain. The findings show that the migration behaviour of Bulgarian citizens is similar to that of the average EU citizen. There are a number of factors, which explain why Bulgarians cannot be considered as exerting pressure on the labour market of EU Member States. The two most important factors are the stable economy and the low unemployment rate in the country – 8.76 per cent, which is similar to that of the EU generally. The macro-economic indicators in BG have also risen and a high rate of economic growth has been observed, living conditions in the country have improved as have the opportunities for professional fulfilment.

Other factors have to be borne in mind. There is the high 'price' of the psychological stress, which always exists when adapting to a foreign country and coping with a new culture. There are considerable financial expenses involved in settling down in an unfamiliar environment often a long way from the country of origin. The language barrier deters quick integration, high immigration flows in the accepting state might prevent further immigration in that country, because of problems with integrating the first wave of migrants, the lack of attractiveness of the jobs on offer, which usually do not correspond to the high educational levels and predominantly young profile of Bulgarian emigrants (most of the available jobs are more labour intensive than knowledge intensive). For the sake of clarity, we produce here two tables to demonstrate the attitudes of Bulgarian citizens to work in the EU countries.

In pursuance of the policy for managing migration, from the end of 2005 the Ministry of Labour and Social Policy (MSLP) started creating a net of advisers on social and labour issues in Bulgarian embassies in the EU Member States. Currently, there are advisers in Madrid, Berlin and Athens and appointments will also be made in France and Italy. Their main task will be to protect Bulgarian workers outside national borders but they are also expected to explain the legal rules in the receiving state concerning employment and social security. Furthermore, they will inform nationals from the receiving state about their employment rights in Bulgaria and assist the exchange of information and know-how between the MLSP and the respective institutions in the receiving state.

Since Bulgaria now provides an external border for the EU, it is keenly interested in creating instruments for an integrated management of the migration process. Its migration policy aims to ensure respect for all basic human rights by balancing the freedom of movement of persons with

3 BBSS Gallup-Bulgaria, http://www.gallup-bbss.com.

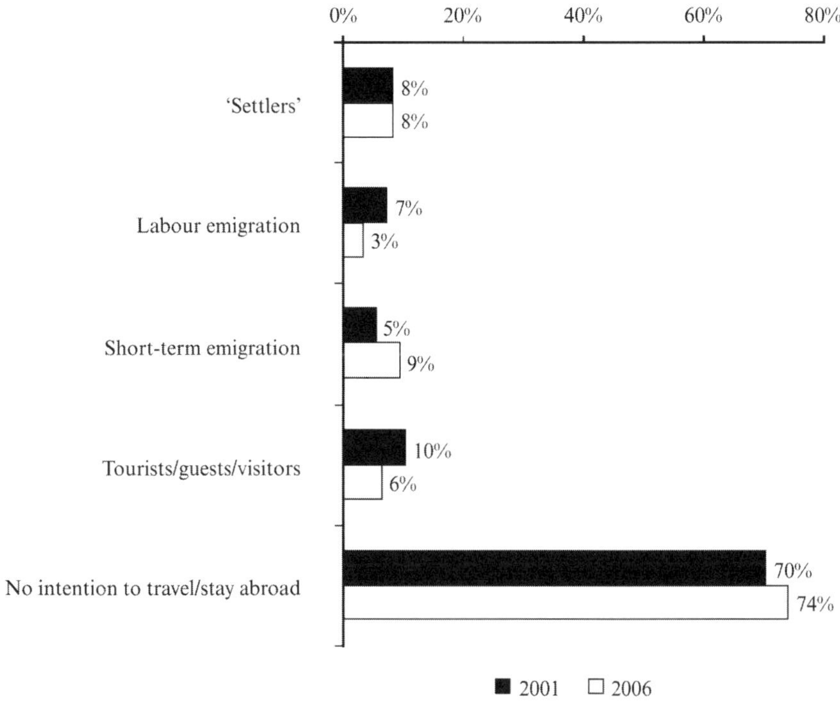

Figure 3.1 Overall situation comparison 2001–2006

Source: data gathered from Gallup International (2007).

controlling and ultimately abolishing illegal migration. In pursuance of these objectives the following pieces of legislature have been adopted:

1. *EU Citizens and Members of Their Families Entry and Residence in and Departure from the Republic of Bulgaria Act*. With this new law Directive 2004/38 has been transposed. Article 2 introduces the notion of the 'citizen of the EU' in BG legislature, as distinguished from the notion of 'foreigner' (citizen of a third country). The former category of foreigner in this new act remains in force for citizens from third countries outside the EU. This is an important step since the Bulgarian government is clearly declaring its commitment to the principles of the free movement of persons across the EU. Bulgaria is clearly complying appropriately, therefore, with EU law and does not intend to impede the free movement of EU citizens.
2. *Law on Employment Promotion and the Special Rules for its Application*: opportunities have been created after accession to the EU so that nationals of other EU Member States, who are actively seeking work,

Table 3.1 Estimation of the factual emigration flow 2001–2006

	Total	Labour emigrants	Settlers
EU total	31,600–34,500	14,000–15,300	18,300–20,000
Spain	9,200–10,000	4,600–5,000	6,000–6,600
Germany	7,000–7,700	3,200–3,500	3,700–4,000
USA	4,400–4,800	1,900–2,100	2,100–2,300
Italy	3,900–4,300	350–390	2,300–2,600
Greece	3,500–3,800	1,600–1,700	2,900–3,100
UK	3,100–3,400	1,400–1,500	2,300–2,600
France	2,200–2,400	530–580	1,300–1,400
Turkey	1,800–1,900	–	1,000–1,100
Canada	1,300–1,400	530–580	1,000–1,100
Ireland	530–580	530–580	–
Total	43,800–47,900	17,700–19,400	26,100–28,600

Note: Rounded figures based on the first mentioned destination.

Source: data gathered from Gallup International (2007).

can now register at Bulgarian Employment Offices and take advantage of public services, which help people find work;

3. *Ordinance for the terms and conditions to allow posted workers in Bulgaria in the framework of the service provision* – it sets out equal working conditions for both nationals of EU Member States and Bulgarian nationals;
4. *Ordinance for the terms and conditions for performing a mediating activity to secure work* – it confers the right to nationals from the EU and the EEC to perform a mediation activity to secure employment; the terms for which registration lasts in this case has been increased from three to five years. The previous requirement that mediation could only be provided by legal entities with more than 50 per cent Bulgarian participation has been revoked.

The development of Bulgaria's migration policy has reached a new stage through the establishment of an administrative unit within the European Integration and International Relations Directorate at the MLSP called the Free Movement of Workers and Management of External Labour Migration Unit. It was in charge of preparing the country for the free movement of workers after Bulgarian accession to the EU and is also in charge of the acceptance of third country nationals by Bulgaria for different kinds of employment, including social and cultural emigrants and immigrants.

Because of the increasing relevance of migration for both national policy and bilateral and multilateral diplomacy, in 2005 an inter-institutional working group was established within the MSLP to deal with issues such as migration and integration of immigrants in Bulgaria. This decision was taken in response to a recommendation in the Report of the EU Commission about the migration environment in 2005. The working group is in charge of harmonizing Bulgarian law with EU law, including the compliance of Bulgarian policy with the whole framework of EU policy in the field of migration. Some of the issues overlap with those in the Migration section of the Justice and Internal Affairs department. The group is required to analyse periodically the state of both legislative and administrative practice in Bulgaria across the field of social and cultural integration.

At the beginning the migration group consisted only of representatives of institutions, which were dealing with migration and integration issues. During 2006 it was expanded to include representatives from social partners and local authorities and currently consists of 37 persons. An extensive forum has, therefore, been set up for the initial discussion of every pressing question in the field of migration and integration and the debate continues among the wide public as well. The inclusion of such a diverse range of stakeholders promises to lead to an informative, deep and mature discussion on migration issues.

This working group will start working on the National Strategy of Migration and Integration of Migrant-Workers. The strategy will outline the current situation regarding the emigration of Bulgarian citizens with the aim of finding employment for foreign nationals. While preparing the main document, the working group also intends to explore the trends in labour force shortages in particular professions and fields. In the framework of this Strategy a review will be made of the approach and the results from the information campaigns, which have been carried out in Bulgaria for legal work abroad. Particular attention will be paid to the opportunities for Bulgarian nationals to be consulted and advised about their reintegration within society after their returning to Bulgaria. The Strategy will also explore the idea that resources should be set aside to provide attractive social inducements and incentives when there is a shortage in certain professions.

Steps should also be undertaken to assist the integration of citizens of Bulgarian origin, who are living outside the country but who want to settle permanently in Bulgaria. The National Strategy will take into consideration EU policy in this respect – the existing and proposed EU secondary laws as well as the practice of the separate EU Member States. Here it should be noted that in 2006 the Basic Common Principles for Immigrant Integration Policy in the EU were translated into Bulgarian. They were discussed initially in the framework of the Working Group on migration and afterwards a lot of publicity and scholarly effort went into explaining the need for their inclusion in the implementation of the integration policy.

At the moment the number of foreign nationals with permanent residence in Bulgaria continues to be just over 52,000. Most are concentrated in the major Bulgarian economic and cultural centres. Thirty-five per cent live in Sofia, 9 per cent of them live in Plovdiv and its region, 8 per cent live in Varna and its region while 5 per cent are also found in Bourgas and its district. The data, which concerns those foreign nationals with long-term residence permits, shows that the largest numbers come Macedonia, Turkey, Great Britain and the Russian Federation; then come those from Greece, USA and Germany. Of these groups those from the EU show the strongest interest in establishing permanent residence within the country.

As for accepting EU citizens within Bulgaria's labour market, after an extensive debate the government decided to apply European Community law in the field of free movement of workers thereby opening up the market. On 12 December 2006 the Council of Ministers of Bulgaria declared its decision to apply European Community law in the field of free movement of workers without restrictions, by adopting Regulation (ECC) N 1612/68 of the European Council. Article 5 (4) of the Constitution of Bulgaria in relation to the EU Accession Treaty of Bulgaria, which came into force on 1 January 2007 and the directly applicable Regulation (mentioned above), ensures that citizens of the EU Member States can legally enjoy free movement within Bulgaria without having to apply for a work-permit and are exempt therefore from any labour market test. As for the regulations concerning their residence is concerned, the new law adopted recently in Bulgaria – the *EU Citizens and Members of their Families Entry and Residence in and Departure from the Republic of Bulgaria Act* – is relevant. These matters are within the competence of the National Police Service and EU citizens can reside in the country with an identity card or a passport for up to three months. The act stipulates that EU citizens can reside in the country on a long-term or permanent basis after being issued with a certificate from the National Police Service, which requires them to comply with certain conditions. Long-term residence lasts for up to five years and then a certificate for permanent residence can be granted if the applicant meets certain other conditions. Currently, only 536 EU citizens are officially employed on the Bulgarian labour market, while foreign nationals also employed in the country come from our neighbouring countries – 130 come from Greece and Romania. The influx from our neighbours makes us expect an increase in labour force movement in our border regions.

Another sign of Bulgaria's integration into the EU labour market is the National Employment Agency's involvement from 2007 in the network of the EU employment services (EURES). The National Employment Service has started to provide information to employers and job seekers from the EU about vacancies and employment opportunities in Bulgaria. As for the employment of third country nationals is concerned, according to current Bulgarian law foreigners, who need to work on a labour contract or as posted workers in Bulgaria, need work permits. This is also the practice in the other EU Member

States. The work permit for third country nationals is issued after a labour market test has been completed. This includes a check on whether there is a Bulgarian or other EU applicant, who wants to fill the published vacancy. If there is no such an applicant or a foreigner with a permanent residence then a work permit is issued.

No work permit is required for foreigners, who manage commercial partnerships, who are members of Board of Managers or are representatives of foreign commercial partnerships, for example. There is a simplified (relaxed) procedure (without a labour market test) for foreigners when their employment is related with the execution of international treaties – high management staff, specialists who possess special knowledge concerning production technologies, equipment and management; staff of an international company involved in coordinating activity, specialists introducing special technologies and know-how as well as applying specialized and unique techniques.

At the moment about 1,000 citizens from third countries have been issued work permits in Bulgaria – 211 from Turkey, 165 from Macedonia, 125 from the Ukraine, 77 from India, 64 from the USA, 53 from Serbia, 47 from Russia and 35 from China. In brief, if the business requires human resources, which are unavailable at the moment and Bulgarian nationals cannot become qualified to an acceptable level, there are no legal obstacles for the employment of third country nationals. However, it should be remembered that from January 1, 2007 EU citizens have priority over third country nationals. The government wants to emphasize that it is up to Bulgarian businesses to encourage the engagement of the Bulgarian workers in the country – and here we do not have in mind only remuneration. Proper career schemes offered by the employers could encourage a lot of potential Bulgarian workers, especially young job-seekers, to enter the domestic labour market.

As noted earlier, it is expected that the number of workers from third countries will increase. Bulgaria may well become like some other countries in southern Europe – a country, which attracts migrants (a 'receiving' country). Recently, a question has been raised by the employers in Bulgaria and is under discussion: whether there could be a larger acceptance of citizens from third countries in Bulgaria working on labour contracts in areas where there is a labour shortage such as tourism. The employers insist on defining a quota for such workers – something which has not been the practice in Bulgaria so far. The country is trying to conduct a balanced policy with the aim of preventing the eventual increase of workers from third countries from putting Bulgaria into a difficult position. Its ability to absorb these new workers has to be very carefully analysed so that integration failures are avoided.

The statistics show that actually there is a significant *unused labour resource within Bulgaria's labour market.* While there are 5,245,000 people of working age, there are only approximately 4,500,000 actively employed. In 2006 356,054 were unemployed and of these 117,307 had received secondary vocational and secondary general education, i.e. 33 per cent of the registered unemployed have the requisite education and could, through short-term professional qualifications, update their knowledge and skills and start working. Furthermore, 22,687 people or 6 per cent from the unemployed have enjoyed a higher education and we can also add a proportion of the inactive people who are of working age.

The average number of those not trying to find work during the first six months of 2006 was 299,000. Of these 99,400 had received a secondary general or secondary vocational education, while 16,900 possessed higher educational qualifications. This means that a total of 116,500 people have sufficient educational qualifications to be quickly retrained. Indeed, the MLSP has introduced measures to help the unemployed gain qualifications and encourage them to enter the labour market through the payment of bonuses, for example. In 2006 47,376 people have been drawn into training programmes. The training of the unemployed is carried out according to a list of professions, which is updated annually in accordance with information about the particular professions at a regional level. In 2007 it was envisaged that more than 43,000 people would take part in different qualification courses. At the moment a new study is being conducted among 2000 employers to update information about the employers' needs from the labour force with regard to particular qualifications. At the end of 2007 the limited period (up to 18 months) for receiving monthly social assistance from the unemployed, who are of working age, will finish. These people are a potential labour resource reserve, who need to be drawn into Bulgaria's labour market.

Conclusion

Bulgaria keeps statistics about the labour resources across the country, identifies the trends and updates the measures related with them. It defines the migration policy in accordance with the commitments, which arise from EU Membership, with the policies and practices of the EU and with the national interest. One strategic objective of Bulgaria's migration policy is to assist the Bulgarian nationals as citizens of the EU so they can fulfil their right to free movement and also to facilitate the movement of other EU nationals in Bulgaria. The other very significant part of the policy making with respect to migration in Bulgaria is to manage effectively the migration process and integration of third country nationals. The situation in Bulgaria after the first year since accession has to be analysed carefully so that new trends are identified and the state of the labour market has to be studied with a view to satisfying the needs of the employers in certain sectors where a shortage of indigenous is evident. Based on the projections emerging from these statistics, further steps can be taken to develop Bulgaria's policies concerning the labour market.

Inevitably, since Bulgaria's accession to the EU its labour market is gradually becoming part of the EU labour market, the government believes that it took a mature decision when it decided to open the labour market. It is willing to cooperate with all institutions and partners in the EU in order to analyse the migration flows between Bulgaria and other EU Member States. Hopefully, the results emerging from this cooperation will show clearly what is going on and the impact of these migration flows on Bulgaria and its partners. It is clear nowadays that no one country can cope on its own with the challenges of migration and free movement without sharing data, expertise and best practice. Definitely, the spirit of solidarity as a prevailing principle in the EU should be applied in the field of migration too. This will bring coordination and consistency and, finally, it will help the Member States and the whole EU to maximize the benefits of migration and free movement.

Migration will become even more important in the forthcoming years. Therefore, planning appropriately for future migration developments is vital for the achievement of the added value brought by migration. Moreover, the correct regulation of the migration process is an important instrument for achieving progress in the globalizing world economy. All this makes the issue of migration into a national, regional and a global one.

The labour market aspects of migration also need to be considered. A lot of the current migration policy is driven by the recognition that migrant workers occupy gaps in certain domestic labour markets. Their mobility contributes to a healthy labour market and their role is well recognized by major stakeholders such as employers. Nowadays, when global competition for talented and highly qualified experts is increasing, governments have the responsibility to manage labour migration wisely – protecting the interests of the migrants as well as the interests of host and home countries.

Chapter 4
Stemming the Flow? The Causes and Consequences of the UK's 'Closed Door' Policy towards Romanians and Bulgarians

Dhananjayan Sriskandarajah and Laurence Cooley[1]

Introduction

Whereas public debates about immigration to the UK prior to 2004 were typically concerned with the dramatic increase in the number of people claiming asylum that occurred in the late 1990s, recent concerns have instead revolved around the large number of labour migrants who have moved to the UK since the enlargement of the European Union in May 2004. Against this backdrop, the UK government decided in late 2006 to impose restrictions on the number of Romanians and Bulgarians who could move to the UK following their accession to the EU in January 2007. This was in contrast to the decision to grant free labour market access to nationals of the eight Central and Eastern European countries that joined in 2004. One of the aims of this paper is to explore whether this policy reversal was informed by evidence of negative impacts of migration from the A8 states, or whether it was made in response to other factors, such as pressure from the tabloid media.

Having explored the causes of the UK's decision to impose transitional restrictions on Romanian and Bulgarian migration, this chapter then presents two possible consequences of this decision – irregular working (since, as EU nationals, Romanians and Bulgarians can travel freely to the UK) and a diversionary effect into self-employment (both genuine and quasi self-

1 The authors would like to thank participants at the IMILCO workshop on 'EU Enlargement, Informal Economy and New Migratory Landscapes', Istanbul, 14–15 December 2006, the IMISCOE seminar on 'EU Enlargement and Labour Migration within the EU', Warsaw, 23–24 April 2007 and the interdisciplinary one-day workshop on 'Migration in the Enlarging European Union: Interrogating transitional arrangements', Liverpool Law School, University of Liverpool, 17 September 2007, for their comments on previous versions of this chapter. We are also grateful to Catherine Drew for her help on initial drafts of this paper and to Maria Latorre for her assistance with the Labour Force Survey. Responsibility for any mistakes or omissions rests with the authors.

employment), since it is not possible under EU law to prevent nationals of the new Member States from being self-employed in the UK. We examine early data on flows of Romanians and Bulgarians and demonstrate that transitional arrangements may not have substantially reduced post-accession migration flows to the UK.

The Decision to Grant Free Movement in 2004

The UK government's decision to allow workers of the eight Central and Eastern European accession states (A8) unrestricted access to its labour market as soon as they joined the European Union,[2] announced in December 2002, initially received little attention. As accession day drew closer, however, there was considerable public concern over the potential numbers of Central and Eastern Europeans that were expected to 'flood' into the UK.

One of the reasons that the government chose to take a liberal approach to labour market access for accession nationals was the small predicted flows of migrants from Central and Eastern Europe to the UK. Several studies estimated the possible migration flows from the new Member States into the existing EU15 (Boeri and Brücker 2000; Brücker et al. 2003). These studies, and one commissioned by the UK Home Office (Dustmann et al. 2003), predicted that flows into the UK would be relatively small. The UK study predicted net annual inflows of A8 migrants of between 5,000 and 13,000 to 2010, based largely on previous flows of A8 nationals to the UK. For example, the UK's International Passenger Survey showed that prior to enlargement, flows from non-EU Europe were much smaller than those from other regions, and were indeed negative in net terms in 2001 (Sriskandarajah 2004). Similarly, the 2001 Census revealed that people born in Eastern Europe (again including the former USSR) numbered around 240,000 and accounted for only 5.6 per cent of the foreign-born population.

Predictions of small inflows of accession state nationals did not prevent rising public anxieties as May 2004 approached. There are a number of explanations for why this was the case. First, while Eastern European migration to the UK before 2004 was relatively small, fears over rising post-enlargement flows played into wider concerns about rising immigration since the late 1990s. According to one regular survey (MORI 2006), those identifying race and immigration as being of concern rose from less than 5–10 per cent during the 1970s and 1980s to range between 35–40 per cent in recent years. Another poll

2 Under accession treaties, existing EU Member States have the right to restrict labour market access to workers from the so-called A8 countries that joined the EU in 2004 (the Czech Republic, Estonia, Hungary, Latvia, Lithuania, Poland, Slovakia and Slovenia) for up to seven years. Workers from Cyprus and Malta, which joined at the same time, enjoy unrestricted access.

conducted prior to EU enlargement suggested that 85 per cent of people did not think that the government was in control of immigration (MORI 2003).

Secondly, Eastern Europeans had been central in the construction of public myths and fears around migration. In 2000, around a quarter of all asylum applicants came from Eastern Europe (including war-torn Kosovo) (Home Office 2004a). In 2003, Romanians and Bulgarians were at the centre of a scandal over fraudulent visa applications, which eventually led to the resignation of the immigration minister a month before the 2004 round of enlargement. Perceptions that immigration was 'out of control' and that certain immigrants were trying to 'beat the system' were firmly planted.

Thirdly, sections of the UK media focused on the impending arrival of 'hordes' of Eastern Europeans, and particularly Roma people. Headlines such as 'See you in May: Thousands of travellers are on their way' (*The Sun* 19 January 2004, 4–5), 'Blair's bid to save UK jobs from EU gipsies' [sic] (*The People* 1 February 2004, 2) and 'Stop the invaders' (*Daily Star* 12 February 2004, 6) are indicative of the anxiety that the media both reflected and exacerbated.

In the event, the UK government stood firm and granted accession workers unrestricted access to its labour market. Some commentators have suggested that this was due to labour demand rather than a liberal attitude to immigration on the part of the government (Hardy and Clark 2005). The UK had one of the lowest unemployment rates in the EU (4.8 per cent in May 2004) and appeared to be experiencing skill shortages in certain areas, particularly low-skilled sectors. By welcoming accession migrants, the UK government also believed it stood to gain an advantage in attracting the best highly skilled and entrepreneurial migrants from these countries. The government was also explicit about role the policy of free movement would play in reducing the demand for irregular workers. The then Home Secretary said of the decision: 'These measures will enable the workers we need to work here legally rather than fuelling the sub-economy – a modern-day slave trade, exploiting migrant workers and undercutting UK employees' (Home Office 2004b).

Some sections of the government also pushed for free movement by emphasising the diplomatic gains that could be won through fully engaging with the spirit of EU enlargement and building on the perception of the UK as a 'champion of enlargement'. Finally, and perhaps most importantly, the UK government based its decision on the relatively small numbers predicted by experts rather than the larger flows envisaged by the press.

The UK government did, however, make minor political concessions to quell public fears. It inserted a last minute clause into the European Union (Accessions) Act 2003 that allowed free movement of workers provided that newly arrived accession nationals (and those who had been working in the UK for less than 12 months) register under a Worker Registration Scheme (WRS) for a £50 fee (which has since increased to £70). Data generated from the WRS (jointly published by several government departments in quarterly *Accession*

Monitoring Reports) have been a crucial source of information about A8 migration and is referred to extensively below.

In order to calm worries about 'benefit shopping', the government also required that A8 migrants had to prove their 'right to reside' in the UK before they could access UK state benefits. Until they have been in continuous employment for over a year (with breaks of fewer than 30 days), A8 workers are only legally entitled to reside in the UK if they are in employment and registered on the WRS, are self-employed and/or have sufficient funds not to seek state benefits. This effectively precludes them from income-related benefits for at least one year, although they do have access to in-work benefits such as tax credits and child benefits throughout.

The Post-enlargement Experience

Migration Flows

Estimating the exact scale of migration from the A8 is made difficult because existing data sources are unable to capture either total or net flows. Here, we consider the four main sources of data on A8 migrants: the *Accession Monitoring Reports*, National Insurance Number (NINo) allocation data, the International Passenger Survey (IPS) and the Labour Force Survey (LFS).

According to the government's *Accession Monitoring Reports*, which are based on data collected from the WRS, there were 766,000 approved applications between May 2004 and the end of December 2007, running at between 39,000 and 63,000 per quarter since enlargement (Figure 4.1). These figures are gross application numbers rather than net figures and hence do not reflect return migration and so may overestimate the number of A8 nationals working in the UK at any one time. On the other hand, the figures exclude inflows of the self-employed, estimated to number approximately 105,000 people by September 2006.[3] Nor do the data include 85,265 dependants of A8 migrants, of whom 55 per cent are under 17 years old (Home Office et al. 2008). Of course the figures also exclude those who do not register at all, whether that be through ignorance, cost[4] or the perception that they will not be in the UK long enough to 'make it worthwhile' (Anderson et al. 2006).

A second administrative source of data on A8 migrants comes in the form of statistics on National Insurance Number allocations, which show that 717,100 A8 nationals registered over the period 2004/05 to 2006/07 (Table 4.1).

3 Home Office Minister Tony McNulty estimated that if self-employed workers were included the number of A8 migrants who entered the UK between May 2004 and September 2006 could be nearer 600,000 (BBC News 2006a), compared to 495,375 successful WRS applications in that period.

4 There is currently a fee of £90 to register on the WRS.

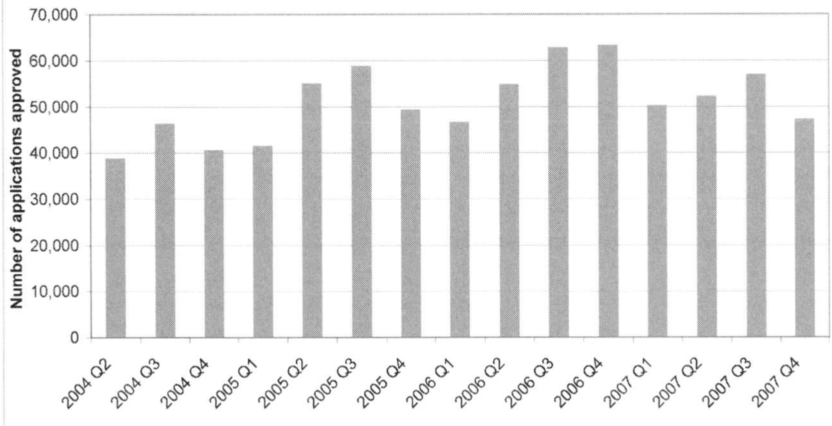

Figure 4.1 Successful applications to the Worker Registration Scheme, May 2004–December 2007

Again, since there is no requirement to de-register when leaving the UK, NINo data cannot capture net flows; nor can they include people who do not register for NINos. However, the data do help illustrate the scale of A8 migration to the UK. However, unlike the *Accession Monitoring Reports*, NINo data include the self-employed.

Table 4.1 Overseas nationals allocated a NINo, by year of registration and source region, 2003/4–2006/7

	2002/03	2003/04	2004/05	2005/06	2006/07
A8 states	17,900	28,700	119,200	276,700	321,200
Other EU	80,700	84,900	81,300	97,600	103,700
Non-EU Europe	14,800	15,800	14,100	15,500	16,300
Asia and Middle East	114,500	115,000	110,000	134,200	145,400
Australasia and Oceania	27,300	24,200	23,400	32,500	33,200
Americas	26,600	31,200	26,700	31,400	31,800
Africa	66,600	70,100	64,500	73,900	61,400
Others/unknown	800	800	600	600	500
Total	349,200	370,700	439,700	662,400	713,500

Note: Values may not sum to totals due to rounding.

Source: data gathered from Department for Work and Pensions (2007).

According to the UK's International Passenger Survey (IPS), which provides estimates of gross and net flows of long-term migrants (people intending to move for a year or longer), net immigration from the enlarged EU has risen since 2004. In the years 2004, 2005 and 2006 combined, net immigration of accession nationals was 181,000 (Office for National Statistics 2007) – representing 32 per cent of WRS registrations during that time.[5] In comparative terms net immigration from the EU has gone from 14,000 per annum (from the EU15) in 2003 to around 100,000 (from the EU25) in 2006, suggesting that Europe is on its way to becoming the most important region of origin of immigrants to the UK (Figure 4.2). Poles, who account for an increasing proportion of WRS applicants,[6] were already the single largest nationality of immigrants to the UK in 2005 (Office for National Statistics 2006a). Yet, these figures are also incomplete because they are based on a relatively small sample and refer only to those people who are intending to migrate for one year or longer.

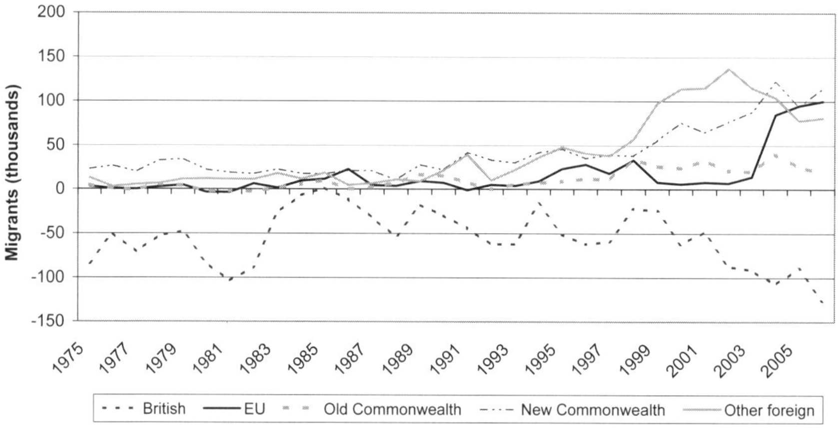

Figure 4.2 Total net migration to the UK by citizenship, 1975–2006

5 Between May 2004 and December 2006, there were 558,705 successful WRS registrations.

6 71 per cent of approved WRS applicants in 2007 Q4 were Polish, compared to 60 per cent in 2005 Q2 and only 57 per cent in 2004 Q4. Indeed, while the number of Polish applicants continues to rise, the number of successful applicants from Estonia was 63 per cent lower in 2007 than 2005. Registrations from Latvians fell by 52 per cent, Lithuanians 39 per cent and Czechs 30 per cent between 2005 and 2007 (Home Office et al. 2008). This is perhaps explained by the more rapid falls in unemployment in these countries and their higher economic growth rates in comparison to Poland, since unemployment and GDP are good predictors of A8 migration (Cooley et al. 2005; Gilpin et al. 2006; Blanchflower et al. 2007).

IPS data also indicate that outflows of A8 migrants have started to increase, indicating that at least some migration from the new EU Member States to the UK is temporary, although since returning migrants are only captured by the IPS if have been in the UK for a year or more, it will take some time before patterns of return migration of A8 nationals arriving since 2004 become clear.

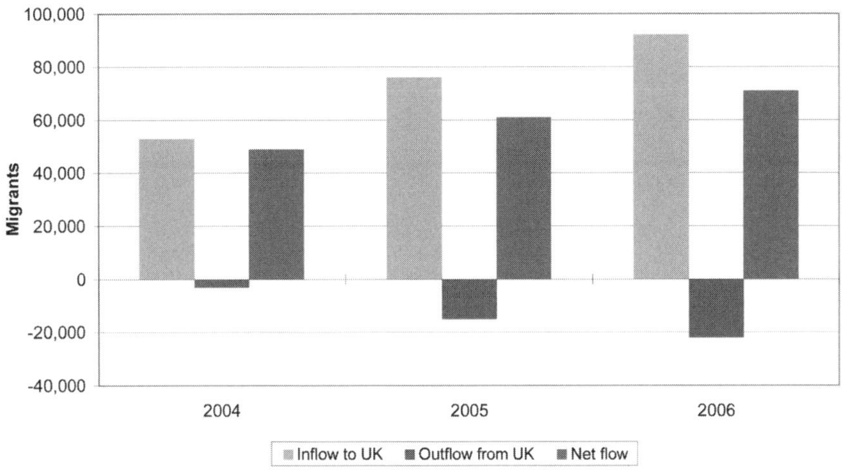

Figure 4.3 Net flows of A8 nationals to/from the UK, 2004–2006

Yet there is considerable evidence to suggest that most A8 migrants will not even appear in the IPS migrant data. For example, IPS visitor data show that between June and August 2006, 92 per cent of A8 visits were planned for less than three months (Office for National Statistics 2006b). It is also likely that many A8 workers are engaged by employment agencies to work in temporary jobs (39 per cent of WRS registrants fall into the 'administration, business and management' category in which employment agencies sit). Some 22 per cent of Polish migrants in the UK are reported to be seasonal workers (CRONEM 2006). Figure 4.1 above suggests that a slight increase in applications occurs over the summer, suggesting seasonal employment. Recent *Accession Monitoring Reports* have included information on migrants' intended length of stay in the UK, as specified at the time of registration – although it is worth noting that migrants' plans often change and so their initial intentions may not reflect their actual length of stay. Table 4.2 shows the intended length of stay of A8 nationals registering during 2007.

In a survey conducted by Spencer et al. (2007), 24 per cent of A8 migrants stated that they intended to settle in the UK permanently. While this suggests that initial intentions to stay for shorter periods may change, it also

Table 4.2 **Intended length of stay, A8 migrants registering during 2007**

	Number of registered workers	Percentage of total registered workers
Less than 3 months	121,550	59%
3–5 months	3,450	2%
6–11 months	6,350	3%
1–2 years	8,645	4%
More than 2 years	16,465	8%
Do not know	50,505	24%

Source: data gathered from Home Office et al. (2008).

indicates that the majority of A8 migrants still intend to return to their home countries.

If we turn to the change in stock of A8 migrants collected from the quarterly Labour Force Survey,[7] the rises since 2004 are relatively small in comparison to WRS figures. Between spring 2004 and spring 2006, Walling's (2007) estimates[8] indicate that the stock of people born in the A8 states and in employment in the UK rose by 178,000. The stock of economically active and working-age A8 migrants rose by 194,000 and 214,000 respectively. Taking spring 2003 as the base year (in order to capture migrants who may have moved to the UK in anticipation of May 2004's enlargement), the increase in the stock of working-age A8 migrants was 237,000 by spring 2006. Updating these figures using more recent LFS data reveals a further jump of 211,000 in the year to the second quarter of 2007. This is likely to be a reflection not only of continuing migration from the A8, but also of the chances of migrants being captured by the LFS increasing with length of stay.

In summary, while it is clear that migration from the A8 to the UK since 2004 has been on an unprecedented scale, it is difficult to estimate accurately the increase in A8 nationals living and working in the UK at any one time. The LFS suggests a net increase in the A8-born population of around 140,000 per year since enlargement, certainly larger than official estimates but smaller than what many newspaper headlines report. The most comprehensive LFS-based study of A8 migration to the UK suggests that around one million A8

7 It is important to note that while the LFS can be used to collect data on country of birth, there is no indication of respondents' immigration status or route of entry. Data on people born in the A8 therefore include previous waves of immigrants, including refugees and European Volunteer Workers who came to the UK during and after the Second World War, as well as recently arrived migrant workers.

8 While there are concerns that the LFS under-samples minority groups (Ruhs 2006), Walling's analysis uses updated population weightings, improving the accuracy of these estimates. These population weightings are now included in LFS datasets.

Table 4.3 LFS-based estimates of stocks of people born in the A8 states, 2002–2007

	April–June 2002	April–June 2003	April–June 2004	April–June 2005	April–June 2006	April–June 2007
In employment	36,000	41,000	75,000	151,000	253,000	424,000
Economically active	39,000	45,000	77,000	163,000	271,000	451,000
Working age	57,000	71,000	94,000	190,000	308,000	519,000

Source: data gathered from Walling (2007) and LFS.

workers had migrated to the UK by the end of 2007, but that around half of these had returned home (Pollard et al. 2008). That rates of return migration are relatively high amongst A8 nationals seems to be consistent with the Irish experience (see FÁS 2006). Yet the LFS remains an imperfect measure of A8 migration since it is unlikely to record migrants who only plan to stay in the UK for a short period. Without an accurate measure of return migration by A8 migrants, the 2011 Census is likely to be the best opportunity to capture the size of the UK's new migrant population.

Economic Impacts

Unsurprisingly, the impacts of A8 migration on the UK have been the subject of much scrutiny. Again, there seems to be a divergence between assessments made by academics and policy makers (which have tended to suggest that the experience has been largely positive) and public discourse (which has been dominated by concerns over the negative impacts of A8 migration). We run through some of the elements of this debate briefly below.

Since post-enlargement migration has been dominated by working-age people (82 per cent of WRS registrants are aged between 18 and 34 (Home Office et al. 2008)), the employment rate of A8 migrants in the UK rose quickly following enlargement from 57 per cent in 2003 to 80 per cent in 2005, taking it above the non-migrant average (Gilpin et al. 2006). There is also evidence to suggest that A8 workers are complementing UK workers. The 2003 National Employer Skills Shortage Survey identified that there were 271,000 hard-to-fill vacancies, mostly in elementary occupations, health and social work, hotels and catering, construction and retail (Learning and Skills Council 2004).[9] These tend to be the occupations in which A8 migrants are found working. Unsurprisingly, many employers, particularly small enterprises, recruiting low-skilled labour feel that EU enlargement has benefited their businesses.

9 Although note that the absolute figures should be treated with some degree of caution since there may be incentives for employers to over-emphasise the extent of skills shortages.

Where employers have experienced difficulties in recruiting from the local labour force, A8 migrants have been praised for their work ethic and reliability (Anderson et al. 2006; Dench et al. 2006).

There is evidence that many A8 migrants are underemployed in these low-skilled occupations. A higher proportion of A8 migrants to the EU15 have medium and high-level qualifications than members of the host country populations (European Commission 2006a), yet they are concentrated at the lower-end of the employment spectrum in the UK. Drinkwater et al. (2006) find that although Poles who entered the UK after May 2004 have a higher average age of leaving education than almost all other post-enlargement immigrant groups, they are overwhelmingly employed in low-skilled jobs at low rates of pay.[10] Many migrants are prepared to accept this trade-off as they see low-skilled work as a 'stepping stone' to more professional employment (Anderson et al. 2006). However, this brain waste may mean that the UK is missing out on the additional skills of these migrants (Drew and Sriskandarajah 2006).

The effect A8 migration has had on the wage and unemployment levels of non-migrant workers has become one of the most controversial debates around EU enlargement. For the UK economy as a whole, migration from the A8 would seem to have been beneficial. Assessments by the Ernst and Young ITEM club (2006) and the Bank of England (2006) have found immigration from Central and Eastern European to be advantageous for UK businesses and consumers by easing inflation, allowing the Bank of England to lower interest rates by an estimated half a point. There have been suggestions that this necessarily means that for workers, migration has been detrimental. Yet while unemployment rose steadily rising to reach 5.6 per cent in August 2006 (its highest level in six years), reinforcing anecdotal claims that Eastern European migrant workers were undercutting wages and taking jobs, it subsequently fell to 5.2 per cent in the three months to January 2008 and wage growth remained buoyant, fluctuating around the 4 per cent mark over the course of 2006 and 2007 (Office for National Statistics 2008a; 2008b). While unemployment has since risen once more, there is little to suggest that this is linked to immigration. Rather, it is a result of the British economy heading into recession in late 2008.

Causality between immigration and wages and unemployment is far from established in the literature. For example, Gilpin et al. 2006 find no statistical link between the rise in the claimant count unemployment and A8 migration. Dustmann et al. (2005) and Manacorda et al. (2006) find no discernible impact of immigration on native wages, although they do suggest that the earnings of previous immigrants may be affected. A meta-analysis of studies of immigration into a range of developed countries finds the impact of

10 The exception is post-enlargement immigrants from non-A8 European countries where the average age of leaving education was 20.7 compared to 20.6 for Poles.

immigration on wages to be very small (Longhi et al. 2005). An April 2008 report by the House of Lords Select Committee on Economic Affairs, which considered the economic impacts of all immigration to the UK, not just that from the A8, states that '[t]he available evidence suggests that immigration has had a small negative impact on the lowest-paid workers in the UK, and a small positive impact on the earnings of higher-paid workers', and that the evidence 'is insufficient to draw clear conclusions about the impact of immigration on unemployment in the UK' (2008, 28–9).

The contention that migrants 'steal jobs' from locals is problematic since it assumes that there is a fixed 'lump of labour' – or set number of jobs in the economy, whereas, in reality, total employment continuously rose from around 27.5 million in the first quarter of 2000 to just under 29.5 million in the three months to January 2008 (Office for National Statistics 2008a; see also Goodridge 2006; Ruhs 2006). As Dustmann et al. note:

> Immigration may depress wages and employment of natives. However, it is by no means inconsistent with economic theory to think that long run responses to immigration may involve no effect, or that immigration increases wages of workers complementary to immigrant labour. (2005, F327)

Indeed, immigration of A8 migrants into certain sectors of the economy, such as fishing and agriculture, has increased output and expanded the demand for labour (Portes and French 2005; see also Dustmann et al. 2005). A Bank of England report (Blanchflower et al. 2007) argues that migration from the A8 has actually served to reduce the natural rate of unemployment. That overall vacancies are still high and hard-to-fill vacancies down only slightly from 2001 (Ruhs 2006) provides further evidence to suggest that the UK labour market continues to grow because of, rather than despite, EU enlargement.

Irregular Working

Portes and French see the increase in employment rates for A8 nationals described above as evidence 'that illegal or unreported working amongst [A8] groups may have been reduced as a direct result of access to the formal labour market' (Portes and French 2005, 15). Around 18 per cent of A8 migrants registered between May 2004 and June 2005 were in the UK prior to accession (Drew and Sriskandarajah 2006). Alongside legal workers, studies have found significant proportions of A8 nationals were in the UK before May 2004 either illegally or in states of semi-compliance (Anderson et al. 2006; Ruhs and Anderson 2006). The latter category is made up of people who had entered the UK legally but were in violation of their permitted work conditions. The 40,000 A8 nationals who were either in or working in the UK illegally would have been able to legalize their status through registration and starting to pay tax and National Insurance contributions.

By contrast, evidence from other countries in the EU15 suggests that applying restrictive labour policies has at best delayed migration flows, or at worst encouraged undocumented migration, which is likely to be detrimental for both the irregular and regular workforces (Farrant et al. 2006). We consider the implications for irregular working by Bulgarians and Romanians of the transitional arrangements put in place for the 2007 enlargement later.

Public Services

At the time of the decision to restrict labour market access for Romanians and Bulgarians, there was no rigorous empirical evidence of any adverse effects on public services resulting from the decision to grant freedom of movement to A8 nationals. Fears of benefit tourism had not been fulfilled, with only 21,759 applications for income-related benefits (78 per cent of which were declined). Only 6 per cent of those registered with the WRS have dependents under the age of 17, further suggesting that the pressure that A8 nationals place on the public purse is limited (Home Office et al. 2008).

Indeed, A8 migrants may be making important contributions to public services. Although recent arrivals from the European Union may not be as represented at the higher end of the earnings spectrum as previous cohorts of migrants, they still make important tax contributions. Their taxable earnings may be based on a low basic wage (over three quarters are paid the minimum wage) but they make up for this by working longer working hours than the occupational average (Anderson et al. 2006). Furthermore, many A8 migrants are working in public service occupations, for example driving buses or working as care assistants (Home Office et al. 2008).

Yet anecdotally, there have been some concerns that A8 migration is putting a strain on public services. These appear to have been made primarily in places that have not historically experienced large flows of immigration and do not have the resources or institutional knowledge to cope with large inflows of people. Indeed, WRS data suggest that only 12 per cent of A8 workers are based in London, with the rest spread widely across the UK, often in rural areas (Home Office et al. 2008). The Audit Commission has recently published research on the local challenges posed by increased inward migration (Audit Commission 2007), and this adds much-needed empirical evidence to what had otherwise been a largely anecdotal discourse. The research suggests that pressure on local services has not been as great as some commentators have claimed, although it does highlight some specific and perhaps unconsidered impacts, such as increased use of internet terminals in public libraries. The Audit Commission argues that local capacity is not necessarily linked to the scale of recent migration, but more by previous experience of migration and diversity.

It appears that a lack of sufficiently detailed data collection has meant that some local authorities, even those more used to receiving substantial population inflows, were caught unaware, and that resources from central government did not respond quickly enough to changing population sizes. As a response, in August 2006 the Local Government Association suggested that local authority taxes might have to rise by 6 per cent to cover the costs of coping with rising migration in some places (BBC News 2006b; Wintour 2006).

Social Cohesion

A8 migrants appear to have experienced a more positive reception into local areas than other migrant groups, particularly ethnic minority and Muslim immigrants. This is due to the way that the dynamics of race, ethnicity and religion strongly influence how new migrants are received in the UK (Pillai 2007), but should not be taken to imply that the experience of A8 migrants has been entirely unproblematic. Pillai's research also uncovers notable undercurrents of tension around resources. Hostilities are most prominent in economically vulnerable, small, rural communities where changes in population are more apparent. Established communities appear to be concerned about migrant's access to welfare entitlements and social housing as well as the impacts of immigration on wages, unemployment, house prices and public services. For example, there has been concern over the adverse effect that the arrival of migrant children has on Catholic schools, both in terms of access to admission places and the quality of tuition.

Research shows that there is a strong belief among Eastern European migrants that the responsibility to integrate lies with them, and that speaking English is central to achieving this. Being largely white and Christian, those migrants who have experienced hostility generally do not interpret this as racism, and local authorities do not see them as a group that should receive specific resources to encourage integration (Pillai 2007). While social cohesion does not seem to have suffered significantly as a result of A8 migration, we should not fall into the trap of assuming that Central and Eastern Europeans are immune from the racism and discrimination that previous groups of immigrants have faced.

The Approach to Romania and Bulgaria

It is in the context of the experience outlined above that the decision not to grant free movement to Romanians and Bulgarians should be seen. On the face of it, the decision should have been relatively simple: the same principles of, and promises about, free movement were at work, and the populations of the accession countries were smaller this time around. In many ways, flows of people between newer and older members of the EU should be the most regular of migratory flows. For operational reasons too, allowing free movement may have made sense, allowing already overstretched immigration control resources to be directed away from restricting the movement of EU citizens who have right to travel to the UK, and towards people who require visa clearance.

Yet political concerns arising out of the post-2004 experience led to a different outcome. Once again, the debate was played out extensively in the media, with concerns about further 'uncontrolled' immigration being repeated. Some of the counter-arguments that were deployed in 2004 were not as effective this time around. For example, although the number of job vacancies in the UK economy has fallen only slightly, there is the feeling that this labour demand can be met by EU25 nationals without the need for Romanians and Bulgarians. Similarly, many feel that the UK's liberal decision in May 2004 secured its place as champion of EU values and that this time it would not do the UK any harm to follow other Member States' examples.

As a result, UK policy on free movement changed with respect to the 2007 enlargement. On 24 October 2006, the government announced that it would impose restrictions on the numbers of Bulgarians and Romanians allowed to work in the UK (Home Office 2006a). While highly skilled Bulgarians and Romanians are still be able to enter the UK through the work permit scheme or top tiers of the new Points Based System, lower-skilled Bulgarians and Romanians are only able to access a limited number of 20,000 temporary positions per year in the food processing and agricultural sectors. The government has advised that it will review this policy annually and that it will consider extending the low-skilled quota to other sectors, but only if there is sufficient evidence of demand that cannot be met by workers from established communities. In October 2007, it was announced that the transitional arrangements would be extended for a further year. As with the WRS, these restrictions do not apply to students who will continue to be able to take up part-time work while studying (up to 20 hours per week). Nor do they apply to self-employed Bulgarians and Romanians who are free to come and work in the UK (and in fact, they have been able to come for some time under the European Community Association Agreements).

We believe that five key factors arising out of the previous experience of EU enlargement led UK policy makers to override commitments to the principle of free movement and any operational concerns, and instead impose a restrictive approach to the free movement of workers from Romania and Bulgaria. Each is dealt with in turn below.

Anxiety over Numbers

Numbers have played a central role in the policy reversal towards Bulgarians and Romanians. The data on WRS registrations that were collected with the intention to reassure the public has ended up by having the opposite effect. The numbers do appear to be large and unprecedented in recent UK immigration history, especially when deployed in the contexts that they are often discussed. For example, anti-immigration voices and sections of the media have cited these statistics squarely alongside the far lower government-approved estimations of the expected numbers of accession migrants. This has led to headlines about actual flows being several tens of times greater than what was predicted, leading to the conclusion that 'This confirms that the government hopelessly underestimated the likely immigration from Eastern Europe' ('Million migrants flood in', *The Sun* 9 February 2005).[11]

The disparity between government estimates and actual numbers can be *partly* explained by the way the available data are continuously misquoted and therefore blown out of proportion (Sriskandarajah 2006). Very few commentators and political leaders have explicitly acknowledged the difference between gross and net flows. That many migrants who have registered with WRS have gone home is a fact missing from almost every account of this phenomenon.[12] Headlines such as '"Nearly 600,000" new EU migrants' (BBC News Online 22 August 2006) suggested that these people all resided in the UK at the time, which was clearly not the case. WRS data collection methods have exacerbated this confusion. The government predicted *net* immigration flows but collected *gross* immigration flows. With no provision for migrants to de-register from the WRS when they leave the UK, the only sources of gross flows are surveys such as the IPS and LFS.

Other sources have compared data of different time periods. A BBC Online article written two and a half years after 2004 accession states 'Ministers expected up to 13,000 a year to move to the UK, but 600,000 have so far' (BBC News 2006c). As time passes, so the apparent disparity between the figures will grow still further. Another earlier example deliberately confused visitor and migration flows. The article 'Million migrants flood in' (*The Sun* 9 February 2005) opens with 'A MILLION Eastern Europeans have come to Britain since EU enlargement in May last year, official figure revealed today.' However, this figure actually refers to the estimated 923,000 *visitors* and not *migrants* who came to the UK from A8 countries. Sensationalist media reports have been given credence by statements by respected public figures such as Frank Field, a Labour MP and ex-minister, who stated in July 2006:'We foolishly went ahead and had an open-door policy and instead of between 5,000 and 13,000 people arriving, in the first year something like half a million did' (BBC News 2006c).[13]

While clearly significant and larger than government estimates, flows of Central and Eastern Europeans to the UK do not look as striking against the

11 Other examples include 'Eastern European migration "far exceeds estimate"' (*Daily Telegraph* 11 November 2004, 10) and '1M migrants flood Britain' (*Daily Express* 9 February 2005, 2)

12 Notable exceptions are Tahir (2004) and Watt and Travis (2006).

13 The actual number of registered workers in this period was 250,000.

207,000 British citizens who left the UK on a permanent basis during 2006 (Office for National Statistics 2007). We do not want to suggest that the size of migration from the A8 states has not been considerable. However, it needs to be put in a wider context that includes considerable return migration (Pollard et al. 2008) and the high mobility of British people themselves within Europe (Sriskandarajah and Drew 2006).

Finally, while there is anxiety over the numbers at the national level, this is perhaps more acute at the local level and here there is little available data. Sir Sandy Bruce-Lockhart, chairman of the Local Government Association has suggested that it is difficult for councils to find the resources to 'provide services to growing populations that are not recognised by government statistics' (Slough Borough Council 2006). Karen Dunnell, the national statistician, and David Rhind, chairman of the government's Statistics Commission, have also commented on the need for a robust system for measuring internal and external migration (Wintour 2006). There have been calls from senior business leaders, including the Confederation of British Industries' (CBI) Susan Anderson, for pausing before allowing further EU migration until this is in place (BBC News 2006d).

Context of Control

Another emerging priority that explains the change of approach has been the desire of the government to be seen to be in control of the immigration system. While this has been the case for the last few years, a series of events during 2006 have made it political imperative for the government to be seen to be acting tough on immigration. These events included the apparent release of around a 1,000 foreign national prisoners from UK jails without their being considered for deportation, a sex-for-visas scandal and the discovery that the Home Office itself had been employing illegal immigrants to clean some of its buildings. These and other events led to the departure of the Home Secretary and to his successor declaring that the department he had inherited was not 'fit for purpose'.

In order to rebuild public confidence, the new Home Secretary's emphasis has been all about being 'in control' of immigration. This was made clear in a speech he gave in August 2006 where he broke with the government's usually flexible approach to economic migration by talking of wanting only an 'optimum number of migrants' (Travis 2006). Greater importance has been placed on enforcement and removals, the Immigration and Nationality Directorate (IND) has been renamed the UK Border Agency and has been given greater management powers through transfer to agency status, uniforms have been issued to immigration officers, and the enforcement budget has been doubled.

This desire to 'control', or at best 'manage', flows stood in contrast to the principle of 'free' movement of workers within an enlarged EU. Political arguments for restrictions seem to have become more tempting even though, as we discuss later, the restrictions in this case will not necessarily mean more effective 'control' of flows from Romania and Bulgaria.

Concern over Social Impacts

As well as economic impacts, labour migration has brought with it some challenges that if not addressed could have serious social implications. Policymakers will undoubtedly have listened to these genuine concerns over the welfare of established communities and the calls for a 'pause' in migration that went with them. The setting up of a Migration Impacts Forum clearly signals the Home Office's concern that migration is resulting in negative social impacts, and will consider impacts on community cohesion and public services (Home Office 2007).

John Denham, a Labour MP and Chair of the Home Affairs Select Committee has been vocal in his concern that A8 migrants have pushed down the wages of bricklayers in his constituency and forced many out of work. He also asserts that the existence of cheap and young labour is also hampering the government's target of getting those on welfare to work (Swinford 2006). The CBI Director, Richard Lambert has said that while relatively cheap migrant labour has been good in filling skills gaps in the short term, if there is no investment in upskilling the established community, it could lead to unemployment, poor health and crime in the long term (Eliot 2006).

There are also concerns within government about public service provision which partly derive from resource allocation based on inaccurate population data (discussed above) and A8 access to welfare entitlements. A leaked Home Office document entitled 'Migration from Eastern Europe: Impact on public services and community cohesion' discusses how hospital beds are being blocked by A8 migrants who are unable to leave since they are barred from social care benefits. Inability to access housing benefits or be housed in a shelter has led to large rises in A8 homelessness, particularly in London. This trend has led Homeless Link to advocate a pause on allowing Eastern Europeans who could end up in the same position coming to the UK (Homeless Link 2006). These concerns are real but it is doubtful whether imposing transitional arrangements will alleviate them. Restricting further migration will not make them go away; rather it may aggravate some of them – for example, if Romanians and Bulgarians move to the UK by exercising their right to visit as EU citizens and then stay on, and are unable to access the labour market, they may end up destitute.

Perceptions of Romania and Bulgaria

It would seem that public perceptions about Bulgarians and Romanians are less favourable than those of other Eastern European nationals. These perceptions revolve around criminality and corruption, but also the large Roma populations of Romania and Bulgaria. As in the rest of Europe, Roma are the subject of much prejudice in the UK (see MORI 2001). A briefing paper issued by MigrationWatch UK (2006), an anti-immigration pressure group, carefully notes the large number of Roma and ethnic Turks living in Romania and Bulgaria.

The visa scandals that occurred in Bulgaria in 2003 also confirmed in many peoples' minds that there would be large numbers of immigrants 'trying to beat the system'. Some of the perceptions were apparently confirmed in a leaked Home Office document of July 2006 that warned of '45,000 undesirable' criminal migrants expected to arrive in the UK from Romania and Bulgaria after accession (Cracknell 2006). While the strength of these opinions are difficult to test, their existence will have at least contributed in part to the tough stance taken by UK policy makers, either because they themselves believed them to be true or because they knew their room to manoeuvre was limited by public perception.

Other Countries' Policies

The government announced its decision to allow free movement in the case of the 2004 accession states three years before enlargement. When it came to the 2007 enlargement, though, existing Member State governments played their cards much closer to their chests. The 'diversion effect' that restrictive policies in four-fifths of EU15 states had on the UK has been clear. While the UK government announced its decision on the 2004 accession countries early, other Member States waited as long as possible in order that they would know each others' decisions.

If other countries had announced their intentions to open their labour markets to Romanians and Bulgarians before October 2006, there is the possibility that the UK's decision may have been different. There is much evidence to suggest that Romanians and Bulgarians will migrate to Spain, Italy or Greece rather than the UK, if given the choice (Drew and Sriskandarajah 2006). There are stronger previous migration networks and bilateral labour agreements between these countries. Romanians are Italy's largest foreign-born population and Spain's third largest (before Britons). In contrast, there are around 10,500 Romanians living in the UK.[14] If Spain and Italy had said 'yes' prior to the UK's decision, perhaps the government would have followed suit. In the end, Italy placed some restrictions on Romanian and Bulgarian workers and Spain is operating a work permit scheme which will be replaced after two years by an open-door policy (BBC News 2007b).

---

14 7,500 Romanian-born people were recorded as living in the UK in the 2001 Census. The Labour Force Survey shows that this number increased by 41 per cent between 2000 and 2004 (IPPR 2006a).

The Consequences of a Closed-door Approach

It is quite possible that the UK's policy turnaround could exacerbate many of the problems that it was intended to alleviate. The announcement of transitional arrangements failed to convince those on the right who are critical of the government's record on immigration, and created fears on the left that it could provide opportunities for irregular working and exploitation of migrants. Indeed, it could be argued that the seemingly tough decisions will neither calm public fears over immigration nor show the government to be in control of immigration.

Opportunities for Irregular Working

The most important implication is that by restricting the labour market access of people who can freely enter the UK as EU citizens, the UK government risks creating more opportunities for irregular working. As of January 2007, Romanians and Bulgarians can travel without a visa to the UK for a period of up to three months. Once they are here, it is possible that those who do not have a legal right to work will slip into the irregular workforce. There are also greater possibilities for semi-compliance or 'disguised working'. Romanians and Bulgarians may claim to be self-employed but become, in effect, sub-contracted employees. A2 students could quite easily work more than their permitted weekly hours. Some of the problems that have in the past led to the closure of visa regimes, namely that participants do not leave when their visa has expired, are likely to apply to the low-skilled quotas for Romanians and Bulgarians (Ruhs 2006).

As the A8 countries' economies grow, aided by EU structural funds, the incentives for A8 citizens to migrate will be reduced and many will return to take up opportunities at home. The unemployment rates of all of the A8 countries apart from Hungary have fallen since accession in 2004,[15] economic growth rates have been impressive (ranging from 3.9 per cent in Hungary to 10.9 per cent in Estonia in 2006),[16] and wage growth has also been high, reaching 27.2 per cent in Latvia, for example (Eurostat 2007). At the same time, events in the UK, such as the 2012 Olympics construction project, could further increase the demand for low-skilled workers. Although the government

---

15 According to Eurostat data on total unemployment rates, available at epp.eurostat.ec.europa.eu/portal/page?_pageid=1996,39140985&_dad=portal&_schema=PORTAL&screen=detailref&language=en&product=STRIND_EMPLOI&root=STRIND_EMPLOI/emploi/em071.

16 Eurostat data on growth rate of GDP volume, percentage change on previous year, available at epp.eurostat.ec.europa.eu/portal/page?_pageid=1996,39140985&_dad=portal&_schema=PORTAL&screen=detailref&language=en&product=STRIND_ECOBAC&root=STRIND_ECOBAC/ecobac/eb012.

has the flexibility to extend the quota system to other sectors, employers may turn instead to the informal labour market, whether that be wittingly or due to confusion surrounding the immigration status of accession nationals.

Migration Flows

Data for other EU15 states indicate that restrictive policies do not automatically curb labour migration flows. The European Commission's report (2006) on the effects of transitional arrangements showed that A8 nationals accounted for only 0.4 per cent of the total British working population in 2005. Proportionally, this is smaller than in Austria (1.4 per cent) and Germany (0.7 per cent) where free movement of workers was *not* granted. While these countries had larger initial populations of A8 nationals, there have been reports of undocumented working, bogus 'self-employed work' or sub-contracting to get around restrictions. An increase in irregular migration will do nothing to allay the public's fears about large numbers of arrivals.

The approach taken towards migration from Romania and Bulgaria also has implications for the availability of statistics on migrants from those countries. With no equivalent of the Worker Registration Scheme for the 2007 enlargement, the Home Office reports on Romanians and Bulgarians rely on compiling several different sources of administrative data, and it is likely that researchers and policy makers will have to wait until the release of International Passenger Survey data for 2007 before a more accurate measure of the scale of migration from the two new Member States becomes clear.

Administrative data on the number of Romanians and Bulgarians registering to work in the UK since their countries' accession are presented in Table 4.4. The table indicates that the largest group of migrants applying for registration certificates are the self-employed. Indeed, the proportion of self-employed Romanians and Bulgarians amongst those registering would seem to be higher than the proportion of A8 nationals who are self-employed, which is not surprising given that this is the only truly free route through which they can access the UK labour market.

The data pose the question: would this number of Romanians and Bulgarians have taken up self-employment in the UK if transitional arrangements not been put in place, or have they been diverted into self-employment by the restrictions, as we anticipate above? One way of answering this question is to compare total inflows to the UK against estimates of likely migration to the UK from Romania and Bulgaria under the assumption of free movement. IPPR's research has suggested that, based on the A8 experience, 41,000 Romanians and 15,000 Bulgarians would have come to the UK in their first year of EU membership had they been granted free access to the labour market (Drew and Sriskandarajah 2006).

A total of 22,930 Romanians and 14,930 Bulgarians registered to work in the UK in 2007. This is a total of 37,860, compared to the IPPR estimate of

Table 4.4 Successful registrations by Romanian and Bulgarian nationals, 2007

		January–March 2007		April–June 2007		July–September 2007		October–December 2007	
		Romanians	**Bulgarians**	**Romanians**	**Bulgarians**	**Romanians**	**Bulgarians**	**Romanians**	**Bulgarians**
Registration certificates	Exempt	1,315	925	735	425	470	335	345	245
	Highly skilled	20	25	15	15	25	20	35	20
	Student	215	115	380	270	660	320	695	420
	Self-employed	1,920	735	4,005	1,115	2,705	930	1,635	680
	Self-sufficient	115	85	135	95	120	65	90	45
	Family members	1,005	630	825	295	575	225	565	210
	Total	*4,590*	*2,515*	*6,095*	*2,215*	*4,550*	*1,895*	*3,365*	*1,625*
Accession worker cards	Work permit	255	245	270	325	215	335	190	430
	Other	155	20	175	35	230	30	140	20
	Family members	115	25	180	45	145	50	60	15
	Total	*525*	*290*	*625*	*405*	*595*	*415*	*390*	*470*
SAWS	Total	890	1,535	875	3,105	95	100	335	360
	Grand total	*6,005*	*4,340*	*7,595*	*5,725*	*5,240*	*2,410*	*4,090*	*2,455*

Note: Values may not sum to totals due to rounding

Source: data gathered from Home Office and Department for Work and Pensions 2007a; 2007b; 2007c; 2008

56,000 without transitional arrangements. Taking into account people who do not register, we might surmise that the transitional arrangements have only had a limited impact in terms of stemming inward migration. The high proportion of self-employed workers in the data suggests that the restrictions have diverted people into self-employment. Of course, an alternative explanation is that the IPPR estimates of migration flows were wrong, and indeed other estimates were as high as 620,000 for the first two years of Romania and Bulgaria's membership combined (Open Europe 2006) and 290,000 in the first 20 months (MigrationWatch UK 2006), but these alternative estimates seem unfeasibly high.

The data do not, of course, include those working in the UK illegally. There is the potential for investigative journalists to find Romanians and Bulgarians working illegally in the UK, which will create yet another crisis in public confidence. The government has proposed on-the-spot fines for A2 nationals found working illegally and heftier charges for their employers, but whether this will be effective is questionable. Research in other countries has found that while undocumented migrants are scared of the authorities, they are not deterred from migrating (Lazaroiu 2003).

Exploitation

The government has also announced its intentions to extend efforts to crack down on exploitative businesses. This will be essential if the government is to protect both British and foreign, regular and irregular workers from exploitation and possible wage depression in the short term. It needs to extend this enforcement campaign to employment agencies that recruit A8 migrants. After accommodation and travel costs are subtracted, often even legally registered Central and Eastern European workers do not receive the minimum wage and many go without entitlements such as sick leave and holiday pay (see Anderson et al. 2006). In Sweden, free movement of workers was permitted in 2004 on the condition that monitoring systems were in place to ensure that local and migrant workers had the same working conditions. Some argue that this highly regulated labour market explains the lower numbers of A8 migrants who entered Sweden compared to the UK post-accession (Tamas and Münz 2006; Ruhs 2006), although it may also result in diverting migrants into self-employment.

Despite the 2005 Immigration, Asylum and Nationality Bill[17] giving authorities greater powers to tackle exploitative employers, there are still doubts that the government can effectively prevent abusive employment practices. Ruhs (2006) finds that its track record has not been commendable. Although the number of 'successful enforcement operations' against irregular

17 Available at www.publications.parliament.uk/pa/cm200506/cmbills/013/2006013.htm.

workers has increased (from 390 in 2003 to 1,098 in 2004), the prosecution rate of employers has remained extremely low – only reaching 21 Section 8 prosecutions in 2004/05. Penalties have also been low. More than half of those prosecuted received a fine of less than £700 – which hardly amounts to an effective deterrent (Ruhs 2006).

If commentators and others are concerned that Eastern Europeans may undercut wages and be favoured in the low-skilled job market, then they should be most concerned about illegal immigrants. Irregular migrants are thought to be concentrated in high-demand and low-wage sectors (Farrant et al. 2006), most likely undercutting the minimum wage. Irregular workers are also extremely vulnerable to exploitative working practices. The inability to regulate the health and safety of this sector has had tragic outcomes, for example the death of 23 Chinese cockle pickers in Morecambe Bay in February 2004 (Casciani 2005). There is some anecdotal evidence that Romanians and Bulgarians, who have come to the UK since January 2007, are being exploited by gangmasters (Lawrence 2007). Because of their limited immigration status, these workers are often unable to escape the conditions they find themselves in.

Public Perceptions

The decision to restrict labour market access has done much to endorse and even intensify already negative perceptions of the newest EU nationals. Concerns about 'undesirables' and 'criminals' coming from Romania and Bulgaria have been acted on and legitimated. There is also the possibility that the signal that the restrictions sends out will damage community relations. Many will see the restrictions as an official admission that A8 migrants are pushing down wages and 'stealing jobs'.

Finally, arguments that placing restrictions on A2 workers will keep criminals out of the UK seem to be misplaced. If anything, traffickers and employers of irregular workers now have a larger population of people to play with. Despite the restrictions, ministers are still concerned that criminals from the two newest Member States will come to the UK. A leaked memo states that 'there is a concern that free movement will encourage people from Romania and Bulgaria to come to the UK, drawn towards organized criminal activities already well established in the UK' and cites figures suggesting that Romanians are responsible for 80 to 85 per cent of UK cash point crime (Hickley 2006). The transitional arrangements also appear to have done little to prevent other people perceived to be undesirable by the British public coming to the UK and featuring in the news media – for example, Roma children in Slough (BBC News 2007c).

Furthermore, the government's decision to place restrictions on access to the labour market by Romanians and Bulgarians does not appear to have satisfied the demands of sections the media for a tougher immigration regime.

The Sun newspaper, for instance, criticised the restrictions as both unworkable and not 'tough' enough, and the anti-European UK Independence Party leader described them as 'a sham' (Porter 2006). Headlines in the run-up to 1 January were also reminiscent of those in May 2004, and included '£4 flights to bring EU invasion' (*The Sun* 30 December 2006).

In the absence of comprehensive evidence on post-enlargement migration flows from Romania and Bulgaria, we are reliant on anecdotal evidence of the impact of the more restrictive regime, often supplied by the very same newspapers that have sensationalized the UK's experience of A8 migration. Tabloid newspapers have reported how easy it is for Romanians and Bulgarians to come to the UK and either register as students and gain the right to work part-time or become self-employed (Lewis 2007), and have run headlines such as 'Pickpocketing on the increase as Eastern European gangs trawl London's West End' (*Daily Mail* 16 February 2007).

Conclusion

The UK experience before and since the 2004 EU enlargement demonstrates clearly some of the fundamental challenges facing migration policymakers. On paper, allowing free movement of workers within an enlarged EU seems straightforward. The movement of relatively small numbers (compared to the total EU population) of workers across largely uncontrolled borders seems true to the principle of free movement upon which the EU was built and true to the promise of EU integration given to acceding members. Yet, as we have seen, the political context in which domestic decisions are taken has meant that what was a bold and beneficial decision in 2004 became an almost impossible option in 2007.

In the two and a half years between the two decisions being taken, there has been a curious interplay between evidence and public opinion. The government may have taken the bold decision of allowing free movement of workers but, driven by the need to reassure people that things would be under control, it created the WRS in 2004. Yet the larger-than-expected (gross) flows revealed in WRS data have simply served to undermine confidence further. This seems to have made the UK government even less trusting of estimates of likely flows from Romania and Bulgaria, and even keener to ensure that public concerns are seen to be addressed. Yet we remain sceptical whether the measures taken to address these concerns are likely to be successful.

The government's approach to the 2007 enlargement was more restrictive, but much of the evidence available on inflow of Romanians and Bulgarians to date is anecdotal and supplied by the very same media outlets that helped create the hysteria that contributed to the government's decision to operate a closed-door policy. This risks feeding a vicious cycle whereby media reporting of failed attempts to 'clamp down' on migration drives ever more desperate, but no more effective, attempts by policy makers to reduce migration flows.

As we have discussed above, in the short term, restrictions on Romanian and Bulgarian workers may lead to the unpalatable situation of promoting irregularity. Although the move to restrict free movement of workers from these countries may have allowed the UK government to reassure the British public that it has immigration 'under control', there is a risk that public confidence may be further undermined if irregular flows increase or if large numbers of Romanians and Bulgarians come to the UK as self-employed workers. Early data suggest that transitional arrangements may not have had a significant impact on migration flows from the new Member States to the UK, although we can only speculate on this point since there is such a large disparity between estimates of inflows under conditions of free movement, and because data on migration from the EU's two newest Member States are still scant.

The challenge of managing migration into the UK raises the broader question of how effective UK employer enforcement is and will be over the next few years. If the UK government can live up to its promise of cracking down on irregular working, then some of the real and political dangers can be minimised. However, going on past experience, this may not happen as effectively or as quickly as leading politicians would like.

SECTION 2
Going East:
The British in Bulgaria

Chapter 5
Property and Transnational Neoliberalism: The Case of British Migration to Bugaria

Deema Kaneff

Introduction

According to the Office of National Statistics in Britain, British citizens now own approximately a quarter of a million second home properties abroad, which is more than twice as many as ten years ago (Aspden 2005, 55). During the same period, 1994/95 to 2003/04, the total level of UK household investment in foreign property increased three times (Aspden 2005, 56). The largest proportion of this activity by far has been expended in Europe so it seems to me that the question, which needs to be asked, is: why this huge rise in property ownership abroad, especially in the last decade? The answer, I suggest, needs to be sought, at least in part, in terms of the effects of neoliberalism across Europe. This general statement needs immediate qualification, since neoliberal policies have been implemented quite differently in different parts of Europe and at different times – even within countries considerable variation exists between regions.

My focus in this chapter will be on British property buyers in rural Bulgaria. In the previous seven years, there has been a boom in the sale of properties in Bulgaria and the property market has strengthened further since EU accession in January 2007. Indeed, in 2007 apparently 35 per cent of all financial investments in Bulgaria were property related.[1] Foreign involvement has played a prominent role since 30 per cent of all property deals were made by foreigners, mostly by British citizens and companies.[2] While the market is most developed at the Black Sea, ski resorts and particular cities (such as Varna and Sofia), there are also pockets of interest in some of the picturesque rural regions of the country, including the northern central provincial region of Veliko Turnovo – the focus of this chapter.

Below I look at why British people move – either seasonally or permanently – to rural Bulgaria. We might expect that this mobility is encouraging a pattern of increasing inequality as 'rich' foreigners displace 'poor' Bulgarians. Indeed,

1 www.chambersz.com/index.php/content/view/10303/109.

2 www.sunnyvillas-bg.com/bg/faq.php.

in the tourist areas the exclusion of Bulgarians due to impossibly high prices is a feature of the local property market. Yet in the rural area discussed here, that is, an area which does not attract pure investors and prices are still modest, the issues are not so clear cut. Are the Bulgarians really the 'poor victims' in this equation and the Britons really the 'wealthy exploiters'?

The first section, below, provides background information concerning the property market in Bulgaria and discusses the importance of property in the neoliberal context. The following two sections focus in turn on the British buyers and then the Bulgarian sellers. In the former case, I argue that 30 years of neoliberal policies have pushed many potential British second home owners from the more exclusive areas (France etc.) to the more affordable, cheaper Bulgarian market. It is downwardly mobile Britons, who are buying in rural Bulgaria. As for the Bulgarian sellers, neoliberal reforms since 1989 have produced increasing levels of economic and social insecurity (as elsewhere in Europe) and, as a result, selling second homes is one response by asset 'rich' people strapped for cash. The conclusion to the chapter returns to raise some more general points on the issue of property and transnational neoliberalism.

The Growing Importance of Property in Bulgaria

It has been argued that neoliberal policies contribute to an 'accumulation by dispossession' whereby wealth is amassed by a relatively small part of the population and through the expulsion of others from their resources. These resources can be either material, such as land or even common/collective/state resources – e.g. state pensions, access to education or health care. (Harvey 2005, 159–60). Such accumulation processes are at the centre of new social inequalities, which are increasingly excluding sections of the middle and working class (Dumenil and Levy 2005; Friedman 2004; Harvey 2005; Thornton 2004; Turner 2004).

Property ownership is one concrete and therefore particularly useful way of exploring this link between neoliberalism, accumulation and inequalities. Furthermore, there are both national and transnational dimensions to this accumulation process – the property market is a useful tool for trying to gain an overview of how national and international processes are interconnected. In the case discussed here, I suggest that national UK neoliberal policies have international consequences, since downwardly mobile sections of the British middle class are responding to their declining position by 'relocating' to another country (an 'escape' made possible by the deregulation of markets and revolutions in technology, which have created new opportunities for transnational responses to national problems). Thus accumulation and inequalities need to be studied transnationally. Indeed, a study of downward mobility and increasing inequalities, which is restricted to the national arena, would miss an important sector of the population – those who manage to move away. A study of foreign engagement in the Bulgarian property market allows us to look at transnational responses to declining national living standards.

The role of property as a form of security seems to be a central, but often ignored dimension in understanding transnational responses to neoliberalism. The privatisation of property was a fundamental platform of postsocialist neoliberal reforms across eastern Europe. However, the significance of private property as both a reform and ideological tool[3] has distracted attention away from the importance of property as a form of security. While 'neoliberalism' is a term that can refer to a wide range of policies, which get played out differently in different contexts, one constant is the inevitable reduction in state welfare provisioning – as state assets and resources get transferred to the private sector as a result of privatisation. This leads to diminishing social protection for citizens (irrespective of the context). At the same time, neoliberal doctrine encourages individuals to take over the responsibility of his/her own welfare (rather than relying on state assistance). I suggest that as the state has withdrawn from many areas of social provisioning, people have become increasingly 'obsessed' with property buying/selling as a way to secure their retirement and realise economic security. This has both national and transnational implications, in both Bulgaria and Britain.

Furthermore, revolutions in communication technology have accompanied the expansion of transnational property markets. New technologies have been particularly important in establishing, developing and enabling the expansion of the market. The importance of the media and internet have played a particularly prominent role in the Bulgarian property market. British buyers to whom I spoke identified one TV programme as the original source of their knowledge about Bulgaria – Channel 4's programme 'A Place in the Sun', which followed a British couple who were looking for a place to buy in a foreign country.[4] The programme was screened on British TV in September 2001. Afterwards the information was

3 Privatising property was the first and probably most important step in dismantling socialism and establishing a market economy. Indeed, it was viewed as a precondition for the creation of a successful market economy. Private property was also a central political and ideological tool. Property was, and still is, a 'flagship' for identifying a 'democratic' system (the reality is, of course, much more complicated, with all political systems made up of different combinations of and emphasis on private and public ownership).

4 Sharpley (2004, 24, 30) also notes the importance of TV programmes in influencing British tourism. The market is clearly shaped by the media. For example it was not until 2005 (some four years after the first programme on Veliko Turnovo was shown in Britain) that a programme was made featuring the city of Plovdiv. Non-coincidentally, a foreign market in Plovdiv began developing soon after. In the late summer of 2005, I interviewed an Irish estate agent who had set up the first Plovdiv-based agency to sell houses in the region. What has been happening in Veliko Turnovo is a sign of what developed in Plovdiv. Clearly the media acts as a trigger for social movement (a topic beyond the focus of this chapter, but nevertheless worth noting, see Verdery 2003, ch. 2).

published as a book, leading to a flurry of other TV programmes specifically about Bulgaria, as well as numerous articles in newspapers and journals. A large number of buyers on the internet also claim to have bought properties in Bulgaria 'blind' – simply bulk buying from internet sites (although this was more characteristic to investors buying in other parts of the country). There are also countless internet sites where properties are advertised and sold, while chat forums bring together buyers and sellers in conversations that cover various topics; everything from advice about reliable lawyers to moral issues relating to wealthy foreigners buying up cheap Bulgarian properties. New forms of technology have made the property market more accessible to 'ordinary' people and constitute the foundation for a core site of market activity that brings together buyers and sellers enabling the expansion of trade.

It is precisely with such 'ordinary' investors that I am concerned below. The process of accumulation is often thought about as involving large players, such as commercial developers in the case of property. While commercial developers and big individual investors are undoubtedly active in particular regions of Bulgaria, for example, the Black Sea and ski resorts, in the rural region which is the focus here it is individual actors that are prominent. I attempt to ground my analysis of transnational neoliberalism by showing how global players need not be big international organisations nor faceless players;[5] often they are 'real' individuals, sometimes themselves victims of neoliberal policies at home who, in trying to address their own precarious positions by seeking security abroad, become, en masse, a significant force in the process of the expansion of neoliberalism across Europe (often with negative repercussions for those in the destination regions). It is precisely such individuals, rather than commercial developers, who are the focus in this chapter.

Bulgaria has developed a new reputation as a relatively cheap and desirable location for British property buyers.[6] A number of factors have contributed to this interest in Bulgaria: the end of the socialist state leading to the incorporation of Bulgaria into the (capitalist) global economy; plus the country's sunny climate, red wine, beaches and ski facilities; as well as its accession to the EU. Indeed, a recent study shows that for Britons buying a

5 Global actors are often represented, in social science literature, as faceless and nameless players, abstract entities referenced only as coming from 'international financial organisations', see, for example, Verdery 2003, Introduction.

6 Of course, there is a long history of north Europeans buying in southern Europe (e.g. Dwyer 2000; Sharpley 2004; Waldren 1997). In the British case, for example, Spain, Italy and France are traditional locations for property buyers and particularly popular destinations. Clearly, second home ownership is not only triggered by neoliberal reforms. Nevertheless, I suggest that the huge increase in the second home market in the last decade, and the particular interest shown by British buyers in rural Bulgaria, is a process closely connected to neoliberalism, unlike parallel processes of some 30 years ago that took place in other regions of Europe.

holiday home abroad, Bulgaria has become the third most popular destination after Spain and France (and unlike Bulgaria, both these other locations are declining in popularity).[7]

The Bulgarian property market, established in 1998, was initially chaotic and transactions and sales only gained momentum after 2000–2001. Ownership of land by foreigners is not currently permitted. In recognition of the uneven playing field, a seven year moratorium following EU accession was put into place, which was designed to protect Bulgarians from exclusion in a market where foreigners have far greater capital resources. However, there are ways to circumvent such laws which are widely publicised in the media.[8] The most common method is for the foreign buyer to register as a Bulgarian firm, since companies can legally own land. Most estate agents provide an all-inclusive service with lawyers, who handle these technicalities for the buyer.

The now booming market is proving to be a good investment opportunity, with properties in certain areas increasing in value by 20–30 per cent annually over the last four to five years, a situation that estate agents predict will continue for the next few years. Many thousands of Britons now live permanently in Bulgaria, others are spending the summer months in their newly acquired properties. The number is increasing rapidly: according to a BBC Radio 4 report (24 February 2005) – in 2004 alone over 10,000 British people brought properties in Bulgaria.[9]

The areas, which are proving most popular, are the Black Sea (now reaching western/Spanish prices) and Bansko (in the mountains). While much of the foreign investment has focussed on these areas and is often carried out on a large scale by commercial developers, there are other pockets of interest, including in certain rural areas. The focus here is on precisely such a case, that is the Veliko Turnovo region, where I have been carrying out research for 20 years, and which now, in the last few years, has become a 'hot spot' for foreign property buyers. In fact, as the sea and ski resorts become so expensive that they are moving out of the price range of many westerners, Veliko Turnovo, amongst other places, is increasing in popularity. A provincial capital, the medieval town has a developed tourist industry, which is much smaller than

7 *The Herald* 'Britons find Bulgarian Prices are right for holiday homes', 29 December 2005.

8 See, for example, the *International Herald Tribune* (Thursday, 13 April 2006, article by M. Brunwasser).

9 In should be noted that in the previous six months, since writing this chapter, circumstances have changed, reflecting trends in the global economy. With the global financial crisis and recession in Britain, British investment has slowed down considerably in Bulgaria (although other investors, such as Russians, are still active players). However, the fact that British buyers in the rural parts of Bulgaria are not simply investors means that this group's activities have not been curtailed to the same extent as those buying in Bulgaria purely for investment purposes.

the other better known areas of Bulgaria. Its rural character also determines the type of investors it attracts and the development that is taking place. Rural property is not considered as safe an investment as coastal or mountain properties, or as the urban centres of Sofia or Varna. It is much cheaper, partly because there is an abundance of land and run-down, deserted houses and demand is much lower than for other select locations in Bulgaria. So it is a different type of buyer, who is attracted to the Veliko Turnovo region – one whose main concern is not necessarily a good investment; at least of equal importance is the desire to find a home to live in (seasonally or permanently). Those looking for properties solely for investment purposes continue to buy in the prime coast and ski resort locations.[10]

British Buyers in Rural Bulgaria

From the interviews I have held with Britons looking for, or already owners of property in the Veliko Turnovo region, it is clear that a majority move to Bulgaria – seasonally or permanently – because of the better life conditions offered in the country. Internet site participants reveal a similar viewpoint: people move because of a wide range of dissatisfactions with life in Britain from rising insecurity caused by state welfare reforms (such as pension reforms[11]), to lack of cohesion and solidarity in terms of social relationships. I have cited several examples elsewhere (see Kaneff forthcoming) and here simply wish to emphasise this point, by quoting Nick, a British estate agent living and working in Veliko Turnovo since 2002. Of his own situation he said that he came to Bulgaria 'not out of bravery but out of desperation' and went on to say that '99 per cent' his clients migrated to Bulgaria for similar reasons, 'because they are fed up with life in Britain'. He continued that 'the ones that come are those wanting something better than what the UK can offer them, those wanting to better their lives'.

What is evident from the statements made by buyers is a feeling of disenfranchisement with life in Britain. In other words, what is being experienced is the destruction of forms of 'social solidarity' (Harvey 2005, 23[12]): people

10 See also *The Independent*, 'Bulgaria enchants Britons', 15 March,2006.

11 Described as the biggest shake up to the UK pensions system since the creation of the welfare state in the 1940s: http://news.bbc.co.uk. (Sunday, 21 May 2006), the reforms include restoring links between pensions and earnings, the raising of the pension age, as well as plans to encourage people to take responsibility and save more for their own retirement.

12 In describing the revolutionary turn away from Keynesian policies following Thatcher's election in 1979, Harvey reminds us of the new Prime Minister's famous declaration that there is: 'no such thing as society' (2005, 23). He continues that: 'All forms of social solidarity were to be dissolved in favour of individualism, private property, personal responsibility and family values' (2005, 23).

feel disempowered. They witness chaos and disruption all around them – in their relationships, neighbourhoods and at work. There are many dimensions to this uncertainty – both material and also emotional (rising mistrust and so on). Anger is expressed at the apparent unfairness in the social security system that cannot/will not guarantee people, who have worked all their lives, a secure retirement. Substantial changes to the welfare system have been a persistent feature of British governments from Thatcher's to the present and are commented on and experienced by British buyers in terms of declining state pensions, evident erosions to health services and to social welfare (see www.mybulgaria.info, 14 October 2004). In short, people feel uncertain about their present and are worried about the future.

One solution – for those who can afford it – is relocation to another country, where a person's spending power is higher, saved money will bring more security in the form of property ownership, and where the quality of life both materially and in other ways is judged to be far better. The 'British obsession with property', to quote a term used by a second British estate agent in Veliko Turnovo (and widely repeated in internet discussions) is about achieving greater security. As the estate agent explained, properties are not only 'homes' to the British, they are also 'investments' – guarantees for the future.

Significantly, almost without exception those buying in Veliko Turnovo are not from the southeast of England, but from the more economically and geographically peripheral areas of Britain – Scotland, the Midlands and Wales.[13] These buyers can be divided into two groups. The first is made up of those who have, to date, been excluded from the foreign second home market because of prohibitively high prices. The cheaper east European prices appear to have made second homes accessible to a broader sector of the population, which was previously excluded from the second home market abroad. This view is supported by a newspaper article that triggered a considerable amount of internet discussion in 2005. When the journalist Rosie Murray-West, writing for *The Times* newspaper, accuses British buyers in Bulgaria of 'land-grabbing', she raised a lot of resentment amongst British property owners, who debated her article for many days on the internet. One internet writer retorted:

> For the 'Torygraph' to talk about land-grabbing does sound just a tad hypocritical surely. I wonder how many holidays Rosie spent at Daddy's place in the French Alps … now that the secret is out and there are opportunities for 'ordinary' people to purchase a second home abroad … The paper has come across all moral and high and mighty. (www.mybulgaria.info, 28 March 2005)

13 I leave aside the question as to whether this means that the demographically wealthier investors from southeast Britain are still buying in Tuscany, France and the Caribbean.

Other buyers make it clear that while once they could have afforded the west European markets, they can no longer do so; eastern Europe is the only place that they can afford a second home. For example: 'We initially became interested in BG because as far as buying property abroad goes, it was our one and only chance because our limited spending power had priced us out of places like France' (www.mybulgaria.info, 24 March 2005). A couple from Manchester I interviewed in Veliko Turnovo during 2004 said that they were interested in property because 'it's cheaper here than in Spain or Portugal and also less commercialised'.

In all the above cases, the 'ordinary people' (to borrow the term from a previous quote), who can now engage in the cheaper end of the foreign property market, can be distinguished from wealthier property owners, who buy second homes in the Caribbean, France and other exclusive European locations. This view is reinforced by a Veliko Turnovo estate agent, who reported that: 'Many buyers come from the north of England, they may be on lower incomes and leading stressful lives, so they opt to go and live where the cost of living is so much cheaper'.[14]

Another group of buyers comprises those Britons, who are totally excluded from the British market: eastern Europe is the only place they can afford to buy property at all. One such case cited in the internet was of a divorced man, who lost his home following legal separation and now finds himself unable to re-enter the British property market. It also includes younger families, who are unable to buy in Britain at all, that is, first home buyers. One internet user describes the situation in the following way:

> In Britain the kids brought up in coastal villages, nice bits of London or the Lake district etc can't afford to live there when they come to buy. They have to move to live in places that are not their ideal. You can't change that. You can't go back in time. It is simply a fact … It's capitalism. (www.mybulgaria.info, 26 April 2005)

Across the board, the younger generations are struggling, unable to buy the same types of property that were available to their parents' generation.

Both the above groups – those excluded from the British property market and those excluded from the more exclusive and expensive foreign second home market – are buying in the Veliko Turnovo region. The vast majority are small investors, who do not have large amounts of capital to risk. Indeed, many pointedly note that the opportunity to buy in Bulgaria is their only chance to buy a house with no mortgage (a couple of others confess to having taken out loans in order to buy in Bulgaria). For many of these people, owning Bulgarian property is their 'nest egg' for retirement. In this sense buyers in rural Bulgaria are distinguished from, for example, Irish buyers, who have increasing amounts

14 *The Independent*, 15 March 2006.

of capital to spend and can engage in a foreign market that, until recently, was occupied by more wealthy Britons. There is no evidence of Irish clients buying in rural Bulgaria. Instead, they buy in the more expensive touristy areas – the Black Sea, ski resorts etc. – where investment is a primary concern.

If we wish to go beyond simply identifying our British investors as 'small-time' and coming from the economically and politically peripheral regions of Britain, then we need to link this discussion to the issue of class (a theme very much present in some of the above quotations). Marxist-influenced writings on class in a new global order agree that globalisation, as 'the international face of neo-liberalism' (Saad-Filho and Johnston 2005, 2) is a world wide strategy of accumulation (Saad-Filho and Johnston 2005; Harvey 2005). These neoliberal policies worldwide are creating an increasingly wide rift between the 'new global elite' and the downwardly mobile middle and working classes (Friedman 2004). While the welfare policies adopted by western nations between World War 2 and the early 1970s were viewed as having largely achieved their main objectives of promoting upward social mobility, increasing economic equality and the expanding the middle class (Turner 2004, 86), most authors agree that a reversal of these processes has been in progress ever since (for reasons why this is happening, see Turner 2004, 90-1). 'One of the primary effects of neo-liberalism was the restoration of the income and wealth of the upper fractions of the owners of capital ...' (Dumenil and Levy 2005, 14; see also Harvey 2005). The middle class is now contracting in size: with some individuals moving up into the globally privileged classes, while many more slide down into the ranks of the lower classes and underprivileged (Friedman 2004; Thornton 2004; Turner 2004). The increasing polarisation of classes – for example, evident in terms of incomes and social conditions – is a process exacerbated by the loss of provisions previously provided for by state welfare.

Once amongst the relatively 'secure' property owners in Britain, members of both the middle and working class have experienced a decline in their standards of living (Friedman 2004; Turner 2004). New patterns of property ownership – whether one can buy and if so, where – becomes one of the ways in which downward mobility can be tracked and studied transnationally. Those buying in rural Bulgaria come from the downwardly mobile population in the UK, individuals struggling to maintain their standards under increasingly difficult circumstances. The British buyers quoted above talk about their weakened position in terms of an erosion in economic/social security and entitlements. Foreign property ownership is one way in which such downward mobility is being addressed: it is a strategy adopted by particular sections of the British population in an attempt to reduce their own precarious positions.

The rural Bulgarian property market has, therefore, developed as a response to the declining situation of a certain segment of the UK property owning classes – those that can no longer afford the more traditional (and expensive) markets abroad for second home ownership (often retirees who can make their pensions stretch much further in Bulgaria); and those who have been totally squeezed out of the British market with Bulgaria providing their only chance of home ownership. The underlying reason for engagement in the Bulgarian market – of both groups – is the need for greater security (financial, emotional and social) in the context of increasing British uncertainty and downward mobility.

The Bulgarian Sellers

So much for the 'wealthy' British investors. How about in Bulgaria, where neo-liberal policies have a shorter history (post-1989) and a market economy is still in the process of being developed?

Statistically, Bulgaria shows up as being a poor east European country.[15] At the same time, other statistics suggest that the story is far more complicated, since house ownership is high.[16] In fact, reports state that Bulgaria has amongst the highest levels of home ownership in Europe with over 90 percent of Bulgarians being home owners and at least one third owning more than one home.[17] This is not something that has occurred recently, but is a situation inherited from the socialist past.

Fifty years of socialism brought about a dramatic improvement in living conditions for a vast number of people, not only through a universal and free educational and health system, but also through a social security system, which guaranteed employment for everyone able to work, universal pension schemes and holiday leave (even for agricultural cooperative workers in rural areas). During socialist times, provincial Veliko Turnovo was a relatively wealthy agricultural region that produced various grain crops as well as certain fruits, such as grapes for wine. It was also a centre of light industry. However, the region went into a spiral of decline after 1989, with the state's withdrawal of financial support leading to the reduced operation and closure

15 For example, see http://www.fiw.ac.at/index.php?id=246&L=3 (The Vienna Institute for International Economic Studies) and www.nsi.bg/GDP_e/ECP_e.htm (National Statistical Institute, Bulgaria).

16 This discrepancy raises fundamental issues about how 'poverty' should be understood in Bulgaria (and other east European contexts) where individuals are rich in 'assets' if not in 'cash'. In any case, a western- oriented idea of poverty that focuses on homelessness or hunger is not necessarily the most appropriate criterion.

17 See *Novonite*, 7 March 2006 (citing the European Quality of Life Survey). *The International Herald Tribune* goes even further, saying Bulgaria has amongst the highest levels of home ownership in the world!, 27 March 2006, article by M. Brunwasser. According to the National Statistics Institute in Sofia, almost 95 percent of Bulgarians are home owners (National Statistics Institute 1995) and one third of Bulgarian households also own more than one home (National Statistics Institute 1994). While these figures are over a decade old, they nevertheless still point to high home ownership patterns in the country.

of many industrial enterprises and agricultural cooperatives. Unemployment rose sharply, with provincial towns suffering in particular (in many cases one half of the population was out of work with little prospect of ever working again). Twenty years later many parts of the province, outside the main business belt of the provincial capital, are still in economic decline. It remains a deindustrialized zone.

In the village where I have carried out fieldwork since 1986, which I refer to as Talpa,[18] some 35 km from Veliko Turnovo, the population continues its steady decline. This process, an effect of socialist industrialisation, was initiated well before 1989, but the decrease in population has been accompanied after 1989 by a lack of resources for the maintenance of the infrastructure and services. Concerned with the continued loss of population the village council has been grappling to find solutions to a community in decline. A programme in early 2000, supported by the mayor, gave empty houses (rent free) to homeless Roma in an effort to bring the community back to life. However, this only resulted in new problems and local tensions in the community (see Kaneff 2006).

From the sketchy outline of regional and local history given above, we can identify the elements that have led to the accumulation of house ownership in socialist Bulgaria. Several factors stand out. Firstly, the paternalist socialist system assumed responsibility for costs relating to health, education and so on, and in so doing, provided high levels of social and economic security, thus creating positive conditions for the accumulation of property. This was made easier in a context of an undeveloped property market so that once property was acquired, for example through inheritance, it was unlikely to be sold. The ownership of two or more homes may not have been a goal of socialist policy, but it was an unintended consequence. Nick, the UK estate agent mentioned earlier, recognised this association between socialism and security when he told me that:

> I've never lived in an ex-socialist country before and the people here have taught me quite a bit. I always thought from what I know before that Communism was all bad, but I hear from a lot of people here that this is not so, that during socialist times they had a lot of security. And they miss this.

Secondly, industrialisation resulted in a dramatic shift in population, from rural to predominantly urban areas.[19] This movement of people out of the villages involved an accumulation of property, as village homes became second properties – a process particularly true in the northern-central part of

18 This is not the real name of the village, but a pseudonym.

19 Rural-urban migration from the 1940s to the 1980s reflected a dramatic demographic reversal: from 70 per cent of the population living in rural areas and 30 per cent in the urban areas in the late 1940s, to approximately 30 per cent living in rural areas and 70 per cent in urban areas 40 years later (Kaneff 2002, 189).

Bulgaria where industrialisation from the 1960s onwards resulted in massive rural depopulation, as young people moved to the cities to work. It is not simply that people attained second residences, but often the village home was left unused. In the province of Veliko Turnovo, those that moved short distances – for example, to the provincial capital – were able to return on weekends to maintain the house and work the land. However, for those who moved further – to Sofia or Varna, for example – the house and plot were not maintained.

Thirdly, and associated with the above, are demographic factors linked with modernisation: the characteristically large numbers of siblings of the early 20th century became a thing of the past by the end of the same century. During the latter years of socialism it was common for families to average one child, resulting in a small number of inheritors owning a greater number of properties. Not only has the population significantly declined, but it has also aged. Talpa represents a typical picture. It has seen a massive fall in population over the last 50 years; now only one-quarter of the number of inhabitants live in the village as compared to the Second World War.[20] Since the 1980s Talpa residents are predominantly elderly – two-thirds of the village's inhabitants are pensioners.

This is a common picture throughout the northern Bulgarian countryside. A low birth rate and an aging population, combined with migration to urban areas over the past 40 years, have resulted in the abundance of deserted rural properties. Rural properties are not a scarce resource. It is these empty houses – second (or third) homes that cannot be maintained by the family – that are being put up for sale.

The abundance of housing is evident in web site discussions where Bulgarians and potential British buyers communicate. Multiple home ownership is not uncommon. One Bulgarian woman engaged in the internet discussion with British citizens, wrote:

> Generally speaking, I don't come from a wealthy family, but I haven't had a day of suffering [here she is replying to a previous comment by a Briton that Bulgarians 'suffered' under communism]. By contrast, I have been to East London and witnessed the sufferings of the British working class first hand. In addition – most Bulgarians already have what you're trying to acquire – a house. I personally own 2 apartments and a house in a village. (www.mybulgaria.info, 12 April 2005)

Another Bulgarian also entered the conversation:

20 At the end of the Second World War (1946) Talpa's population was almost 2000 but this had declined to half of that by 1975 (i.e. to 1075). In 1985 the population was approximately 750 (Natzionalen Statisticheski Institute 1994, Tom: III: 90) and by 2001 it had fallen to 520 inhabitants (a figure provided by the village mayor).

> Bulgarians may be cash poor … but they are asset rich … I am 30, I own a flat in Sofia, a house in the country, land in Sofia and half of my parents' house will come down to me in due course. Does this make me rich? I don't think so. (www.mybulgaria.info, 12 April 2005)

One case I know of in Talpa was of a house that was sold to an Englishman (from the Midlands) approximately two years ago. The house is close to the central village square and was, until the late 1990s, occupied by an elderly widow. Her son lived in Veliko Turnovo and with his family came almost every weekend in order to help in the garden, growing fruit and vegetables that were preserved for the winter and shared between them. After the widow's death, her son tried to maintain the house and garden, returning regularly on weekends and the summer holidays. However, with his mother no longer present to contribute her full time energies to the garden, it became increasingly difficult. The situation came to a head following the death of his mother in law, as the family was then left with caring for two village homes. The financial and monetary costs involved in travelling between two houses in two different villages, and the inability to care properly for both properties or tend to the crops, resulted eventually in the son selling his mother's house in Talpa.

This story is not uncommon. Owners usually live in the towns/cities and the rural house remains empty – the previous generation having died. Sometimes pensioned urban residents return to live full time, or seasonally, in the village, leaving the city property to children or grandchildren. However, even in cases where the elderly couple leave the urban home to take up residence in the village, things are difficult if the couple has responsibilities for two or more rural homes and often one property is left in a state of disuse.

As noted earlier, the phenomenon of deserted houses was already a feature of the late socialist period, during which time people would normally hang onto homes. However today, with the new dominance of the market and accompanying decline in the role of the state leading to increasing insecurity amongst the population, owners consider the option of selling their rural properties. In many cases, owners are stretched for cash, even in debt, and getting rid of an unused rural property is an obvious solution. In Kaneff (forthcoming) I have cited one case of a pensioner whose wife died some three years earlier from throat cancer. He sold his home in a village neighbouring Talpa to a Scottish couple last year. The pensioner took this action because he needed the money to pay off debts incurred as a result of the many months of medical care for his wife (treatments no longer covered by the state). In any case, the village home had remained empty during the previous decade following the death of his parents. The pensioner's situation was common: with a low pension/wage and strapped for cash while at the same time carrying an increasing burden of costs once borne by the state, there was little choice but to sell off part of the assets accumulated during socialism.

Engagement in the market is a strategy adopted by Bulgarians forced to sell their land in an attempt to secure their increasingly vulnerable economic situations. If not motivated by debt, then often it is the need for capital in order to fulfil family financial obligations that is the driving force behind putting a property up for sale, for example, securing the material well-being of a child through the provision of urban housing (often the funds from a sold village house were used to place a deposit on an urban dwelling) or covering educational expenses.

It is somewhat ironic that it was under a socialist economy that home ownership flourished in Bulgaria, and that now, under neoliberalism which trumpets the importance of private property ownership many, at least in provincial Bulgaria, are having their property assets whittled away. It is also a sign for future concern, as the once 'ordinary' property owners in Bulgaria shed some of their resources, thus exposing themselves to greater risks in times of future crises and a higher level of insecurity in the present. After all, second homes can only be sold once.

Conclusion

The present buying and selling of Bulgarian property needs to be seen in the light of neoliberal reforms, which were initiated at different times in both Britain and Bulgaria. In response to the long term consequences of a shrinking welfare state and increasing insecurity, British citizens engage in the foreign property market for a number of reasons, including: as a way of achieving greater financial and social certainty in old age; or in order to enter the property market as first home buyers, having been excluded from the domestic market due to prohibitive prices. In short, property ownership in Bulgaria is a response to rising insecurity as well as exclusion from both the local and more lucrative foreign market. People, who buy in rural Bulgaria, are not from the wealthier property classes, but come from the increasing number of downwardly mobile Britons desperately seeking to consolidate their present and secure their futures – it is no coincidence that Bulgaria is referred to as 'the poor man's Tuscany'.

At the same time, 'ordinary' Bulgarians sell property accumulated before 1989 as a response to their increasingly precarious and vulnerable economic position. They sell assets in order to maintain living standards that are being threatened, or in order to stave off increasing poverty and debt in the new market economy. In both the British and Bulgarian cases, property is an important source of economic and social security, which in the neoliberal context has become part of the 'market forms of social security' mentioned by von Benda Beckmann and von Benda Beckmann (2000: 10).

There is considerable evidence that implementation of neoliberal policies increases social inequalities, concentrating wealth and power in some sectors and excluding a 'vast majority' (Harvey 2005, 118–19; Thornton 2004; Friedman 2004; Turner 2004). My case study underlines the importance of exploring how engagement in the market creates inequalities not only within a nation, but also between nations and global regions. Inequalities need to be understood transnationally: this can be achieved, in part, through tracing the long term effects of policy in one country and how it impacts on another part of the world. Nor is this process carried out solely by large or faceless international organisations/consultants. This is not to say that such conglomerates do not shape localities but transnational neoliberalism is also propagated by small players, 'ordinary' individuals, often themselves victims of neoliberal policies at home, who are trying to escape its worst effects by moving abroad. From such a perspective the picture becomes more complicated, one that cannot simply be conceptualised as between 'wealthy' British property owners and 'poor' Bulgarians. Such inequalities do exist, but adding the transnational perspective reveals the complexity and relativity of the story, which involves both British and Bulgarian citizens marginalised from their respective local markets. Those, who exclude, are also excluded.[21]

To finish, I raise the question of why it appears to be predominantly British buyers involved in the Bulgarian property market. After all, the phenomenon of foreigners buying properties is not confined to British citizens. Other nationalities also buy properties in Bulgaria and form their own communities within the countryside. Belgians also live in the Veliko Turnovo region and the settlement of Japanese near Shipka in the mountains has been widely reported in the Bulgarian media.[22] At the same time other east European markets have also become the target of foreign interest – for example, Croatia and Montenegro are important sites for the foreign property market. I have also collected anecdotal information about Germans buying in neighbouring Poland and Swedes in Estonia. Again, as in my Bulgarian case, there is evidence which suggests that foreign investors in these locations are also from the downwardly mobile sectors of the respective populations. Beyond Europe,

21 It is precisely because global phenomena are played out differently in specific local contexts (see also Nijman 2002), that my conclusions cannot be assumed to be relevant for other areas in Bulgaria where foreigners are buying property. In rural Bulgaria, I have shown that it is not a clear cut case of 'wealthy Brits' and 'poor Bulgarians', because the British buyers themselves are displaced and sometimes the buyers are a property-less class from their own countries. Of course, the really poor cannot even engage in the property market and do not have the option of buying abroad. However, had I looked at either the Black Sea or the ski resorts my conclusions may well have been quite different, because of the presence of wealthy individuals or multinational developers whose concern is pure investment.

22 See, for example, http://ide.li/modules.php?name=News&file=article+sid=40 , www.chamberszcom/old/index.php?option=news&task=viewarticle&sid=435&Itemi d=2, www.standarnews.com/archive/2005/03/03/reportage/index.htm.

a similar trend of US citizens buying property in Mexico is also apparently common.

So a tentative conclusion can be put forward that in situations where poor countries border wealthier ones, or at least are within travelling range, westerners, increasingly marginalised from their home markets, invest in cheaper property across the border. Returning, however, to the European context, my impression is that British engagement in Bulgaria is far more significant than that from other European countries. This is borne out in statistics, which show that Britons make up by far the largest number of foreign buyers (67 per cent), followed by the Irish (13 per cent), Spanish, Russians and others.[23]

In trying to offer an explanation as to why, I can suggest two reasons (both of which demand further investigation). Firstly, while home ownership in the UK is a relatively new feature for the majority of the population (Finch (1997, 132) notes that it was only between the 1960s and 1980s that a majority gained ownership of their homes), distinctive patterns of a social, economic and legal character give particular historical importance to the position of property in the British context. Property is 'multi-functional', associated with social prestige and status and 'a major factor in constituting the identity of individuals and groups' (von Benda Beckmann and von Benda Beckmann 2006, 2), as well as being associated with citizenship rights and entitlements (Verdery 2003, 16). This is not an aspect of property I can explore here: I simply wish to acknowledge that in Britain property ownership appears to hold particular historical significance that goes beyond neoliberal reforms of the post-1970s period and this is a dimension of the story that needs further examination.

Secondly, even assuming this is so, I would suggest that we need, once more, to return to the question of neoliberal reforms. Britain, along with the US, is singled out as having embraced neoliberalism to a greater extent than other European countries and in the process has become a society of greater social inequalities (see Turner 2004, 93; MacGregor 2005, 144; Arestis and Sawyer 2005). This suggests why other west European countries, which have not adopted neoliberal policies to the same degree, do not have such large numbers of disenfranchised – and de-property-ised! people – seeking security in the form of property ownership outside their own countries. It is a matter of degree: neoliberal policies were introduced most 'emphatically' in the UK (MacGregor 2005, 144) and it is, in the end, the repercussions of neoliberal policies on 'ordinary' British people searching for social and economic security, that is a major driving force of foreign involvement in the rural Bulgarian property market.

23 www.sunnyvillas-bg.com/bg/faq.php.

Chapter 6

From Foreigner to Neighbour: A *Standart* View of the Changing Patterns of Communication with British Settlers in Bulgaria

Irina Chongarova

Introduction

In the process of removing existing boundaries and creating new ones, the European Union project established new understandings of space, which form part of a whole institutional language. The terms 'Eurolect' or 'Eurospeak' were coined in the early 1990s to designate the language of European legislation (Goffin 1994; Cheshire 2002). This language or, more precisely, jargon, affects the meanings and connotations of words and concepts, which we use in our daily lives. Officially, Europeans are no longer foreigners in any EU country[1] – they are neighbours. However, to what extent is this formal interpretation reflected in the reality of a contemporary Europe in flux?

Mobility has been an integral part of social life across the Balkans since antiquity (Baldwin-Edwards 2006). Bulgaria was and is no exception (Bekiarova 2004; Krasteva 2005). It shares with its neighbours the destiny of a land situated at a crossroads – for centuries a destination for immigrants. However, one of the key differences in recent immigration to Bulgaria comes from the arrival of a particular kind of migrant – newcomers from Western Europe. This chapter will explore British migrants, especially those settling in Bulgaria. This settlement is clearly part of a global process of British migration. Reference will be made to this wider context but the focus will be on those British people, who choose to invest their capital – financial, social, and often emotional – in a small and still hardly known country on the southwest periphery of Europe.

1 'A foreigner in the understanding of this law is every individual person who is not a Bulgarian citizen, or citizen of another member state of the European Union, of a state who is a party in the Agreement on the European Economic Area, or of Switzerland Confederation' – The Law on the Foreigners, Art. 2. (Amended State Gazette, No. 29 of 2007).

Political and social scientists usually focus on large numbers and structural forces and, in the process, there is a tendency to neglect the migrants' agency. As a result migrant experiences of and reactions to cultural, economic and social inclusion and exclusion are relatively less explored in academic, media and political discussions. The media has played a key role in shaping public opinion towards the process of migration and towards the migrants themselves. Furthermore, it has been a very important factor in encouraging British property buyers to take an interest in Bulgaria.[2] All the new media channels, as well as the conventional ones, participate in constructing images of the migrants and in shaping attitudes towards them – both in the migrant countries of origin and in the host countries (Boomgaarden and Viegenthart 2007; Mazzoleni et al. 2003).

In the first section of this chapter, I will discuss images of the British in the Bulgarian national and regional press in order to understand the process by which the British have been represented in the Bulgarian media between 2001 and 2006, highlighting patterns that are revealed by that data. This period covers the five years before Bulgaria joined the EU when there was an effective balance between relatively low property prices and a relatively high degree of security (both personal and financial) for Western buyers. The second section will then closely explore one of these patterns, which is associated with the idea of being 'neighbours'. This pattern involves ways in which the process of mutual learning and discovering or failing to discover a common language is represented in the Bulgarian press.

Theoretical Framework

Given the focus on communication patterns in media representations, this study will operate at the intersection between media studies, intercultural communication and anthropology. Media and communication theory explores how the newspaper articles, as public discourse, do not simply address 'the public' but also create certain realities (Wimmer and Josef 2005; Robinson and Reeve 2006). As Stuart Hall (1997) argues, the media appears to reflect reality while, in fact, it constructs it. The theory of social representations (see, for example, Moscovici 1972; Bauer and Gaskell 1999), which is the wider theoretical framework for this study, emphasizes how society constructs social representations and the commonsense meanings which evolve from those representations. Representations can be textual and visual discourses, communicated through the media, as well as through the collective social cognitions of social groups created by shared social and cultural experiences, for example. The mass media provides the major source of these representations, and both cultivates and reflects them.

2 See Chapter 5 in this book, pp. 57–74.

A social representation consists of knowledge shared by members of a community about a given subject. It can be examined through the methodical study of the 'commonsense' knowledge of non-specialists. As Bauer and Gaskell note, '[r]epresentations are embodied in communication and in individual minds, shared in a way similar to language' (1999, 167). However, here I do not attempt to measure what 'the general public' or even the '(newspaper) reading public' think, since my focus will be on the media representations themselves. They will be explored in the context of how British settlers in Bulgaria are represented in three Bulgarian newspapers (predominantly *Standart*) between 2002 and 2006.

The study will draw on Critical Discourse Analysis (Kress 1990; Kaplan 1990; Weiss and Wodak 2007). The critical use of discourse analysis in applied linguistics is creating a different approach towards the understanding of media messages. Stressing the multidimensional structure of the text, Robert Kaplan argues that the understanding of grammar and lexicon does not constitute the understanding of text (Kaplan 1990). The comprehension of meaning lies not in the text itself, but in the complex interaction between the author's intent and his/her performative ability to encode that intent, and the receptor's intent and his/her performative ability not only to decode the author's intent but to mesh his/her own intent with the author's (Kaplan 1990, 203).

Critical Discourse Analysis has made the study of language an interdisciplinary tool and is used by scholars from different backgrounds. Most significantly, it provides the opportunity to adopt a social perspective in the cross-cultural analysis of media texts. As Gunter Kress points out, Critical Discourse Analysis aims to provide accounts of the production, internal structure, and overall organisation of texts (Kress 1990). In using this approach I will draw on content analysis techniques (see, for example, Krippendorff 2004; Wimmer and Dominick 2005)

Source of the Data

My study of the representation of British newcomers in the Bulgarian press began in early 2007. Initially, it was conducted as a collaborative study of certain national and regional Bulgarian newspapers. (Chongarova and Katsarska 2007). Here I will focus on data from the national daily newspaper, *Standart*, as well as two local newspapers – *Borba* and *Viara* – in areas where significant British settlements have appeared. Searches were limited to the articles published between 2001 and 2006 when there was a vast increase of interest in buying Bulgarian property among British nationals.[3]

3 The data for the research was discussed at the Intercultural Communication workshop within the MA Programme 'Media Communications' at the Paissii Hilendarski University of Plovdiv. Three MA students took part in identifying the

Why *Standart*?

There were several reasons for choosing *Standart* as a source for this study:

a. It is a national daily newspaper with the third largest circulation in Bulgaria (WAN 2007). It was established in 1992 and survived the turbulent years of political change since then due both to the professionalism of the managerial staff and journalists[4] and the ambition of being the 'newspaper for everybody' with the widest readership possible.
b. It is a politically neutral newspaper – it is neither red or blue. Red traditionally signifies the former Communist Party, renamed after 1989 as the Socialist Party, while blue is the colour of the Democratic movement, which has operated on the right of the political spectrum after 1989. It fragmented during the last decade into separate parties associated with different shades of blue – for example, the dark blue of the party Democrats for Strong Bulgaria.
c. The last but not least argument for *Standart* being used is the existence of an online version and free access to its archive. According to the World Association of the Newspapers data, it has the highest online readership among all the Bulgarian newspapers (WAN 2007, 823,675).

Standart was also the first online daily newspaper, which had an English version – *Standart News*. The choice of the materials for translation into English shows which topics are considered significant for communication to *Standart News* readers in English. I will comment on the *Standart*'s translating policy and strategy later in this chapter.

As for the local newspapers, *Borba* (Struggle) is the local newspaper of the Veliko Tarnovo region, where the earliest British settlements were registered. The electronic archive for year 2005 of the National Library was available for use and an MA student selected the relevant articles. The electronic version of the other newspaper – *Viara* (Faith) – which served the Blagoevgrad region, was also accessed and the relevant articles for 2006 were selected by another MA student.

potential articles for the research from the regional newspapers (acknowledgements in the footnote). Data collected from these sources was analysed to understand the process by which the British have been represented in the Bulgarian media between 2001 and 2006, highlighting patterns that are revealed by that data.

4 The professionalism of several *Standart* news journalists was acknowledged by the Bulgarian Pulitzer – an annual award for journalism named after a prominent Bulgarian medieval writer, Chernorizets Hrabar, http://www.sib.bg/news1.html.

Methodology

The archive of *Standart News* for the years 2001–2006 was electronically searched using the key words 'English' and 'British'. The hypothesis, confirmed by further research, was that the Bulgarian contributors to the newspapers used 'English' and 'British' predominantly as synonyms during this particular period. The choice of these keywords allowed us to observe a wide range of themes concerning the British and Britain. As a result of this search, clusters of articles, presented by their titles/headlines, were compiled for each of the five years. Within each year the articles were divided by month of publication, allowing us to observe the ways in which coverage of 'British issues' changed.

Inclusion and Exclusion Criteria

Explicit inclusion and exclusion criteria were created to identify the potential relevant articles for this research. For an article to be included in the review, it had to fulfil the following timeframe and topic criteria:

> *Criterion 1: Timeframe* The article is published within the five year period (2002–2006)
> *Criterion 2: Topic* The article deals with the British settlers (rather than British tourists or investors) in Bulgaria. This second criterion is more difficult to monitor, since it is connected with people's intentions, which might vary and have a particular dynamic.

O'Reilly, in her study on the British in Spain, which was based on different patterns of residence and mobility, distinguishes four different categories of migrants: full residents, who regard themselves as permanent residents in Spain and do not consider ever returning to their previous home country; returning residents, who are registered as legal residents in Spain and live there most of the time, but spend a few months, mainly during the summers, in their country of origin; seasonal visitors, who spend less than six months each year in Spain and hence are not officially registered; and, finally, peripatetic visitors, a diverse category of people who own second homes in Spain which they visit more or less regularly (O'Reilly 2000, 52). In this chapter we will treat O'Reilly's first two categories as settlers.

The exclusion criteria were respectively: Criterion 1: Not published between 2002 and 2006, Criterion 2: Not about the British settlers in Bulgaria. To identify relevant newspaper articles for the research, a two-step screening was conducted. The first stage was based upon the titles/headlines of the articles. Each was rated as 'include', 'exclude', or 'more information'. Where a title or a headline was marked either as 'include' or 'more information', a full text of the article was retrieved. The second stage of the screening was based upon full-text articles. The full texts of these articles were screened again and articles for an in-depth review were identified. The next stage of the study was an in-depth review of the articles which drew on critical discourse analysis including qualitative text analysis and content analysis techniques.

Findings

When applying the two key words 'English' and 'British' in the electronic search of the *Standart* archive within the timeframe of the study (2002–2005) 1,988 articles were identified (1,281 for the key word 'English' and 707 for the key word 'British'). Lists of titles/headlines were prepared for each of the five years, separated by the month of publication. Hence, all the articles satisfied the time-frame criterion. The retrospective analysis of *Standart*'s coverage of 'British issues' from the start of 2002 until the end of 2006 showed that this coverage considerably increased in terms of the number of articles written. The number of headlines referring to British/English doubled from 2002 (total 225: British 101; English 124) to 2005 (total 499: British 151; English 384), with a further considerable increase in 2006 (total 623: British 196, English 427).

The first stage of the screening, which identified the relevance to the topic criterion based upon the titles/headlines of the articles, produced the following results: 178 articles were rated as 'include', 523 articles were rated as 'exclude' and 1,337 articles were rated as 'more information'. Among the excluded articles were those in which the key words were accidentally used. Other excluded articles covered sports news (predominantly football), British 'partying' tourism, British celebrities etc. One thousand five hundred and fifteen titles/headlines were marked either as 'include' or 'more information' and the full text of these articles was retrieved.

The relevant articles from the additional sources (the regional newspapers *Borba* and *Viara*) were identified using both electronic and manual methods of searching. Due to limited access to these newspapers' archives, the timeframe for the research on the additional sources was respectively year 2005 for *Borba* (14 articles) and year 2006 for *Viara* (13 articles).

Headlines

The headlines of the relevant *Standart* articles present a lively picture of local attitudes towards those British people, who were interested in buying property and/or settling in Bulgaria. In the results of the searches for the first two years (2002–2003) British appear either within all those 'foreigners' approaching the Bulgarian property market: 'Foreigners Seeking out Villas near Varna' (*Standart*, 22 July 2002), 'Westerners Invade the Southern Coast' (*Standart*, 11 June 2002), or separately – 'Brits Buy Houses on the Black Sea Coast' (*Standart*, 31 August 2002); 'Brits Eager for Houses on the Coast' (*Standart*,

13 April 2003); 'Owning a House in Bulgaria – The Latest Hit for the Brits' (*Standart*, 5 June 2003); 'The Brits are Crazy about our Villages' (*Standart*, 21 July 2003).

The next three years (2004–2006) reveal new tendencies within the narratives such as individualisation and personalisation with specific names of people and places appearing in the article headlines: 'An Englishman Exchanges Essex with Vetren Dol' (*Standart*, 18 April 2004); 'The Village of Vruv Expecting Neighbours from England' (*Standar*t, 27 August 2004); 'The English Ambassador in Search of Property in Turnovo' (*Standart*, 22 March 2005); 'A Brit Learns to Cook Kavarma in the Bolyars' Manner' (*Standart*, 11 February 2005). These headlines indicate the process of British settlement in Bulgaria and the ways in which locals were getting used to the newcomers. 'Brits' are not simply numbers but people, who have bought a house on the same street or who own an apartment on the same floor. They are people who have names and faces.

An analysis of the words most frequently associated with English/British in *Standart* news headlines reveals the thematic emphasis and particular patterns in the collective image of the British in Bulgaria. I will briefly discuss here three emerging patterns: *the Invaders*, *the Saviours* and *the Neighbours* and will focus particularly on the last one.

The Invaders The IPPR report on Brits abroad (2006) analyses the scale and nature of contemporary British emigration. It suggests that around 5.5 million British nationals live overseas permanently (equivalent to 9.2 per cent of the UK's population). In addition, an estimated 500,000 British people reside abroad for part of the year, mainly through second-home ownership. This means that nearly one in 10 British nationals lives partly or all of the year abroad (IPPR 2006). For obvious reason these figures were mentioned far less in the UK media than the figures of the immigrants, who came to live in Britain and work in the UK labour market. The headlines in the British media threatening UK citizens with the Bulgars, who were coming, corresponded to the headlines in the Bulgarian media, showing concern and even panic about the British 'invasion' of Bulgaria.

Standart's headlines show a wide range of attitudes – from neutral (informative) to aggressive: 'Westerners Invade the Southern Coast' (*Standart*, 11 June 2002), 'The Last Piece of Land on the Coast is Being Bought' (*Standart*, 10 October 2005), 'Bankers from the British Isles Invade Pirin' (*Standart*, 3 September 2006), *The English and the Irish Occupy Pamporovo* (*Standart*, 02.01.2006), 'The Brits are Crazy about our Villages' (*Standart,* 21 July 2003), 'Englishmen Paying EUR 30 000 for a House in Rogachevo' (*Standart*, 14 April 2004). Even when the headlines reveal considerable indignation and hostility towards the British newcomers, there is also a degree of pride that the Bulgaria has been chosen as an attractive place for investment and settlement.

The Saviours The IPPR study reveals that about 12 per cent of the UK émigrés say they would like to leave because they do not like what Britain is becoming. As a number of headlines suggest, they feel saved from the vanity of the big city in Britain and revived by the Bulgarian countryside: 'Englishmen Seek Refuge in Our Villages' (*Standart*, 19 October 2004), 'British Citizens Find Paradise in Kableshkovo' (*Standart,* 13 November 2004). However, British settlers are both saved and saviours, since they often settle in depopulated areas and restore houses and whole abandoned villages: 'An English Businessman Buys Dilapidated Houses' (*Standart*, 21 April 2005), 'Englishmen Became the Mascots of Kurdzhali' (*Standart*, 3 April 2005). This pattern is much better revealed in the full text screening, where remarkable stories are told about villages, where the local Bulgarian population is the minority and the majority are the British newcomers.

The Neighbours Britons living in Bulgaria are not a homogeneous group, of course. They come from different demographic and socio-economic backgrounds, and have moved at different times and for different reasons. However, the majority of the settlers are those who were attracted by the relatively low prices of the properties and the most intensive period of the settling is 2004–2006 when cheap travel and European Union integration make the EU countries, such as Spain, France and Portugal but also Bulgaria and Romania, more accessible to British emigrants.

Bulgarian newspapers tell stories of British and Bulgarian 'ordinary' people living next to each other, such as 'The Village of Vruv Looking Forward to Neighbours from England' (*Standart*, 27 Aigist 2004), but also about those neighbours who are in the spotlight – 'British Citizens Living Next Door to Zorka Parvanova'[5] (*Standart*, 16 January 2005) and 'Businessmen and Aristocrats Living Next Door on the Coast' (*Standart*, 12 July 2006). The newspaper headlines reveal how different could be the relationship between neighbours since many things can happen in the neighbourhood – 'British Subjects Damage Cars in Local Potholes' (*Standart*, 25 May 2005), 'English Drama in Our Village' (*Vyara*, 30 October 2006) and 'An English Divorce Shocked Bulgarian Village' (*Standart*, 4 October 2006).

The headlines give us the feeling of the active interest of the British property buyers towards Bulgaria, which will be further explored in the full text of the articles.

Full Text Articles

The second stage of the screening was based upon full text articles. The total number of the publications envisaged for the second screening was 1,515. Full

5 Zorka Parvanova is the current Bulgarian First Lady, the wife of the Bulgarian President, Georgy Parvanov (since 22 January 2002).

text documents of these papers were obtained and were screened again using the same inclusion/exclusion criteria. One thousand three hundred and twenty of the articles were excluded, because they were not relevant to the topic focus (Criterion 2) and the number of articles excluded by both stages of screening is 1743. Consequently, 245 remained for in-depth review. The review of the articles involved the use of critical discourse analysis including qualitative text analysis and content analysis techniques.

The communication between the British and the local people and the potential for the development of their relationship is bound up with the potential for cultural adaptation between both parties in this relationship. As the IPPR 2006 study reports:

> the majority of British expatriates slip easily into their new communities. However, a small but significant minority are finding the settlement experience much more challenging. Often these Britons come up against linguistic and cultural barriers that they have not prepared for, and have, in response, clustered together away from the host society. (2006, ix)

The British abroad often display a low degree of cultural adaptation, which is very evident in the case of language skills. As research on British settlers in Spain shows, many British speak little or no Spanish and very few become fluent Spanish-speakers (Casado-Dıaz et al. 2004, 367). King, Warnes and Williams point out two reasons for this 'linguistic laziness' (2000, 135). One reason is that most social life occurs within national/linguistic communities, so there are few opportunities to speak the local language. A second reason is that help with interpretation is widely available for English-speaking settlers (see O'Reilly 2000).

This situation is even more relevant in the context of British in Bulgaria since Bulgarian, unlike Spanish, is not a language offered in the British educational system and is rarely offered by language teaching institutions. Acknowledging the fact that the British are the most monolingual nation, those who consider emigration from the UK as a possibility for the future are concerned about the decline of foreign language education in Britain. As one person noted when commenting on the IPPR report:

> With more and more people emigrating to non-English speaking countries, the decline of the foreign language learning at British education system has serious implications. It is extremely difficult to integrate into a new society if you do not speak the language. It makes filling out a form for a driver's licence much more challenging, let alone socialising with the locals. … The current focus on French is too narrow and could be widened to include Mandarin and Portuguese. With greater numbers of Brits moving to Bulgaria, should this language also be offered at school? (*Brits Abroad*)

Obviously, offering Bulgarian language as a foreign language in the British schools is extremely unlikely and British settlers in Bulgaria, who want to study the local language, have to rely on other possibilities, such as the method offered by the former Bulgaria jazz singer Marinella Pashova, who teaches in a church in London what a *kebapche* and *shopska salad* is:

> *Englishmen Studying Bulgarian in Church*
> An emigrant jazz singer wrote a Bulgarian language textbook for English settlers in Bulgaria. For the last two years the linguist Marinella Pashova teaches about what a Bulgarian village is like, how to become acquainted with their new neighbours, what's a *kebapche* and *shopska* salad and grape *rakiya*. The teacher from Pernik wrote the textbook in 2004, when she came across a site where Englishmen, who bought property in our country, desperately sought someone to teach them the language. She contacted them and organized a group of eight people. She rented a room in the local church next to her home and started the lessons. She first used a textbook published in the USA, but both the vocabulary and grammar proved too difficult. So she had to write her own textbook *Bulgarian for Brits* in 10 lessons with the most common phrases needed by foreigners in our country. (*Standart,* 23 December 2006)

Finding themselves in a Bulgarian village, British settlers meet the older generation of Bulgarians, who are familiar with only one foreign language – Russian – since this was the foreign language taught most widely in the Bulgarian schools during the socialist period. Because the idea of the neighbourhood and typical Bulgarian hospitality excludes the possibility of no communication, the Bulgarian village grannies are trying their best to communicate with their new English neighbours in the only foreign language they know:

> *British Citizens Find Paradise in Kableshkovo*
> Mahala Kableshkovo has become British. 'They are all mild and kind people, though we don't engage socially, we can't understand each other, anyway', 75-year-old Irina, living in Edelvais Str. comments with concern. In order to bridge the communication gap, the old ladies resolved to learn the 'damn' English language. Every evening at the village centre this is the main topic of discussion. The retired women enthusiastically demonstrate their knowledge, which so far amounts to 'good morning', 'goodbye', and counting to three. Self-education is hard to pursue but the enthusiastic ladies will not give up. They dream of teaching the foreigners to cook beans and stuffed peppers. Until then, they will rely predominantly on body language and Russian 'spasibo' and 'zdrastvui'. They are convinced, God knows why, that this will suffice. (*Standart*, 13 November 2004)

The *Standart* articles show different strategies by the British and Bulgarians for finding a common code to communicate. These strategies vary from ignorance to a strong interest in the language and the culture of the other: 'Englishmen Learning to read Bulgarian in Ustrem' (*Standart*, 22 June 2004), 'British Citizens Shopping in the Village via Dictionary' (*Standart,* 24 August 2005), 'Grannies from Buntsevo Discuss Politics in English' (*Standart,* 10 October 2005), 'Old Grannies Choose to Study the Language of Shakespeare' (*Standart*, 4 December 2005) and 'Communication in the Language of Gestures' (*Standart*, 29 August 2006).

> Margaret and Michael are one of the twenty British families who are in love with our Kosharitsa village … The British live in Bulgaria during the last 4–5 years, but they are not very enthusiastic about learning Bulgarian. The inhabitants of Kosharitsa, in turn, are not eager to learn English. The language of gestures, however, works perfectly well for both parties. As for class differences, nobody in Kosharitsa is fond of this topic, because, as locals say, nobody speaks about a rope in the house of somebody who has hanged himself. (*Standart*, 29 August 2006)

In other cases, learning each other's language becomes a matter for competition:

> There were three English settlers – Jamie, Stanley and Allen – among the Bulgarian pensioners celebrating the first anniversary of the Pensioners Club in Beliaskovets village. They are competing for who will be the fastest in learning the language: Bulgarian pensioners learning English or the English settlers learning Bulgarian. (*Borba*, 28 December 2005)

Cultural adaptation also includes an interest in local culture and participation in local rituals. The local Veliko Tarnovo newspaper reports the story of a 60 year old Englishman, who bought the former school building, since the local school was closed due the lack of children in the village. He plans to make it a hotel for motor bikers and to open a local museum of education – an exhibition of authentic school furniture and text books from the Bulgarian revival period, *Borba*, 10 August 2005.

An avenue for mixing British and Bulgarian everyday culture is provided by festivities and food preparation:

> *United Europe Invades the Largest Municipality of Varna*
> No one can keep track of all the surprises the foreigners living here have in store. They are more than 500 along the Kamchia River. More than 120 of them live in Avren and the neighbouring villages. There are over 20 nationalities in the area. Local citizens are proud to declare that their municipality is a miniature model of United Europe. On Christmas Eve

> Joy and Frank West opened a gaming hall in the first Bulgarian English pub. The new pub is located in a 300-year-old house, which the couple saw and liked. They bought it within a week after wavering between Bulgaria and Turkey for their choice of refuge for life. Joint preparations were made for the unique culinary competition entitled Avrena Pie – English Pumpkin Pie. The municipal jury overate while selecting the tastiest Christmas dishes. (*Standart*, 23. December 2006)

British migration to Mediterranean countries, especially to Spain, was bound up with the development of mass tourism but this was not the case with Bulgaria. British people arriving in Bulgaria had little or no knowledge (and, respectively, few expectations) about what life was like in the country. This 'ignorance' had, in some respects, positive consequences: without the burden of many stereotypes, British people were more flexible and more open to the locals. They found Bulgarians to be very kind and cheerful people, despite the results of the 'European social reality' survey, describing Bulgarians as the bluest people in Europe (see, Eurobarometer 273).

> 'We knew about your country only through pictures on the Internet. Actually, it is much nicer. The people are unlike the English. Kinder.' – says 32-year-old Angela Baruk, adding that for her and her husband Ron, the Bulgarian village Ustrem has become a very special place. 'We have everything we need in England, but in the big city, we seem to be losing ourselves. In the village here, we are stimulated'. (*Standart*, 22 June 2004)

The Bulgarians, on the other hand, were equipped with more preliminary information about Britain from different media channels. Nevertheless they had little chance to travel or meet 'living' foreigners in Bulgaria and this was especially true for those inhabiting the small Bulgarian villages. The limited range of stereotypes influencing communication between Bulgarians and British helped them to develop 'intercultural sensitivity' and to discover what Milton Bennett defines as 'ethnorelativism' – 'the assumption that cultures can only be understood relative to one another and that particular behavior can only be understood within a cultural context' (Bennett 1993, 46).

Developing the concept of the intercultural sensitivity as one of the main tools of intercultural communication theory and practice, Bennett defines integration as 'the attempt to integrate disparate aspects of one's identity into a new whole while remaining culturally merging' (Bennett 1993, 60). As *Standart* shows, Bulgarians recognised the efforts of the British settlers to integrate into the local life developing their status from Foreigners to Neighbours.

The Neighbours and the neighbourhood Many Bulgarian newspapers tell stories about the village of Sokolovo as the most English village in Bulgaria (see also Zhivko Ivanov's chapter in this volume). *Standart*, 13 March 2006 reports:

> Apart from the Bulgarians, Roma and Turks, who have lived peacefully for centuries, there are now new settlers from England. These subjects of HRH the Queen own at least 50 new houses in the village. Others are building yet 20 others. Considering the rate at which the houses are being sold to foreigners, they will be 700 in the next ten years, say the local people.
>
> Michael, who is English, together with his wife, Jessie, and daughter, Holly, live in one of the best houses in the village ... The upper side of the village seems to be becoming 'the English mahala', says the Mayor. The local parliament has voted a site for a new church, where the funds for building it will come from donations. (*Standart*, 13 March 2006)

Writing about the British newcomers settling in the Bulgarian villages, the journalists use a number of Turkish words: *komshii* – a word from Turkish origin for neighbours sounds more intimate than the more neutral Bulgarian word, *sasedi*, since it implies sharing much more than a common fence. The word, *mahala,* stands for a neighbourhood and brings the intimate feeling of domestic life, the local community gathering in the village streets, and children playing till late outside their houses. As for the neighbours, there is a universal saying that God might see everything but the neighbours know everything! The British become the source of gossip:

> *English Divorce Shook our Village*
> The family drama of the British settlers shocked everybody in Sushitsa village. Sean and his wife, Kate, bought a house some years ago, which accommodated them and their two children. The English family grew close to their neighbours and became the local people's favourites. Sadly, Kate and the two children were extradited last week[6] and Sean was left in Sushitsa to drown his sorrow in beer. (*Standart*, 04 October 2006)

The author goes on with further details about the British couple's children: Tiffany (12) and Brad (9), who were very fond of Bulgaria, especially the Bulgarian cuisine. They loved to eat at their neighbours' houses, since they liked the home-made Bulgarian dishes (*mandzhi*) prepared by the locals. The story ends with Sean's plan to go to the UK to complete his divorce and to return to Bulgaria with his son. He likes it in Bulgaria, because he does not lack money there; he only complains about the burglars, who visited his house several times. All these details are reported in a reportage style, with author forwarding the gossip without any comments or sign of judgement.

---

6 She had entered the country illegally.

The feeling of home In the context of migration the word 'home' is often used to describe the migrants' country of origin (Parutis 2006; Robinson and Reeve 2006). Nevertheless, mobile people can develop an attachment to a new place, which they call home and which provides them with identity. This is happened in the case of Michael, who *was* originally from Cleveland but *is now* from Kosharitsa:

> Margaret and Michael are one of the twenty British families who are in love with our Kosharitsa village. They live in a modest one-store house, which they bought four years ago for a very good value. They arrived from Cleveland with the intention to stay 2–3 months and they hadn't been back to their country since then. 60 year Michael Hill also does not plan to go back home. Home for me is already here, in Kosharitsa, loves to say the Englishmen. (*Standart*, 29 August 2006)

The intermarriages Bulgarians and Britons become not only neighbours but also relatives. The British-Bulgarian marriages are not new phenomena but their numbers rose with the increasing flows of people between Bulgaria and the UK. The first British-Bulgarian marriage noted by *Standart* was between the one of the prominent Bulgarian intellectuals, Petar Uvaliev, and Sonia Rouve. The headline, introducing the interview with Sonia Uvalieva-Rouve, declares: 'He Never Became English' (*Standart* 14 November 2005).

> In London he lived like a Bulgarian. Actually he never became English. He always said we were too different. A difference that he would often quote sounds like a joke: 'If a Bulgarian door says "No Entry", a Bulgarian has to knock and enter. In England this could never happen – what is private is private. If a sign says "No Entry", then you must not enter. If one wants privacy, others must respect it.' He used to joke that in your country there was no discipline in parking and he admired the English for it.

Sonia Uvalieva-Rouve made the effort to learn Bulgarian language. Yet this does not happen in the most of the new British-Bulgarian marriages, where the only Bulgarian word known by the British spouse is *Da* (Yes) needed for the ritual of the wedding:

> Patrick Wain Turley (37) arrived in Bulgaria for his wedding in Hissarlaka to Rumyana Kostadinova (32) from Kyustendil. The British groom, who doesn't speak a word of Bulgarian, is obliged by law to say 'Yes' in Bulgarian. Patrick really liked Bulgaria and insisted on marrying in Kyustendil on St Valentine's Day. For the sake of that Bulgarian 'Yes' he took a course in the difficult language of ours. The English-Bulgarian family lives in a small town north of London, Stoke-on-Trent. We live

> next door to the estate of the teenage idol – Robbie Williams. (*Vyara*, 16 February 2006)

The second British-Bulgarian marriage in this small Bulgarian town on St Valentine's Day created a relationship between locals and the British nobility:

> *Telephone Love Brings Together a British Lad and a Bulgarian Girl*
> This is the second English wedding in town, after the translator, Rumyana Mihailova, married a British man on St Valentines Day, February 14th.
>
> A descendant of an English lord said 'Yes' to his beloved, Ivona Lazarova, in the City Hall of Kyustendil. Duncan Edward Nichol came to the wedding ceremony dressed in a black tuxedo. Also present at the ceremony were his father, Simon, in a tuxedo too, and his wife, Jane. (*Vyara*, 13 June 2006)

Newspaper discourse Much journalistic work involves the careful monitoring of a range of news forums to find the stories, which will sell the newspaper, and respond to the mass of information and the publicity coming in every day. The Bulgarian journalists writing on 'British issues' see their relationship with their sources (from villagers, property agents through to official institutions) as mutually beneficial.

The British in Bulgaria are seen as newsworthy items. They were still enough of a novelty during the research period (2001–2006) and also became a point of reference for reporting news about the other 'others' in Bulgaria. The headline '1152 British Moved to Live with Us' (*Standart*, 27 July 2006) refers to a report on international migration to Bulgaria in 2005. It gives routine information on the numbers of those (both Bulgarians and foreigners), who crossed the Bulgarian borders during the year, the numbers of foreigners who applied for Bulgarian citizenship and residence permits and also the numbers of Bulgarians leaving the country. The growing numbers of British people in Bulgaria are more flattering than worrying during this period, since they were only the third largest group applying for Bulgarian residence permits:

> 1152 British settled in Bulgaria in 2005. They are 46% more than those in 2004. The UK citizens, who received long-term residence permits, are the third largest group after the citizens of Republic of Macedonia and Turkey. They are followed by the Russians, Greeks and Germans. (*Standart*, 27 July 2006)

The stories about British property buyers are mingled with news about Bulgarian celebrities and politicians. The status of being British is high enough to elevate them to the ranks of the Bulgarian political and intellectual elite in the eyes of the media. This mixture of British middle- and (mainly) working-class newcomers rub shoulders in the newspapers with foreign celebrities, Bulgarian MPs and ministers, their associates and close relatives, who are building luxury hotels and villages for the rich. One example is the story about how the business partner of a Spanish football 'boss', a Swedish count and the former British bodyguard of the Hollywood star, George Clooney, became neighbours on the northern Black Sea coast near Kavarna (*Standart*,12 July 2006):

> The Swedish count bought 100 hectares of the coast, a place which had been for years the Mecca (Makkah) for romantics and the Bulgarian hippy. The former bodyguard of George Clooney lives in Krupen village with his girlfriend. He has a business project – building a holiday village near Kavarna.

The text here sounds detached – purely informative; there is no sign of judgement, no comments about the 'British Invaders' like those appearing in previous years. The British and other foreigners have come and they are staying.

The comparison between the Bulgarian and English versions of *Standart News* shows that much more attention is paid in the English version to the experience of Bulgarians in Britain. As for the 'British in Bulgaria' topics in the English version of *Standart*, the Bulgarian journalists have to be more careful. They feel pressure from certain directions, especially from property sellers, to frame news stories in particular ways or, in some cases, to encourage British property buyers.

The most noticeable change between the texts of the 2002–2003 and the more recent period was a change in the them/us opposition: from the muted 'us' (the Bulgarians occupy an almost exclusive position as the grammatical object/target of the British and other foreigners) to a much more active position as the subject/agent of various actions. This move resulted in a change of perspective from what was being done to the Bulgarians to what Bulgarians themselves articulated as important issues needing to be addressed.

The discourse analysis of the texts confirmed the patterns discovered during the Headlines analysis. Nevertheless, some differences between the tone of the headlines and the articles were noticed. While the headlines (predominantly those headlines in 2002 and 2003 and especially those related to the 'Invader' pattern) conveyed some sense of conflict, crisis and problems with the 'British, who are coming', there was a significant difference in the overall language and tone used when describing these conditions in the stories themselves. This confirms what we have already noted – the attitudes towards the British, when negatively stated, are subject to significant ambivalence. Yes, the British are coming, they are buying our land, but this is the same land abandoned by us. Mixed feelings are revealed: both surprise and pride. How could people deliberately come to live to Bulgaria, when so many Bulgarians are leaving the country?

Conclusion

The chapter has focused on media reactions to the latest twist in a long tale about migration within Bulgaria. This twist has a more global dimension since it has been shaped by the political and economic changes wrought by '1989', post-socialism and EU accession. Newsworthy stories are not the more familiar ones of migration from Bulgaria's neighbours (Macedonia, Greece, Turkey, Romania and Serbia) but from the 'West'. The British are the most noted of these Western newcomers – an expression not only of numbers but their symbolic significance. They enable Bulgarians to tell stories to each other about how the subjects of the British queen are abandoning their country for the charms of Bulgaria! In other words, there is an element of pride and satisfaction that a new member of the *European* Union is so attractive despite the socio-economic problems. Even foreigners from the north-western fringe of Europe are becoming real neighbours.

The North-Western European migration to Spain is well documented (O'Reilly 2000; King et al. 2000; Helset et al. 2004). As for the British and other North-West European migration to Bulgaria, it is a much more recent phenomenon, not enough data has been collected and less scientific effort has been invested in analysing the process (see the chapters by Deema Kaneff and Zhivko Ivanov in this volume).

This chapter focuses on communication between the British settlers in Bulgaria and the locals primarily through the lens of one of Bulgaria's major daily newspapers. I have drawn on media and communication theory to explore how the newspaper articles, as public discourse, do not simply address 'the public' but also create a certain reality. This emerges, to some extent, through textual discourse, which involves media representations as well as the collective social understandings of groups formed by shared social and cultural experiences.

The newspapers discussed here provide a rich source for these representations, both reflecting and cultivating them. Although we began this Conclusion by highlighting the positive aspects of Bulgaria's recent migration story, there is a darker side, of course. There are many others approaching Bulgaria (from the neighbouring countries as well as from Ukraine, Moldova, the newcomers from Asian and African countries), who do not enjoy such media comfort. As previous research shows, media portrayals of new immigrants can fuel local tensions and create a hostile environment (see, for example, Robinson and Reeve 2006, 23). However, the stories analysed here show how the media can promote a welcoming environment. Between 2001 and 2006 the Bulgarian newspapers encouraged a sense of neighbourliness between Bulgarians and the newcomers from the West. They show how media can contribute to constructing civic and cultural concepts of Europe (see Sanna 2006), including the widely discussed concept of European citizenship.

Chapter 7

Britons in the Bulgarian Countryside: Social and Cultural Aspects of Adaptation and Intercommunication[1]

Zhivko Ivanov

The British presence in the Bulgarian countryside is part of the general problem of integration and migration, typical for the countries in Eastern Europe, and Bulgaria in particular, after 1989.

The chapter will seek to:

- provide a better understanding of the scale and nature of migration;
- highlight the role of migration as an important social and economic phenomenon;
- explore the increasing interest in the notion of a national identity;
- investigate an important set of questions around how migrants think about Britain and Bulgaria and what they think of themselves.

The following questions are posed:

- How large is migration from the UK to Bulgaria? Where in the world do migrants go?
- What do we know about the British abroad and their experience? What are the key trends?
- How well have they integrated with the host community?

The British in Bulgaria, who reside long term and have the status of property owners, will be referred to as migrants (settlers).[2]

---

1 This chapter has been translated by Yordan Kosturkov, Paisii Hilendarski University of Plovdiv, Department of English, Plovdiv.

2 A settler (colonist) is often used in a historical context and is built on the theory of colonialization and postcolonial practice. A settler is a person who has migrated to a less occupied area and established permanent residence there, often to colonize the area. It is not a very precise term, since its meaning is to a large degree related to the mobility of people who are relatively young and are looking for work.

Bulgarian Population Decline

Why is Bulgaria so open for residence to foreign citizens, who can purchase property, participate in the social, economic and political life of the region without interrupting their continuing links with their motherland? The first step in finding an answer to this question is to look at how depopulated Bulgaria has become. Among the 241 nations around the world Bulgaria ranks 131 in terms of population density – between Ethiopia (130) and Iraq (132), and in Europe, just above the Baltic states, Iceland, Montenegro, Belarus and Finland (United Nations World Population Prospects 2005). Around the time when the Bulgarian state was restored (1878) there were over 6 million Bulgarians but from the mid-1950s the population began to steadily decline (Bekyarova 2004).

From the 1980s scholars and journalists have primarily focused on the way in which this population decline has been bound up with emigration, especially by Bulgarian Turks leaving for Turkey. After 1984–1985 more than 400,000 Bulgarian Turks were forced to leave the country, and then again, after the fall of the Communist regime, another 200–300,000 Bulgarian Turks left, this time mainly due to economic and humanitarian reasons. This emigration flow was complemented by a continuous stream westwards, resulting in a slower, yet longer term loss of almost one million more Bulgarians (Cholakov 2007, 57).

The demographic crisis, produced by a decline in fertility, was mainly caused by socio-economic factors, but it was further aggravated by these waves of emigration as well as by political changes. These developments, not surprisingly perhaps, overshadowed the process of internal migration to the cities from such regions as Strandzha-Sakar. As a result hundreds of Bulgarian villages and little towns in different parts of the country became practically devoid of social life. In combination with the economic catastrophe of the early transition period (1989–1997) and the abrupt devaluation of money and of property, huge amounts of real estate were removed from market circulation in these regions

During the past decade the process of population decline has continued unabated. The March 2001 revealed that the total number of the people in the country was 7,977,646 – in other words, between the 1992 and 2001 censuses Bulgaria's population had decreased by about half a million people, since in 1992 8,487,317 people were recorded. The comparison with 1985 is even more alarming because the number of Bulgarians was 9.4 millions (Angelov 2006).

The downward trend has continued. By 2002 national statistics showed that the number had fallen to 7,870,000 people and according to the *World Factbook*, by June 2003 7,537,929 people were recorded and the forecast for July 2008 was even lower – 7,262,675) (*World Factbook* 2008). Hence, the average decline since 1986 has been approximately 0.96 per cent per annum. While populations have been declining generally across the global North, only

Latvia has suffered a faster decline than Bulgaria according to the data of UNO experts (World Population Prospects 2005). Demographic processes, which have been in operation for decades, have been compounded by transition into a qualitatively new state to produce a deep demographic crisis in Bulgaria, which bears all the hallmarks of an imminent population catastrophe.

The Strandzha-Sakar case clearly demonstrates the dramatic dimensions of depopulation in a given region, as well as its impact at both political and economic levels. The case study also reveals the social action, which is designed to surmount the problems created by depopulation. During the early 1980s a decision was taken, which was quite controversial in terms of government policy towards minorities – 'Decree No. 22 of 10 May 1982 for the Accelerated Social-Economic Development of the System of Towns and Villages of Fourth and Fifth Functional Category, from the Borderland Regions and the Strandzha-Sakar Area during the Eighth Five Year Plan and until 1990' (State Gazette 1982, 545–51). Indisputably, the area of Strandzha-Sakar, like other problematic regions in North West and North East Bulgaria and the mountainous regions of South West Bulgaria, was faced with a demographic crisis since from the late 1970s it was becoming almost totally depopulated.[3] The depopulation was the product of both industrialisation and a special military doctrine, which secretly ensured that entire regions would become uninhabited or deserted by controlling residence and access to zones, situated mainly along the southern border of Bulgaria with Turkey. The interaction of a whole group of factors, of which the most important was population reduction, led to a demographic crisis across entire regions.

The British Are Coming!!

The collapse of the 'Iron Curtain' after 1989 meant that Bulgaria both opened its borders to W. Europe and gradually freed its special or neglected zones not only to Bulgarians but also foreign citizens. The affiliation of the Eastern European countries to the rest of Europe also led to the opening up of the property market and the liberalization of migration. Just as the Bulgarians received the right to move across the European Union, foreign citizens also gained the opportunity to live in Bulgaria. The largest group of settlers has been and still is the British community. From the middle of 1997 the process of economic development and the stability of the macroeconomic framework began (Kanev 2000; Angelov et al. 2004). From the beginning of the new

3 The largest population density is to be found in the municipalities of Plovdiv (3500 people/km^2) and Varna (1500 people/km^2) while the least populated region is Strandzha (10 people/km^2) – see *National Strategy for the Regional Development of Republic Bulgaria during the period 2005–2015, Population and Demographic situation* (2008).

millennium economic growth has remained at relatively high levels (5–6 per cent growth in GDP). The development of tourism and economic and financial stabilisation has resulted in the dynamic development of the property market. Between 2002 and 2007 the number of estate agencies increased 14 times and 35 per cent of these agencies operated both within the country and outside. Approximately 8 per cent operate exclusively in foreign markets, selling Bulgarian real property (Ivanov 2007, 137–43).

The accession of Bulgaria into the EU also liberalized the legal framework for acquiring property and provided direct access to property, although in the agreement with the EU Bulgaria adopted a gratis period for the acquisition of land (only after 2014).[4] The data on foreigners residing permanently (for an unspecified period) and long term (up to one year) is unreliable, although during the past few years steps have been taken to bring the keeping of these kinds of statistics up to European standards. The National Institute of Statistics, using the registration system of the Ministry of Home Affairs, has provided a current figure of 56,000 foreigners, among whom the British rank only fourth with 6,778 permanent residents. Since there are also approximately 1,840 British long term residents, the total number of non-tourist British residents amounts to about 8,500–9,000 people. These numbers are much lower than the 40,000 to 45,000 British residents announced by the media and the estate agencies. According to the National Institute of Statistics the number of British citizens, who have requested the status of permanent residents in 2006, increased by 50% compared with the previous year. The situation with the data is also complicated by the fact that with the accession of Bulgaria to the EU, the legal definition of 'foreigner' was changed – citizens of the member states are no longer considered foreigners – yet the old practice of registration and statistical counting has been preserved.[5]

In the village of Sokolovo, Kavarna region, members of the British community expressed their choice of the Bulgarian village in a variety of ways, reflecting generally the range of reasons which inspired them to come to

4 Although the purchase of land by foreigners has been allowed already since 2007 when Bulgaria was expected to become a EU member – in practice the constitutional prohibition may remain in force until 2014. It is then that the agreed seven-year gratis period with Brussels for the complete liberalization of the land market in Bulgaria expires. According to the Euro engagements of our country from 2007, the right to freely purchase land in Bulgaria will be granted only to European farmers, who will become permanent residents of Bulgaria with the goal of developing farming (the so-called self-employed farmers). In all other cases the purchase of land by foreigners remains under prohibition until the expiry of the transition period (Velinova 2005).

5 In the last amendments to the Law on the Foreigners, Art. 2. (Amended State Gazette, No. 29, 2007) (1) the following definition is provided: 'A foreigner in the understanding of this law is every individual person who is not a Bulgarian citizen, or citizen of another member state of the European Union, of a state who is a party in the Agreement on the European Economic Area, or of Switzerland Confederation.'

the country. Climate is an important reason but not the only one. The second reason is the location of the village – near the sea, yet not on the sea shore. The third reason is that a golf course is under construction near the village. The mountainous nature of the terrain so near to the village is impressive and there are also historical landmarks nearby and the houses are relatively comfortable. After remodelling and adapting to the conditions of modern living, the houses have relatively large courtyards. Furthermore, the local people very quickly get used to the foreigners and establish contact with them. So the Britons start to live an integrated life – 'they learn Bulgarian, cook dishes from the village cuisine [and] keep a small farm' (Tsenova 2006).

The British residents create their communities, which connect them both with their motherland and with the local people.[6] These communities are attempting to share experience, seek advice and become oriented to the ways of the Bulgarian countryside. The British website Expat World (http://www.britishexpat.com/Home_page.6.0.html) has a special section on the Bulgarian Britons in different cities and regions.[7] Although the British presence has developed only after 1997, especially since 2001, frequent internet postings remind people that the British now have over 10 years of experience of adapting to the local culture. They are sober-minded, analytical and critical, and at the same time tolerant and moderate. The careful comparisons in the postings with the reality of British expatriate life reveal people's ability to 'translate' between the two cultures ('Brits in Bulgaria' [internet forum posting] 2007). The experienced British citizens explain the new stereotypes and cultural clichés, which are mutual and two-way.

The social adaptation of both the British and the young Bulgarians to village life is an important condition for reanimation and renewal. This adaptation is presented in emblematic form in the village of Mindya, where the first settlers were fatigued young Bulgarians from the capital city and from other large cities, followed by foreigners:

> … the principal reason was the opportunity to live happily with my British state pension; to embark at 67 on the unknown was a challenge; here both me and my friend have been received without any reservations; I could not

6 An expatriate (in abbreviated form, expat) is a person temporarily or permanently residing in a country and culture other than that of the person's upbringing or legal residence. The word comes from the Latin *ex* (out of) and *patria* (country, fatherland), and is sometimes misspelled (either unintentionally or intentionally) as 'ex-patriot' or short 'expat' (because of its pronunciation).

7 In the menu of the forum portal it is specially indicated: 'Bulgaria has its own form of the dedicated forum – you can reach it here …' <http://www.britishexpat.com/expatforum/country/index.php?c=2>. In the 20 topics posted by country only Bulgaria, Malta, France and Spain have such differentiated sites in the 'British Expat Forum – In-country Experts'.

> believe it [that] they will pick out a foreigner to wear their national costume and sing songs in their language; I think the villagers have preserved their community spirit. … the citizens of Mindya receive the foreigners well and say they are quiet and peaceful people. The local people do not miss the opportunity of inviting them to their festivals and holidays, organized in the village. And this is maybe because they think of them as their own kind. (Tomova 2007)

'When in 1999 I renounced the cherished status of being "a Sofiote" and became a citizen of the village of Mindya …' is the story of Professor Evgenii Dainov, one of the most reputed political scientists in post-communist Bulgaria, who found in the village authenticity and balance. His perceptions about and contrast between the village and the city coincides with the motives of the foreigners, who are searching for the spirit and the atmosphere of older epochs, older socio-cultural models, nostalgically present in remote places unspoiled by the 'civilized' corners of the world (Dainov 2007).

The small Bulgarian village is attractive given its low property prices compared with prices nationally. To the rural economy are added the atmosphere, the tranquillity, the climate, the social balance and the comfortable communication environment, characterized by its immediacy, goodwill and mutual understanding. Graham Devers, a 62-year-old brickyard manager, who arrived from Manchester about a year ago with his wife, Marie, paid £11,000 for a house in Rujitza. He said: 'The people here are the most friendly and generous that I have ever met' (Lafan 2007).

There are British, who are exceptions to the mass case of the 'rich retired Brit' and are settling among the poor provincial Bulgarian villagers. These are young, energetic and seek social fulfilment in a new environment. In Khotnitsa Lafan the young Brits, between 20 and 35 year old, who settled here, refute the pessimistic opinion of the Khotnitsa citizens that 'the village would soon die as younger inhabitants moved to cities'. Almost a third of properties in Bulgaria are being bought by foreign nationals with 20- to 35-year-old Britons now a large proportion of Bulgarian real estate buyers ('Bulgarian Homes 4 Sale' 2007). This development shows that people are beginning to think in the long term. They are not just pensioners or people close to the end of their occupational careers and are not just coming to Bulgaria to make a quick profit in terms of investment.

To this type of new, younger residents in the Bulgarian villages, we should also add the so-called alternative settlers, who share environmental and nature friendly ideas of lifestyle. They have chosen villages in order to demonstrate their disagreement with the policy of the official authorities and the tourist business regarding the Black Sea coast zones and the alpine ski centres such as Borovets, Bansko and Pamporovo. They fight for the protection of the environment and the pursuit of an eco-friendly life and they support Bulgarian groups engaged in ecological resistance. An on-line group, for example, was founded on 13 August 2006 and its website declared that:

> This group is for people, who want to live in an alternative and eco friendly way in Bulgaria. Many people are now moving to Bulgaria or buying second homes there and we believe that this a great opportunity to use the natural resources of the country to live in an ethical way that respects the environment and the traditional cultures of the country – its not about the traditional ex-pat community. (Yahoo Groups directory 2008)

As Favell points out (2004, 3), the removal of political and administrative borders does not yet mean complete freedom of movement of people across Europe, since important socio-cultural differences, as well as religious and traditional differences, remain and constitute real barriers to the creation of a socially integrated world between the different ethnic groups. In Favell's words, 'For these prototypical European citizens, the formal legal and political barriers might be down, *but other cultural and practical constraints seem to discourage wholesale relocation*' (2004, 1; our emphasis).

A particularly important element in the political integration has been the participation of foreign citizens (with permanent residence) in European Parliament elections (20 May 2007) and local elections (28 October 2007). Another Bulgarian study in the village of Khotnitsa describes this development in the following way:

> 'After all, I will find the information I need and will vote', Susan declares firmly. 'What's the use of voting?', we ask her with proverbial Bulgarian distrust. 'Everything happening in the European Parliament will reflect on life here', the British lady confidently answers. (Garcheva 2007)

The British residents in Khotnitsa not only took part in the elections but they challenge the Bulgarian voters, who traditionally demonstrate a high rate of detachment, especially with regard to the European Parliament. Six British people came to the ballot-box in the Veliko Tarnovo region village of Khotnitsa, declaring that it is very important for every European to exercise their right to vote. The example of the Britons made many residents of the village come to vote, too.[8]

Similar cases were noticed in a number of other regions where foreign settlers demonstrated their desire to change the social-economic conditions and this citizen activity was demonstrated particularly clearly in the case of

---

8 'Low activity in the elections of Euro-deputies', 20 May 2007 (posted in the Kaldata forum), posted 21 May 2007 <http://www.kaldata.com/forums/index.php?s=ca2fa63f092f33c8b02b098f6c4cb492&showtopic=50050&st=75&p=540618&#entry540618>, accessed 26 June 2008.

local elections. In the mayoral election campaign in Veliko Tarnovo one of the candidates included in his programme a special section oriented towards the British residents in the municipality, which promised the opening of a special department to work with the British settlers. At the same time the British declared their desire to vote, as well as their difficulties in deciding who to vote for due to the lack of information about the candidates and their programmes.[9]

These examples, together with the cases presented in other electronic and print media, illustrate the relatively rapid adaptation and inclusion of the British in local social and civic problems. The problem with the water in the village of Ichera, Sliven region, was taken up with renewed energy thanks to John – the local citizens had long before decided that state institutions would not listen to them and had discontinued their civil pressure. In a Strandzha village a British couple brought an action against a cable television company, which regularly cheated the local people by collecting tax from them and not providing the requisite service. In Sokolovo, a village in the Varna region, British settlers created a club to pose specific issues which needed solution by the local government. As a result a special facility was designated for the club's activities and the construction of a church was begun.

In another village in the Varna region – Klimentovo – the local municipal council unanimously decided to designate for free a school building and 2 decares for a Centre of Culture and Recreation to be used by the British community in Bulgaria. This decision, according to the General Assembly's records, was taken out of respect for Queen Elizabeth II and for the 'love between Prince Charles and Camilla, which has survived over time, and because of affection and respect for the British people'. It was 'also a gesture of gratitude to the dozens of thousands of Britons who have settled in Bulgaria, adopting it as their second motherland'.[10]

The British 'invasion' is now deployed across a relatively wider front, since every British newcomer now stands a greater chance of finding support from his/her already settled compatriots. While the view advanced by the internet during the 1990s that 'Some expats would be great' would only occasionally

9 Dr Ivan Manchev promised a municipal department for the foreigners. The surgeon met the Britons at the Khotnitsa Fan Club. 'Mayor elections 2007' (posting on 8 October 2007). <http://www.etarfans.org/forum/viewtopic.php?t=862&sid=58fb56dc7dbb7004966c45e653046951>, accessed on 3 January 2008. 'A special department to work with the British community will be created in the municipality, if Dr Ivan Manchev is elected mayor of Veliko Tarnovo.' See also Krumova, Kremena (2007). Boyko Borissov wins in the region, 7 'local' Britons also voted. // European elections 2007, BG-Sever newspaper, No. 21, October 2007, <http://www.bgsever.info/br-21_2007/stranici/str-5.htm>, accessed 19 April 2008.

10 'They cheat the Brits in rushing to buy Bansko property'. Posted on 7 February 2008, <http://www.bghelp.net/forums/showthread.php?p=100902>, accessed 12 June 2008.

meet a warm response today, such appeals for a virtual internet meeting gather quite impressive 'crowds' of experienced settlers, who are keen to share their experience and their knowledge with the newcomers. If not in the same location (some village in the countryside), at least in the neighbourhood, there are British residents who would respond, by initially helping to solve the problem of the language barrier.

The appearance of the foreigner as a settler – the foreigner who becomes an owner of land (a house, land) – reminds local people about the purchase and loss of identity. As O'Reilly (2002, 188) indicated, the presence of Britons in France and the rapid growth in purchasing property during the 1990s, generated public feelings of the type 'they buy us out', 'they buy out France', 'France for sale'. Similar fears in Bulgaria have never been expressed about 'civilized' foreigners but have focused on an assumed threat of an invasion by Bulgaria's neighbours seeking to buy property. This apprehension is fuelled by political conflicts with Bulgaria's ethnic minority communities, which after 1989 were exacerbated by the media as well as by particular political actors, such as the 'Attaka' party.[11]

In some studies of national security (Bekyarova 2004), which are closely associated with official national policy, the way depopulation and migration negatively affect social cohesion is pointed out. Bekyarova (2004), for example, claims that:

> Practice demonstrates that when the number of migrants from one and the same country increases sufficiently, they stop conforming to the established order and law in the receiving country and within the framework of their own community create a separate pattern of behaviour and organization of life. There are frequently cases when cultural, educational and even political homogeneity is created [within these minorities] and [they make claims] for adequate participation in the political, economic and cultural life of the receiving countries.

Although the Bulgarian majority is dominant in terms of demography, Bekyarova points to various tensions and fears, which are typical of the process of national self-determination in the Balkans.[12] She claims that careful

11 The political party 'Attaka' has no platform but only a so-called declaration of 20 items. Item one in the declaration reads: 'Bulgaria is a single nation, a monolithic state, not divided by the following principles: religion, ethnicity, culture. The difference in origin or faith cannot be placed higher than nationality.' In '20 Items of the "Attaka" party' (official website), posted in 2004, <http://www.ataka.bg/index.php?option=com_content&task=view&id=13&Itemid=51>, accessed 2 June 2007.

12 Natalia Bekyarova cites the following facts: 'The overall balance of the demographic development for the period from 1880 to 1965 demonstrates that the relative share of the Bulgarians in the country marks an incessant, although slow,

scrutiny of population trends among the Bulgarian Turks and Roma should make us seriously consider the future. In the areas where the population is increasing, '*the quantitative mass of the Bulgarian Turks and the Romas is relatively high*' (Bekyarova 2004).

According to Demmers (2002, 89) settlement in a certain territory is not by itself a reason for emerging conflicts; foreign citizens rather act as catalysts for latent conflicts within the society. A comparison between Albanians in Kosovo and Serbia, on the one hand, and the British in Bulgaria, on the other, provides a sharp contrast in how the presence of a foreign ethnic community works out politically.

British nationalist feelings in their new home appear to be largely nostalgic and have no ideological implications for the Bulgarian majority. Consequently, they do not experience any political aggression. The new locality means for them an environment where they can experience a new social, rather than political-ideological life, for cooperation and intercultural dialogue. The homogeneous space of the nations, interpreted in the context of the European idea of the five freedoms, is completely different from the late formation of nation–states in Yugoslavia where foreign ethnic communities have played such an important role. The invasion of the Britons not only is not interpreted as a threat, but their presence is explicitly referred to by the typical phrase, 'In the village, there are houses purchased by Britons' and by advertisements for sales of property such as the following:

> House in the village of Granitovo. In good repair, one floor, with rough-hewn planks used as insulation above the ceiling, two rooms and a corridor, a lumber room and cellar. In one of the rooms there is a sink. A courtyard with vine-arbour and fruit trees, 971 sq m. External toilet facility and a sink in the yard. In this population centre there are about 70 British families. At a distance of 13 kilometers from the city of Elkhovo and 113 from the seaside.[13]

The presence of these foreigners increases the attraction of the offer and emphasizes the importance of the British presence as a factor which, to a large extent guarantees, the reliability of the purchase and the security of life in a particular rural area.

increase. After the Liberation the Bulgarians were around 68.8% of the population, and in 1965 they were already 88.3%. During the same period the relative share of the Turkish population decreased from 23.1% to 9.1%. The remaining ethnic groups preserve relatively permanent values – around 2.6%, with the largest share coming from the Roma population' (Bekyarova 2007).

13 Eva Real Property Agency. Advertising locations <http://eva-elhovo.50megs.com/Mesta.htm> accessed on 26 June 2008. The agency operates with real property predominantly in the above mentioned region of Strandzha-Sakar.

For the Bulgarians, in general, the British are not only the saviours of decaying villages, houses and life in the countryside, but also of centuries-old traditions. Their presence not only is not a threat to the local, but it also supports it by breathing life into it. This feeling of revival has economic, social, cultural and inter-human dimensions and in a publication by Grainger Lafan on the life of the Britons in Veliko Tarnovo region, the reviving influence on local economy is indicated by the mayor, Krassimir Kostov: 'Thanks to the British, it is like we live in a new village. The first thing they do when they arrive is to renovate their homes, then they start work on the paths, then the roads.'

The main disadvantages of life in the Bulgarian village are the same for both the local Bulgarians, and the British newcomers:

- poor infrastructure – roads built 30 years ago, streets without asphalt, no water supply and sewerage, no communication technology, no Internet etc.
- domestic lawlessness – theft, encroachments, vandalism that cannot be controlled or restricted by the local government and the police
- administrative absurdities – taxes, construction, regulation, bureaucratic procedures that impede the initiative and disturb the day–to–day rhythm

The British presence in the everyday life of the Bulgarian village is the most productive model (despite the British being so different socially and culturally), since shows other newcomers how they can contribute to social integration.

Conclusion

From the above account we can draw the following conclusions:

a. the British in Bulgaria bring civilization to relatively depopulated regions;
b. those buying property are adapting to local society and are becoming permanent residents;
c. there is some movement away from popular areas, such as the seaside and the mountains, to the provincial Bulgarian villages on the plains;
d. a category of permanent residents has emerged. These live in Bulgaria all year round or stay in their motherland for a shorter time than in their Bulgarian second home;
e. a new social and economic environment for the Bulgarians in the villages has been created, since they contribute practically and beneficially to local life through producing services, social activities etc.

Before the large immigrant flow, which is expected from the Asian and African regions in order to satisfy the increasing shortage of labour in the dynamically developing Bulgarian industry, the British settlers are creating specific models and mechanisms of interaction with the local culture, which will be very useful in the establishment of cooperation and cultural interaction with other immigrants, who are ethnically, religiously or civilizationally even more different.

SECTION 3
Going West: The Bulgarians and Other 'New' Europeans in Britain

Chapter 8
Bulgarian Immigration and Community Cohesion in London and Brighton[1]

Eugenia Markova

Introduction, Definitions and Scope

A casual reading of the UK press could easily give the impression that East European immigration to the UK started largely after the accession of new EU member states in 2004. However, Bulgarians, together with Romanians, briefly dominated the media in the spring of 2004 when an alleged visa scam emerged. Soon afterwards they were forgotten again only to make a dramatic re-appearance in the summer of 2006 as the two countries' EU accession approached. The media was flooded with horror stories about HIV positive migrants and criminals arriving from the two countries. At the same time, high powered studies had identified the extensive contribution to the British economy, which immigrants had made after enlargement in 2004 (Ernst and Young 2006; Blanchflower et al. 2007; Gilpin et al. 2006; Iakova 2007) – studies, which implied that an open market policy for the new accession states should be maintained. Nevertheless, the UK government decided to adopt a harder policy stance, and in October 2006 it announced rules which limited Bulgarian and Romanian nationals' access to the UK labour market once they joined the EU. Furthermore, the British government's 'Managed Migration' strategy also sought to limit immigration from other non-EU states, particularly skilled workers, based on the assumption that nationals from accession states were likely to fill the majority of low-skilled jobs for the foreseeable future (Home Office 2006).

Yet, during the past 15 years or so people have been coming to the UK from non-EU East European countries in substantial numbers, both legally and illegally. For example, since 1994 Bulgarians and Romanians have been able to obtain self-employment visas under the European Community Association Agreement (ECAA) and thousands have taken the opportunity to do so. Opportunities have also existed under the Seasonal Agricultural

---

1 This research is part of a bigger study financially supported by the Joseph Rowntree Foundation. It was coordinated by the Sussex Centre for Migration Research at the University of Sussex and co-managed by the author of the article and Prof. Richard Black, both at the University of Sussex at the time of the project.

Workers Scheme (SAWS), and from 2002, the Sector-Based Scheme (SBS). In 2005 SAWS work permits were issued to 3,006 Bulgarian nationals while in the same year, 1,683 Bulgarians were issued SBS work permits. Meanwhile, it has also been possible for highly-skilled people to enter Britain through the regular work permit scheme, as well as programmes such as the Highly Skilled Migration Programme (HSMP) and the Scheme for Innovators. HSMP applications approved to Bulgarians increased from just six in 2002 when the scheme commenced[2] to 59 in 2005 (Salt 2005).[3]

Moreover, despite the significant research attention to nationals from the 2004 EU accession countries – Poland in particular – immigrants from other Eastern European countries such as Bulgaria have remained relatively invisible and ignored by researchers, with some exceptions. Bulgarians were included as a control group in a COMPAS study (Anderson et al. 2006) on the employment of Central and East European immigrants in the UK following the 2004 EU enlargement. The study highlighted the difficult circumstances of immigrants, who were trapped in low-wage occupations in agriculture, construction, and the hospitality and care sectors, suffering instability at work, problematic contracts and low payment. Immigrant workers from the A8 accession countries (Poland and Lithuania) as well as Bulgaria were found to comprise about 10 per cent of the workers in low wage employment in contract cleaning, hospitality and catering, home care and food processing sectors in London (Evans et al. 2005). In an IPPR report on the likely migration implications of the Bulgarian and Romanian accession to the EU, both nationalities were profiled working in sectors that were either unskilled or hard to fill and in which many A8 nationals were currently working (IPPR 2006).

This chapter will attempt to contribute to the scarce knowledge on the Bulgarian migrant community in the UK. The focus will be on the employment, education and housing of Bulgarian immigrants living in Brighton and Hove and in the London Boroughs of Hackney and Harrow, as well as their broader interaction with local communities, particularly focusing on the issue of community cohesion. A cohesive community was defined along the lines of the Home Office/DCLG's (Local Governments Department) definition of cohesion – where there is a common vision and a sense of belonging for all communities; where the diversity of people's different backgrounds and circumstances are appreciated and positively valued; where those from different backgrounds have similar life opportunities; and where strong and positive relationships are being developed between people from different backgrounds in the workplace, in schools and in the neighbourhoods.

2 The HSMP started on 1 February 2002 and so data for 2002 are for 1 February to 31 December 2002.

3 The SAWS and SBS schemes are due to be restricted to Bulgarians and Romanians from 2008.

Community cohesion was measured in the following four ways: 1) in terms of three key contextual factors – employment, education and housing; 2) also in terms of whether immigrants report that they 'belong' in their neighbourhoods, in the borough and in the UK; 3) the extent to which diversity is respected; 4) their expectations for the future and the extent to which they participate in community activities. These measures were translated into questions such as 'Do you have friends from other ethnic backgrounds?', 'Do you talk to your neighbours?', 'Do you think that your neighbourhood is a place where people from different backgrounds and ethnic origin get on well together?'

Study Localities

The three localities of Brighton and Hove, Harrow and Hackney were selected as study localities since they represent three distinctive social contexts where emerging immigrant diversity is being experienced and responded to. Perhaps the most obvious choice was the London borough of Hackney, an inner city borough with a population of just over 200,000, long noted for its very wide ethnic diversity. According to the GLA Ethnicity Index, it is the third most diverse local authority in the UK after Brent and Newham. Hackney has a particularly large proportion of the population in the category 'Other White', which includes the East Europeans/Bulgarians, as well as 'White Irish' (three per cent), and many West Europeans, North Americans and Australians.

In contrast, Harrow is an outer London borough, again with just over 200,000 residents, but not so well recognised as a destination for immigrants. Yet, in recent years it too has experienced growing ethnic diversity, and the arrival of a wide range of immigrant groups. Indeed, Harrow ranks fifth nationally in terms of the proportion of non-white residents and has the second highest proportion of Indian-origin residents in England (22 per cent) after Leicester. The 2001 Census recorded that a third of all residents were born abroad, coming from 137 different countries. The two largest groups of immigrants were those born in India (12,400) and Kenya (10,250), while some 2,040 were born in Eastern Europe.

Meanwhile, the City of Brighton and Hove was selected as a locality with a relatively low rate of ethnic diversity and a predominantly white population but where new immigrant communities were becoming established. There is anecdotal evidence of the growing presence of East Europeans working in the city's hotels and restaurants and attending the city's one Greek Orthodox church. The city has a population of just under a quarter of a million.

Field Methods

Conducting a questionnaire survey with Bulgarian immigrants formed part of a bigger quantitative survey administered to a total of 388 immigrants coming from Albania, Bulgaria, Russia, Serbia and Montenegro and Ukraine and 402 long-term residents, living with them, in Brighton and Hove and in the London boroughs of Hackney and Harrow. Some 85 of the interviewed immigrants were Bulgarians – 29 living in Brighton and Hove, 29 – in Hackney and 27 in Harrow. They were surveyed between June and November 2005. Overall, the sample Bulgarian population was predominantly young, the majority being in the 20–29 age group, and included slightly more women than men.

Table 8.1 Age and Gender of sampled Bulgarian population (number of respondents)

16-19	3
20-29	30
30-39	20
40-49	26
50-59	5
Over 60	1
Male	39
Female	46
Total	85

Source: field survey, 2005.

'Snowballing' with multiple entry points was used to access migrant respondents. It was the only possible and ethically acceptable technique. Access to Bulgarian immigrants was facilitated through personal contacts and through introductions from key contacts in the community, especially through owners of Bulgarian ethnic restaurants and cafes.

It is acknowledged that the sample of Bulgarian immigrants is relatively small and the sampling procedure was unlikely to produce a random sample of responses. In order to compensate to a certain degree for the non-randomness of the sample, a 'tree' or a snowballing diagram was kept on the way each respondent was recruited. Nonetheless, the selection of both immigrants and long-term residents was conditional upon their visibility and their degree of social activity.

Bulgarians Arriving in the UK

The peak year of arrival for 24 per cent of the Bulgarians in the sample was 2003. The next largest cohort came during 2004, when the British consulate in Sofia had issued an excessive number of self-employment visas before the visa scam was revealed. Thirty five people (41 per cent) in the sample came between 2003 and 2004.

Contrary to expectations, much of this immigration appears to have been of couples rather than single men or women. Thus, about two thirds of the immigrants (57) interviewed were married or had a partner – about the same as the UK average of 61 per cent – while more than three quarters (79 per cent) of these partners were residing in the UK. Most of these partners were also from Bulgarian origin – only 12 people (21 per cent) reported having a partner from a different ethnic origin. However, some had come to the UK without their partners – a little over one in seven Bulgarians had left their partners in Bulgaria. Just under half of the Bulgarian immigrants surveyed (48 per cent) also had dependent children, somewhat more than amongst the UK population as a whole (29 per cent). The vast majority of these children (79 per cent) were living in the UK and another 12 people (21 per cent) reported having their children in Bulgaria. Those who had their partners in Bulgaria also had their children there.

Legal Status

There was a great variety of self-reported legal status. The largest group of Bulgarian immigrants surveyed said they were 'temporary, with a right to work'[4] (42 per cent, N=36), followed by dependants (18 per cent, N=15); another 14 Bulgarians said they were permanent residents – they had come during the mid-1990s. Four said they were undocumented and another seven had 'semi-legal status' (13 per cent were semi-legal and undocumented). Five were full-time students and another four were on temporary visas without the right to work, i.e. were awaiting a Home Office decision about heir application for permits.

Reasons for Coming to the UK

Slightly more than half (53 per cent) of the Bulgarians interviewed had left their country of origin primarily for economic reasons, either because they were not earning enough (29 per cent) or they could not see any prospects for improvement of the economic conditions (13 per cent). Only three people were unemployed before emigrating to the UK. Just under a quarter came

4 Includes work permit holders, those with self-employment visas, those with 'discretionary leave to remain.

Table 8.2 Current legal status by country of origin (%)

	Albanian	Bulgarian	Russian	Serbian	Ukrainian	Total
Permanent residence	51.9	16.5	64.6	68.9	32.9	45.6
Temporary, with a right to work	9.9	42.4	8.5	13.1	7.6	16.8
Temporary, not working	17.3	4.7	3.7	4.9	0.0	6.2
Temporary, working without permission	1.2	8.2	2.4	0.0	1.3	2.8
Undocumented	9.9	4.7	4.9	1.6	32.9	11.1
Student	4.9	5.9	12.2	11.5	21.5	11.1
Dependant	4.9	17.6	3.7	0.0	3.8	6.4
Total	100.0	100.0	100.0	100.0	100.0	100.0
N=	81	85	82	61	79	388

Source: field survey, 2005.

to join a family member already in the UK and one person to get married, which contrasts with the results of a survey on the mobility of EU citizens, suggesting that Europeans move more for love than employment.[5]

It also appeared that more Bulgarian women than men had left their countries of origin because of family reasons or marriage, which is consistent with the notion that men had migrated first and that their partners had followed.

Table 8.3 First-ranked reason for leaving the country of origin (%)

	Albanian	Bulgarian	Russian	Serbian	Ukrainian	Total
Economic	45.7	52.9	40.2	24.6	51.9	44.1
Political	28.4	0.0	3.7	37.7	6.3	13.9
Education	8.6	12.9	12.2	14.8	15.2	12.6
Family/marriage	13.6	23.5	24.4	16.4	17.7	19.3
Other	3.7	10.6	19.5	6.6	8.9	10.1
Total	100.0	100.0	100.0	100.0	100.0	100.0
N=	81	85	82	61	79	388

Source: field survey, 2005.

5 http://www.euractiv.com/en/innovation/just-europeans-move/article-153775.

Despite the dominance of economic reasons for leaving the country of origin, it seems that Bulgarians came to the UK mainly because of the ease of entry (e.g. 'able to obtain an entry visa') (45 per cent), followed by family and friends already in the UK (37 per cent), while eight people (10 per cent) came for studies.

In spite of the prominence of media stories about immigration 'scams' designed to allow immigrants to access welfare, it is worth mentioning that none of the Bulgarians in the sample chose to come to the UK because of welfare benefits. Most of them came through the SAWS scheme, as self-employed businessmen,[6] students or as dependants.

Table 8.4 First-ranked reason for choosing the UK as a destination country (%)

	Albanian	Bulgarian	Russian	Serbian	Ukrainian	Total
Family, friends or marriagc	42.0	36.5	42.7	49.2	40.5	41.8
Ease of entry	23.5	44.7	29.3	19.7	35.4	31.2
Economic	23.5	9.4	15.9	4.9	8.9	12.9
Education	7.4	9.4	11.0	26.2	13.9	12.9
Other	3.7	0.0	1.2	0.0	1.3	1.3
Total	100.0	100.0	100.0	100.0	100.0	100.0
N=	81	85	82	61	79	388

Source: field survey, 2005.

Education

As noted earlier, education and housing are two key social factors that underpin community cohesion, at least in theory. Britain has a relatively well-educated workforce and aspires to be a 'knowledge-based society', where educational achievement is prized. At the same time, however, it has a residual section of the population with low qualifications, which also suffers from economic and social exclusion. In turn, housing has long been regarded as a key factor in social integration. Some immigrant minorities are confined to low quality housing and there is intense competition for public housing between immigrants and other low-income communities.

6 Between March 2002 to March 2005 2,422 self-employed ECAA visas were granted to Bulgarians. Following the visa scam at the beginning of 2004, decisions on new applications were suspended but resumed in February 2005 (IPPR, 2006).

Educational Background

In terms of education, those interviewed were relatively well-educated: 47 per cent had completed secondary education or college, 52 per cent had been educated at university and only one person (1 per cent) possessed no qualifications. This cohort is considerably better educated than the general population in all three localities studied, although this may reflect sample bias. Most of the Bulgarians interviewed had completed their education in Bulgaria – only 12 per cent had completed their education after arrival in the UK.

Language Skills on Arrival

Bulgarians like the other immigrant groups in the survey reported low levels of language competence at the time of their arrival. Thus almost two thirds of the Bulgarians interviewed (65 per cent) described their level of English on arrival as 'none' or 'basic', while a quarter said they spoke no English at all. The lowest level of English-speaking proficiency on arrival was also reported by Albanians, of whom 70 per cent of them spoke no English at all.

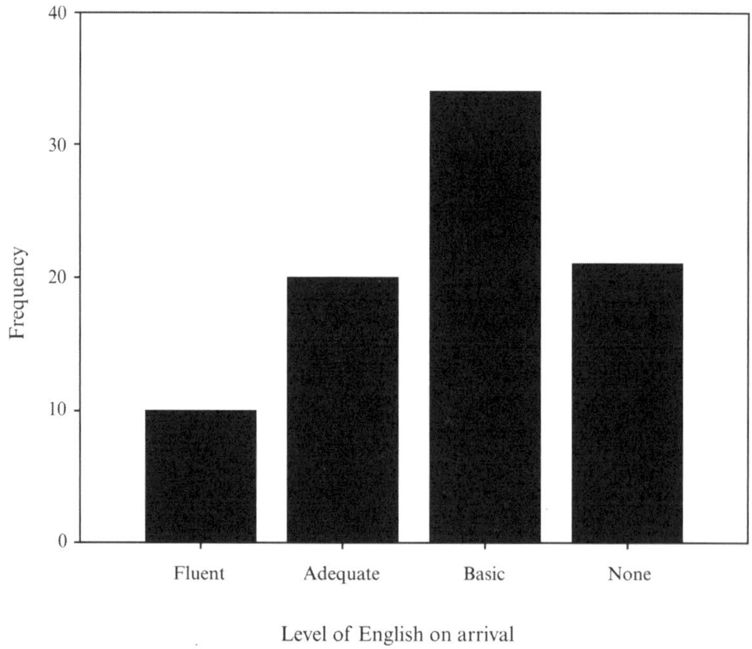

Figure 8.1 Bulgarian immigrants' level of English on arrival

Source: field work, 2005.

A Ukrainian mother in her late 40s, living in Brighton, spoke about the difficulties which immigrant children experience in the UK when they first start school here without knowing the language. She said:

> At the very beginning my son could not speak a word of English at school. Kids started bullying him. He was psychologically traumatised adapting at school. The teacher then explained to the class that it was not that he was stupid but he just did not speak the language and it helped. They stopped bullying him. I know also other Russian and East European kids at the schools of Brighton and Hove that had been mercilessly bullied by their classmates. Kids form groups at school according to their common language.

Current English Language Skills

However, a remarkable improvement in English language skills was reported since arrival, with more than three quarters of the Bulgarian immigrants describing their current level of English at the time of interview as 'fluent' or 'adequate. It should be noted that these are self-reported levels of English competence and my experience showed that this was not always the case.

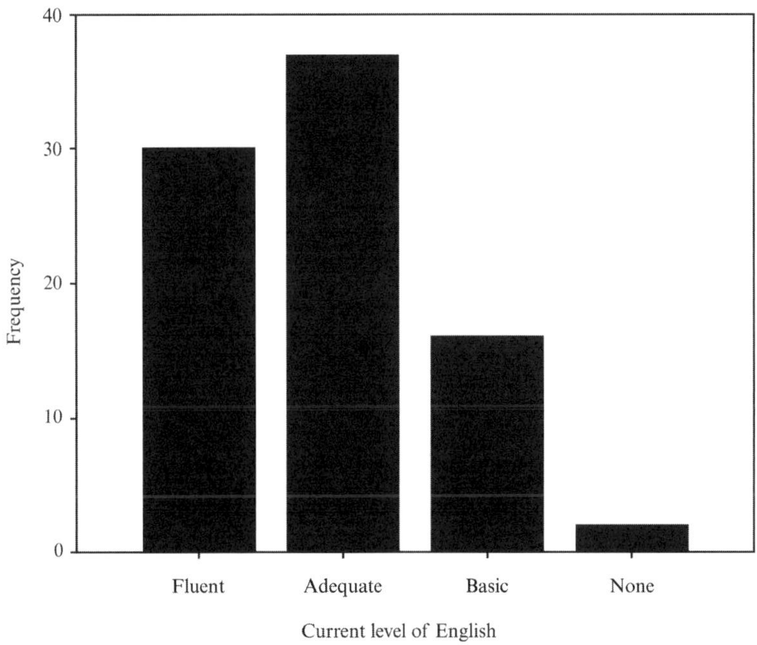

Figure 8.2 Bulgarian immigrants' current level of English

Interestingly, slightly more immigrant women (46 per cent) than men (23 per cent) described their level of English on arrival in the UK as 'fluent' or 'adequate', but this gender gap had narrowed by the time of interview, with 83 per cent of Bulgarian women reporting 'fluent' or 'adequate' English, compared to 74 per cent of men. Some immigrant women who came later to the UK to join their partners said that they had attended English classes at home before emigrating.

Housing

Whilst there might be little basis for social exclusion arising from the educational status of East European immigrants, the same is not true of housing where the dominant form of tenure was private rented housing, often associated with poorer conditions. Indeed, almost three quarters of all Bulgarian immigrants interviewed reported living in private rented housing in all three localities, in spite of the significant variation in housing types between these localities more generally.

Table 8.5 Housing tenure by locality (%)

Tenure	Brighton	Hackney	Harrow	Total
Owner occupied	21.5	11.0	7.7	13.7
Council or other social rented	8.1	23.5	15.4	15.7
Private rented from landlord	37.8	34.6	46.2	39.2
Private rented from letting agent	17.0	19.1	18.8	18.3
Family or friend provided accommodation	11.1	11.0	9.4	10.6
Employer provided accommodation	4.4	0.7	2.6	2.6
Total	100.0	100.0	100.0	100.0
N=	135	136	117	388

Source: field survey, 2005.

Although interpretation of the privately rented statistic is not straightforward, it is noticeable that 57 per cent reported living with non-family members (48 people, of whom 23 were living with another one to two non-family members and another 19 with three to five non-family members, while six were living with six to 10 non-family members). This was particularly valid in London where small flats were not easily available; as a result, they were renting two or three storey houses and sharing with other people, usually other Bulgarians.

Our informants reported finding their accommodation through a variety of routes. The most common route was through support or assistance from family, partners or other Bulgarians, who were not necessarily friends (44 per

Table 8.6 Housing tenure by immigrant group (%)

	Albanian	Bulgarian	Russian	Serbian	Ukrainian	Total
Owner occupied	8.6	11.8	17.1	23.0	10.1	13.7
Council or other social rented	33.3	1.2	13.4	26.2	7.6	15.7
Private rented from landlord	38.3	50.6	26.8	19.7	55.7	39.2
Private rented from letting agent	9.9	23.5	23.2	16.4	17.7	18.3
Family or friend provided accommodation	9.9	9.4	15.9	9.8	7.6	10.6
Employer provided accommodation	0.0	3.5	3.7	4.9	1.3	2.6
Total	100.0	100.0	100.0	100.0	100.0	100.0
N=	81	85	82	61	79	388

Source: field survey, 2005.

cent), followed by letting agencies for privately rented accommodation (28 per cent). It is interesting to note that only 12 per cent (10 people) were owner-occupiers, most of whom had lived in the UK between five and 10 years. Only one Bulgarian occupied council accommodation (in Hackney), while eight were living in accommodation provided by family or friends at the time of the interview and almost all of these people were living in London.

Labour Market Performance of Bulgarian Immigrants

Social factors, such as education and housing, have an important influence on patterns of immigrant integration and community cohesion, but of critical concern, both to academics and policy-makers, is the economic experience of immigrants.

Employment Prior to Reaching the UK

Of those who were working prior to leaving their country of origin, more than a third (38 per cent) reported being in a managerial, professional or associate professional position, followed by those in education. Not all of the Bulgarian immigrants surveyed had been employed before arriving in the UK: just over a quarter had been students (28 per cent), whilst a further 4 per cent (three people) were not in the labour market.

Table 8.7 Employment category in country of origin, by immigrant group (%)

	Albanian	Bulgarian	Russian	Serbian	Ukrainian	Total
Managers, professionals and associate professionals	24.7	37.6	53.7	36.1	36.7	37.9
Administrative and skilled trades	13.6	7.1	11.0	3.3	12.7	9.8
Personal service and sales	4.9	11.8	6.1	8.2	11.4	8.5
Process, plant and elementary	4.9	11.8	4.9	3.3	7.6	6.7
Education	30.9	28.2	13.4	39.3	16.5	25.0
Not working	21.0	3.5	11.0	9.8	15.2	12.1
Total	100.0	100.0	100.0	100.0	100.0	100.0
N=	81	85	82	61	79	388

Source: Field survey, 2005.

Meanwhile, of those who had worked prior to coming to the UK – the clear majority – the highest proportion were occupied in wholesale or retail trade (21 per cent), followed by those in business activities of one kind or another (19 per cent); 10 people (18 per cent) were employed in the health services. Just under a quarter (24 per cent) reported that they had also worked in another foreign country before arriving in the UK. They had worked in a total of 10 different countries with Germany, Greece and Libya being the main destinations. Other countries included Belgium, Cyprus, Hungary, Italy, Russia, Tunisia and Turkey.

First and Current Employment in the UK

When they first arrived in the UK, those interviewed found work in a range of sectors, the most significant being construction (for men), personal services (for women) and the hotel and restaurant sector (for both men and women). This may reflect the periods during which Bulgarians came to the UK. For example, those who had recently arrived came during a period of critical labour shortages in the construction industry or had already obtained ECAA self-employment visas specifically for the construction sector. Just nine people (11 per cent) said they had not worked since they arrived, with women twice more likely not to have worked than men.

Current employment

Levels of current employment were very high amongst those interviewed – only one person amongst the economically active was unemployed. Of those who were working, the majority were in full-time employment, although more men than women were full-time employees. Some 15 of those working (20 per cent) were self-employed and four worked through an agency, which was common practice for recent arrivals, who had a poor grasp of English and weak connections with the Bulgarian community.

Most were working legally but four admitted to working illegally (three in agriculture and one in construction), while another seven were working in breach of their immigration conditions (one in health, three in personal services, one in construction and two in hotels and restaurants). Indeed, those with insecure legal status (undocumented, or with temporary residence) were more likely to be working than those with permanent residence, and were also more likely to be employed full-time.

Overall, those working possessed a wide range of skill levels from management and professional occupations to elementary jobs. Half were employed in process, plant and elementary occupations; some 20 per cent said they were in managerial and professional occupations, followed by 16 per cent (12 people) in administrative and skilled trades and personal services (15 per cent or 11 people).

Table 8.8 Current employment category, by immigrant group (%)

	Albanian	Bulgarian	Russian	Serbian	Ukrainian	Total
Managers, professionals and associate professionals	19.6	19.7	27.3	42.2	17.9	24.1
Administrative and skilled trades	30.4	15.8	16.4	26.7	6.0	18.1
Personal service and sales	17.9	14.5	29.1	11.1	29.9	20.7
Process, plant and elementary	32.1	50.0	27.3	15.6	46.3	36.5
Total	100.0	100.0	100.0	100.0	100.0	100.0
N=	56	76	55	43	67	299

Source: field survey, 2005.

Bulgarians remain concentrated in construction (22 per cent), personal services sectors (21 per cent), hotels and restaurants (18 per cent) and real estate, renting and business activities (15 per cent).

Finding and Changing Employment

The most important way for Bulgarians to find their first job in the UK, was 'through people from own ethnic group' (33 per cent, N=25), followed by 'an agency in the UK' (26 per cent, N=20) and 'an agency in Bulgaria' (9 per cent, N=7). The same question was asked about how immigrants found their current or most recent job, which generally produced a similar range of responses. This suggests some substance to the notion that East European immigrants may be 'trapped' in ethnic employment ghettos.

Table 8.9 How immigrants found their first job in UK (%)

	Albanian	Bulgarian	Russian	Serbian	Ukrainian	Total
People from my ethnic group	48.5	32.5	25.4	24.5	36.0	33.8
Newspaper, internet, notice board	6.1	13.5	22.4	32.7	21.3	18.4
Agency in the UK	16.7	28.8	13.4	10.2	5.3	15.4
Went myself, asking different employers	18.2	5.0	10.4	14.3	16.0	12.5
British friends	3.0	2.5	9.0	4.1	4.0	4.5
Agency at home	0.0	8.8	3.0	2.0	0.0	3.0
Other	7.6	8.8	16.4	12.2	17.3	12.5
Total	100.0	100.0	100.0	100.0	100.0	100.0
N=	66	80	67	49	75	337

Note: excludes those who never worked in the UK

Source: field survey, 2005.

However, two thirds (66 per cent, N=50) of those interviewed, who were working, had a White British employer at their current or most recent job – a slight increase in the proportion whose first employer was White British, and very similar to the proportion of long-term residents, who reported having a White British employer. Another 11 per cent (N=8) were working for a Southern European employer, especially in Hackney. Turks in Hackney were employers of the Bulgarian Turks and Pomaks and 9 per cent (N=7) were working for a Bulgarian employer.

Wages

Information was collected where possible on wages, and in total, 58 Bulgarians reported their gross hourly wage rate, whilst 74 estimated their monthly income.[7] Information was also collected on non-wage benefits. A total of 15 Bulgarians, seven women and eight men (24 per cent of those in employment) reported earning under £5 an hour, which is below the National Minimum Wage.[8] Moreover, no Bulgarian men were working for less than £4 an hour while two women reported working at this rate. Very low wages amongst Bulgarians appeared to be more prevalent in Hackney, and less so in Brighton and Hove, which has largely to do with tougher competition for jobs in London.

Turning to monthly incomes, slightly higher levels of income were reported compared to what might be expected from hourly earnings, reflecting the fact that respondents often worked long hours. On average, Bulgarians, amongst the other immigrant groups under study, were least likely to be trapped in jobs with very low monthly incomes, i.e. below £600 per month. Similarly, a range of fringe benefits were also reported by Bulgarian immigrants, including meals received as part of their job, paid holidays and bonuses. However, both of these can be interpreted as characteristic of the type of employment undertaken by immigrants: the 'bonuses' received were more likely to be the equivalent of piecework in agriculture rather than the large bonuses received by very wealthy workers in the City of London. Indeed, 37 per cent of working Bulgarian immigrants reported receiving no fringe benefits at all – not even paid holidays.

Table 8.10 Monthly wages, by immigrant group (%)

	Albanian	Bulgarian	Russian	Serbian	Ukrainian	Total
Less than £600	11.3	6.8	38.5	27.0	15.8	18.5
£601 – £1,000	30.2	24.3	28.8	13.5	28.9	25.6
£1,001 – £1,500	41.5	45.9	19.2	21.6	42.1	35.4
£1,501 – £2,000	13.2	21.6	9.6	18.9	7.9	15.0
More than £2,000	3.8	1.4	3.8	18.9	5.3	5.5
Total	100.0	100.0	100.0	100.0	100.0	100.0
N=	53	74	52	37	38	254

Source: field survey, 2005.

7 Although some respondents reported both hourly and monthly wages, it was not possible to make a simple conversion from one to the other, since this would depend on the number of hours worked each month.

8 As of October 2005, the National Minimum Wage was £5.05 an hour. However, it is worth noting that some respondents may have interpreted our questions about wages as referring to *net* rather than *gross* wage rates, which would have the effect of lowering the level of reported hourly wages.

It is not unreasonable to assume that immigrants' wages are affected by legal status – in other words, undocumented immigrants or those without a right to work are likely to earn less. Some evidence for this is found from the fact that all undocumented immigrants were earning on average £500 less than legal Bulgarian immigrants.

Working Hours

As noted in the previous section, one strategy adopted by immigrant workers is to work long hours in order to translate low hourly wages into reasonable monthly incomes. The Bulgarian immigrants interviewed were somewhat more likely than the other immigrant groups in the study to be working over 45 hours per week (53 per cent, N=33), with this being particularly true for Bulgarian women (18) compared to 16 men. Interestingly, those Bulgarians with permanent residence were more likely to work longer hours. Anecdotal evidence also suggests that new immigrants are often likely to hold more than one job at the same time, again to maximise incomes. However, only 8 per cent of economically active Bulgarians in the survey were indeed found to be doing more than one job.

Membership of a Trade Union

Bulgarians were the only immigrant group in the survey without even a single trade union member. All the other immigrant groups interviewed included a few trade union members, with Serbians and Ukrainians being the most active (9 per cent and 6 per cent respectively). Some respondents explained this low rate of trade union participation by the fact that they had been organised for too long during the communist era in their home countries, and so had lost interest in joining any type of organisations. This might also partially explain the lack of strong immigrant organisations amongst these groups.

Cohesion in Diverse Communities

Sense of 'Belonging'

Turning first to the Bulgarian immigrants' sense of belonging to their neighbourhood, only 3 per cent (N=2) responded that they were 'very strongly' attached to their neighbourhood, while another 30 per cent felt they belonged 'fairly strongly' to it and 10 said they 'did not know' how they felt about their neighbourhood. This appears to reflect a real lack of identification amongst the Bulgarians and the other new immigrant groups surveyed with the neighbourhoods in which they were living.

However, when Bulgarians were asked specifically if they felt they belonged to the UK, a much higher proportion said they did, either strongly or fairly strongly – 57 per cent, of whom 41 per cent said they belonged 'fairly strongly'. Those in Brighton and Hove felt the weakest sense of belonging to Britain – 18 said they did not feel they belonged to Britain compared with only seven in Hackney and 10 in Harrow.

A number of factors might explain why immigrants were less likely to express a sense of belonging to their neighbourhoods. Most obviously, immigrants might be expected to identify closely with their country of origin. When Bulgarians were asked about their feelings of belonging to Bulgaria, 95 per cent (N=81) said they belonged to their home country and 69 per cent (N=59) said they belonged 'very strongly' to Bulgaria. Only three people said they felt 'not very strongly' to Bulgaria and only one person said 'not at all strongly'. Interestingly, these last four people were all recent arrivals to the UK. None of the Bulgarians in the study were uncertain about their feelings of belonging to Bulgaria unlike the other immigrant groups in the survey. However, those in Brighton expressed a slightly weaker sense of belonging to Bulgaria compared with their counterparts in London: 55 per cent (N=16) said they belonged 'very strongly' to Bulgaria compared to 69 per cent (N=20) in Hackney and 85 per cent (N=23) in Harrow. Interestingly, like the other immigrants in the survey, Bulgarians also reported a higher sense of belonging to the borough, in which they lived, than their own neighbourhood. This suggests that the problem of lack of belonging is one that exists at a neighbourhood level, rather than more widely. Just under half (47 per cent, N=40) of the Bulgarians in the study said they belonged to their borough, while only six did not know how they felt about it.

Another possible explanation is that Bulgarian immigrants, like the other immigrant groups in the sample, live in more deprived neighbourhoods. Yet, this is not consistent with the fact that long-term residents living in the *same* neighbourhoods had a much greater sense of belonging and that the reported sense of belonging to neighbourhood was lowest in Brighton and Hove, which was the least deprived of the three localities (only two Bulgarians said they belonged 'fairly strongly' to the City, compared to 11 people in Hackney and 12 in Harrow). Indeed, in the UK as a whole the level of deprivation of a neighbourhood appears not to affect whether people say they feel they belong to it. Half of the Bulgarians in Brighton chose the city because of employment, while half of those in Hackney and 85 per cent of those in Harrow went there because of family and friends.

Rather clearer evidence is available to suggest that the immigrants' sense of belonging – whether to their neighbourhood, borough or to the UK – increases over time. Thus those who felt they belonged 'very strongly' to their neighbourhood, had been in that neighbourhood on average for about 18 months longer than those, who felt they did not belong to the neighbourhood at all, whilst those, who felt they belonged 'very strongly' to the UK, had been in the the country on average for three years longer than those who felt they did not belong in the UK at all. In contrast, the immigrants' sense of belonging to their home countries was unrelated to the amount of time they had spent in the UK.

Some other factors are found to be associated with a stronger sense of belonging to the neighbourhood, notably whether they planned to return to Bulgaria soon (just 15 per cent of those with return plans in the next three years said they belonged, compared to 57 per cent of those without such plans); whether individuals had children with them in the UK (46 per cent expressed a strong sense of belonging, compared to 30 per cent for those without children, or whose children were living elsewhere); their type of accommodation (owner occupiers had a stronger sense of belonging than private tenants); education (with only 31 per cent of university-educated immigrants expressing a sense of belonging, compared to 38 per cent of those without a university education); and gender (40 per cent of men, compared to 30 per cent of women expressing a sense of belonging). Meanwhile, a number of other factors were not associated with individuals' sense of belonging to their neighbourhood, including age, education, language ability, occupation, and legal status.

Valuing diversity

Community cohesion is not simply about whether people feel they belong – it is also about whether people from diverse backgrounds get on with each other and whether diversity is valued and appreciated. For example, a white British respondent in Brighton, who had previously lived in London, talked about the lack of ethnic diversity in the city; he missed the diversity of some areas in London like Lewisham and Brixton. When he first moved to Brighton in 1990, he said he was shocked to have all white British colleagues and neighbours. This has meant that his pool of friends was much less diverse than before. Most of his non-British friends were from London. Such concerns were not expressed by the Bulgarians or, to a lesser degree, the other immigrant groups; they would prefer predominantly white neighbourhoods and would prefer white homogeneity than ethnic diversity.

Three initial measures were used to explore whether diversity was valued: first, whether individuals believed that their neighbourhoods are places where people get on well together; second, whether they felt that their neighbourhoods are places where people help each other; and thirdly, the frequency with which people reported talking to their neighbours, including those from other ethnic or national backgrounds.

Bulgarian immigrants agreed that the neighbourhoods they are living in are places where different people got on well together, with 81 per cent of them definitely agreeing or tended to agree with this proposition; this was much lower for the other immigrant groups in the survey. Bulgarians in London were more likely to agree with this proposition than those in Brighton. For example, while in Hackney, around 83 per cent of Bulgarians agreed, this figure fell to just 69 per cent in Brighton. Bulgarians were most positive about the proposition when compared with the other immigrant groups in the survey, with one in three agreeing that this was definitely the case (27 per cent, N=23). Nearly half of Bulgarians felt it was a 'mixture' of 'help each other' and 'going their own way', with this view being held most strongly in Harrow.

Overall, Bulgarians, together with Russians interviewed, were less likely than Albanians, Serbians and Ukrainians in the sample to report that they talked to their neighbours frequently, with 17 Bulgarians (20 per cent) never talking to their neighbours. Those Bulgarian immigrants with children living with them were also more likely to talk to their neighbours at least once a week compared to those without children.

Interestingly, Bulgarians reported in higher proportions that they talked to local people – so just under half of the Bulgarians interviewed said they spoke to local people at least once a week, which usually meant greeting them. Only 6 per cent (N=5) Bulgarians interviewed reported that they never spoke to local people. Levels of interaction were lower in Brighton and Hackney, and higher in Harrow. For Bulgarians, contact with local people was mainly reported as being in local shops (67 per cent, N=57), at work (18 per cent, N=15) and in restaurants and pubs (6 per cent, N=5).

In terms of interaction between immigrants and long-term residents the possibility of marriage or cohabitation is a key factor. Over half of Bulgarians (84 per cent, N=48) were married to or cohabited with another Bulgarian, only four (7 per cent) reported being with an English person and the rest were married to a person from the former USSR or the Balkans (Greek, Latvian, Polish, Serbian) (N=5, 9 per cent), which suggests some very small degree of 'intermixing' between Bulgarians and others, including the native British population, unlike Russian, Ukrainians and Serbians. Quite high levels of mixing between people from different ethnic or national backgrounds though were also revealed in terms of friendships, with around 75 per cent of Bulgarians (N=64) interviewed saying that they had friends from different ethnic group to them, usually from the former socialist countries.

Social networks are important for a number of reasons, not least because they provide a source of support to individuals and families when they are in difficulties. However, when they were asked who they would turn to in case of a personal problem, 54 per cent of the Bulgarians interviewed (N=46) said they would turn first to their spouse, followed by 12 per cent (N=10) of people who would turn to other household members and other Bulgarian friends. Three said that they would prefer to either not ask for help or that there was nobody to help, while eight people (9 per cent) would turn to other relatives. Similar responses were received when asked to whom Bulgarians would turn if they were ill in bed, with 52 per cent (N=44) of them saying their spouse. However, the answers to both questions may simply reflect the fact that 67

Table 8.11 'The neighbourhood is a place where people help each other' (%)

	Albanian	Bulgarian	Russian	Serbian	Ukrainian	Immigrants	Long-term residents
Help each other	12.3	27.1	18.3	11.5	11.4	16.5	22.1
Go own way	74.1	8.2	50.0	32.8	68.4	46.9	36.6
Mixture	11.1	47.1	25.6	42.6	16.5	28.1	38.6
Don't know	2.5	17.6	6.1	13.1	3.8	8.5	2.7
Total	100.0	100.0	100.0	100.0	100.0	100.0	100.0
N=	81	85	82	61	79	388	402

Source: field survey, 2005.

Table 8.12 Frequency of talking to neighbours (%)

	Albanian	Bulgarian	Russian	Serbian	Ukrainian	Immigrants	Long-term residents
On most days	30.9	18.8	15.9	21.3	25.3	22.4	39.1
Once or twice a week	27.2	25.9	29.3	34.4	22.8	27.6	29.1
Once or twice a month	13.6	23.5	14.6	21.3	12.7	17.0	13.9
Less often than once a month	13.6	5.9	23.2	11.5	12.7	13.4	8.5
Never	12.3	20.0	15.9	8.2	26.6	17.0	8.0
Don't know	2.5	5.9	1.2	3.3	0.0	2.6	1.5
Total	100.0	100.0	100.0	100.0	100.0	100.0	100.0
N=	81	85	82	61	79	388	402

Source: field survey, 2005.

per cent of Bulgarians reported having a partner; only 4 per cent (N=3) of Bulgarian respondents had no one to ask for help if ill in bed.

Levels of cooperation with work colleagues were also quite high. When asked whether people at their workplace respected each other, only around 5 per cent (N=3) of Bulgarians said they did not. This figure excludes those who said they did not know, those who worked alone, and those whose work colleagues were all Bulgarians. Some 11 per cent of Bulgarians (N=8) said they were working with other Bulgarians, while 71 per cent (N=54) were working with people from other ethnic groups; 12 per cent (N=9) said they were working alone and another 7 per cent (N=5) did not responded. In turn, just under two-thirds (64 per cent, N=54) of Bulgarians reported that they had friends from work. The 'friendliest' sectors for Bulgarians were construction (94 per cent, N=16) and health and social work (86 per cent, N=6). However, when asked to whom they could turn if they had a problem of work, most Bulgarians would turn to their employer (43 per cent, N=33) or other Bulgarians (22 per cent, N=17) or relatives (16 per cent, N=12).

Expectations of Life Opportunities

Age, family status, educational background, length of stay in the country and intentions for repatriation were all significant factors shaping immigrants' expectations of future life opportunities in Britain. What surfaced as most important during in-depth interviews was a stable job that would pay enough for a decent life. Young people also often wanted to get good education and improve their English language qualifications. Having a 'quiet' life was the most often mentioned word in the in-depth interviews with Bulgarians.

> Quiet life, good understanding with neighbours and other people; normal life. (Bulgarian, Harrow, F, 30)

> To be healthy, like life in the UK, that's why I have chosen to live here. I want a quiet life and to be able to travel with my family everywhere in the world. I want everything that a normal person wishes to achieve. (Bulgarian, Hackney, M, 28)

Asking immigrants whether they intend to return home is notoriously difficult, since evidence suggests that they overwhelmingly respond that they *do* intend to return, even if in reality that return is very unlikely. Nonetheless, we did ask whether Bulgarian immigrants intended to return home. In all, around three quarters (73 per cent, N=63) of them reported that they intended to repatriate to their home country at some stage. This intention has been rather higher amongst Bulgarians (73 per cent) and Ukrainians (57 per cent) than the other three groups (all around 40 per cent). Bulgarians living in Brighton were more likely to wish to return (strangely they had the weakest belonging to Bulgaria) than their compatriots in London; they were also the ones feeling the weakest sense of belonging to the UK, neighbourhood and the city.

Yet any view that return is imminent needs to be qualified. For example, people with young children and partners in the UK sometimes reported that they planned to settle in the UK at least until their children graduate from school and find jobs. Meanwhile, of those Bulgarians who reported that they do intend to return, few felt that this return was imminent – just two Bulgarians had already fixed a date, whilst another five expected to return within the next year, last year (should have already returned), 10 – within the next 2–3 years (16 per cent) – whereas more than half (57 per cent, N=36) said they did not know when, and another 13 per cent (N=8) anticipated that they would not return until they retire. Those from Ukraine were the most likely to have a definite plan to return.

Amongst those Bulgarians, who had a plan to return, earning enough money in the UK was the most significant factor given by them to explain their plan to return (44 per cent, N=28), followed by improved economic conditions in Bulgaria (21 per cent, N=13) and family and personal reasons (17 per cent, N=11). Those who have been in the UK for up to three years, who had come for economic reasons, and were working in low-skilled occupations, were more likely to have a concrete plan of return. Half of the Bulgarians (52 per cent, N=13), who had been in the UK between five and 10 years, were certain they would not return. Similarly, all Bulgarians (N=8), who had come for education to the UK, either did not know when they would return or were certain they will not. Those with a concrete plan of return were also more likely to say they did not belong to the neighbourhood, borough, or the UK.

Community Participation

Another element of community cohesion is whether people feel that they can influence decisions at a local level and their participation in local life. When asked if they agreed that they could influence decisions affecting their local area, just over a quarter (28 per cent) of Bulgarians interviewed said they definitely agreed, or tended to agree, while Albanians adopted the most positive stance and Serbians the most negative.

Similarly, around 24 per cent (N=20) of the Bulgarians had attempted to solve a local problem in the last 12 months and, of these, slightly more than half (N=11) had contacted the appropriate organisation to deal with the problem, five had contacted a local councillor or MP, two had contacted a local radio station, and one had attended a tenants' or local residence group meeting. Length of stay in the UK and legal status appeared not to influence either whether immigrants felt they could influence local decisions or the likelihood of them taking action to do so, although those immigrants who were owner-occupiers were slightly more likely to have taken actions, such as contacting a newspaper, organising a petition or attending a meeting.

It is also striking that immigrants, including Bulgarians, were only half as likely as long-term residents to have volunteered (formally or informally) in the last 12 months or to have given money to charity. Only three Bulgarians (4 per cent) said they had volunteered in the last 12 months, this compared to 31 per cent of Ukrainians, 30 per cent of Serbians, 27 per cent of Russians and 26 per cent of Albanians. These three Bulgarians said that they had provided driving, organised and helped with organising a local event. One said: 'Britain is not a socialist country, is it? Why volunteer then?'

Bulgarians were not involved in many community or voluntary activities and, unlike Serbians, Russians and Ukrainians, were not related to their Church either. Some Albanians reported active voluntary participation in their communities.

Despite the relatively low levels of community involvement, it is worth noticing that around 55 per cent (N=47) of the Bulgarian immigrants interviewed said that they were involved in some sort of group, club or organisation – almost half (47 per cent, N=22) reported being involved in sports clubs. None of the Bulgarians was a member of a political party in the UK, religious group, environmental group or trade unions unlike Russians or Albanians in the study. However, Bulgarians together with Russians in the survey were more likely to be members of an ethnic community organisation; some 17 of Bulgarians (N=8) said they were members of a Bulgarian community group.

Conclusion

This chapter has explored the experience of Bulgarian immigrants living in the London Boroughs of Harrow and Hackney, and in the City of Brighton and Hove, focusing on their characteristics, their perspectives on community cohesion, their expectations for the future and their interactions with long-term residents. Although this was not a representative sample in a statistical sense, it is larger than previous studies on Bulgarians in the UK and the first to systematically compare their experiences with these of other non-EU East Europeans.

The study suggests that 2003 was the peak year of arrival to the UK for the Bulgarians in the sample. A significant proportion of them are in the country to work, and they have been quite successful in finding employment even if this is in low-skilled, low-paid sectors, with little upward mobility to date. However, the experience of Bulgarians with community cohesion appears more mixed: one the one hand, high levels of interactions were reported between Bulgarians and long-term residents, while both groups agreed that diversity was respected in their neighbourhoods and workplaces. Yet, in terms of their sense of belonging to the neighbourhood, their levels of community participation and the extent to which they believe they can influence local

Table 8.13 Volunteering in the last 12 months (%)

	Albanian	Bulgarian	Russian	Serbian	Ukrainian	Immigrants	Long-term residents
Volunteered	25.9	3.5	26.8	29.5	30.4	22.7	52.0
Did not volunteer	74.1	96.5	73.2	70.5	69.6	77.3	48.0
Total	100.0	100.0	100.0	100.0	100.0	100.0	100.0
N=	81	85	82	61	79	388	402

Source: field survey, 2005.

things through their own actions, Bulgarians were much more negative about life in the UK, compared both to the other immigrant groups in the study and to long-term residents.

Nonetheless, neighbourhood belonging did appear to depend somewhat on the individual character of the neighbourhoods in the locality where Bulgarians were living: those living in Harrow exhibited stronger belonging to their neighbourhoods compared to Bulgarians that lived in Brighton and Hove. It also depended on the time immigrants had spent in a neighbourhood; the longer they had stayed in a neighbourhood, more likely they were to express a sense of belonging. Moreover, the fact that is the immigrants' neighbourhoods, rather than the UK as a whole, they feel they do not belong to suggests that place-specific policy responses are required if this lack of belonging is to be addressed.

Another important issue is whether the government and civil society should pay more attention to the two new accession countries of Bulgaria and Romania. This is certainly a timely question, particularly given the changed circumstances of the second round of EU enlargement in January 2007, on-going negotiations towards eventual EU entry for some other countries in the region, the development of an 'EU Neighbourhood' policy towards those countries not expected to join the EU and last but not least the current economic climate.

In this context, the most obvious way in which the UK government, and more especially the UK press, has been paying attention to East European migration is by highlighting its illegal even criminal nature – and, by implication, the threats to border control and the rule of law associated with such illegal movements. Moreover, as noted above, steps have also been taken to limit labour market access to non-EU nationals from Eastern Europe. Yet none of the respondents in the Bulgarian sample had arrived in the UK illegally, even if some had broken immigration rules by overstaying on a visa or working in contravention of the terms of their visa. Meanwhile, the study hardly shows heavy competition for jobs amongst the Bulgarian immigrant group, or between them and long-term residents. However, some anecdotal evidence suggests possible competition for jobs between the Bulgarians in the sample and new arrivals following the 2007 EU accession. Yet, a policy stance that needs reconsidering is the UK decision to renew its 'closed-door' labour market policy for Bulgarian and Romanian workers.

It could also be suggested that little policy action is needed more generally towards new European immigrants, and the Bulgarians in particular, since their objective circumstances, and levels of community cohesion, both appear to improve over time. For example, the study shows significant improvements in English language competence, even though those interviewed did not participate in any English language classes in the UK.

Chapter 9
Being a *Rara Avis*: The Educational Experiences of Bulgarian Children in Schools in London

Yordanka Valkanova

Introduction

This chapter is designed to identify key issues in the learning experiences of recently arrived children of Eastern European migrants during their transition to the British educational context. Drawing on a case study of Bulgarian children in London, I will provide a grounded conceptualisation of their educational needs with the aim of informing policy towards creating educational opportunities, which suit the specific needs of these groups. In coming to the UK and adjusting to the educational system here, Eastern European children face many challenges, which need to be recognised. Promoting educational policies, which address the needs of young migrants coming from Eastern Europe, will encourage their socio-educational integration and guarantee their fundamental rights.

The 'unprecedented' (Somerville 2007, 1) migration from Eastern Europe is a topic that is very much a part of the national conversation as we seek to come to terms with the challenges facing the schools and the fact that the school population is becoming increasingly diverse (Green 2007; Favell 2008). For the past decade, government concern has centred on the provision of education to support the adaptation of migrant, refugee and asylum seekers' children to the UK school system. However, the curriculum model developed focuses predominantly on the educational needs of children of South Asian and West Indian origin (Stevens 2007).

Nevertheless, a number of programmes have been developed and some schools have established policies towards Eastern European children's adjustment, which are being used to enhance pupils' learning and to facilitate teaching (Findlay and Stam 2006). Furthermore, there has been an increase of services to migrant children by education charities. This commitment is surrounded by a patchy understanding of the impact which the new migration is having on the local services and budget (see Eade and Garapich's chapter). A recent review of the literature on the Eastern European migration to West Europe indicates that there is relatively little research, which explores the processes of adjustment to the transition and how to conceptualize that transition (Datta et al. 2006). Moreover, not much is known about how the family life of the Eastern Europeans and their socialisation practices shape children's school adaptation (Robila and Krishnakumar 2004).

The study drawn on here is informed by cultural-historical activity theory (CHAT) (Vygotsky 1982; Davydov 1988, 1981; Leontiev 1981, Daniels 1986, 1993, 2004, 2005) and seeks to provide in-depth insights into how the experiences of the young people are mediated through the economic, social and cultural dynamics associated with the transition process. CHAT is a psychological theory based on philosophical inquiry. It is a methodological approach for studying the individual in relation to the activity in which he or she is involved (Daniels 2004a, 2004b). It is important to mention that elaborating his ideas about the interrelationships of learning and development, Vygotsky (1982) paid special attention to the role of adults in children's learning and argued that the mind develops in the course of acquisition of psychological tools under the guidance of adults or more capable peers.

Therefore, to understand the learning experiences of the newly arrived migrant workers' children, it is necessary to examine what subject positions are created within learning and how actual self are both created in and live inside the learning. What this more holistic approach suggests is that isolated strategies, like learning English as an additional language or even the adoption of the series of strategies recommended by the DCSF (2008), may not assist the transition of the Eastern European children. As the analysis of the results of this study on Bulgarian migrant children shows, the transition appears to involve affective consideration of experiences. Hence, the approach should consider more complex strategies addressing the cognitive as well as affective engagement of learners.

Overall, this study explores the children's learning experiences in a naturalistic way and aims to contribute to the understanding of children's learning in the context of family migration. The chapter is organised as follows. The first section briefly reviews the educational system in Bulgaria in order to highlight the educational history of the children. The second section outlines the theoretical framework of the study and uses CHAT to show how children experience the adjustment to the new context. The third section describes the methodology and methods adopted to answer the research questions. The last section presents the results and the discussions of the empirical investigation.

Overview of the Bulgarian Educational System

The educational system in Bulgaria is free and operates within three levels, namely primary (*nachalno*), which lasts for four years (7–11 years old), general secondary (*osnovno*) (11–14 years old), and high secondary school (*sredno*) (14–18 or 19 years old). According to the Law of Public Education (Law 1991) the latest age at which children must start school is 7. Children are permitted to enter school below compulsory school age subject to readiness. Primary education in Bulgaria covers grades 1 through 4 and is completed without exam. A certificate is issued in fourth grade. The curriculum consists of seven compulsory subjects, namely Physical Education, Art, Music, Mathematics, Literacy, Introduction to Bulgarian History, Geography and Natural Science, Domestic Work and Technology. The minimum comprehensive instruction includes 22-25 hours per week.

Secondary education in Bulgaria can be divided into secondary general/ comprehensive and profile-oriented/ and vocational. Secondary general education can be attained at secondary comprehensive schools (the duration of studies at this schools are four years) and profile-oriented schools (duration of studies four and a half years). Students can enter the profile-oriented schools upon completion of grade 7 or 8 after passing entry examinations, according to the profile of the school (mother tongue/literature, mathematics, humanities etc.).

After the successful completion of secondary education and passing written matriculation examinations, a *Certificate of Secondary/Secondary Specialised Education* is issued. Holders of this certificate are entitled to continue their education at a higher educational level without restriction as to the choice of a higher education establishment. Admission to higher education institutions is based on successful entrance examinations. The type and number of these examinations are determined by the higher education institutions and are linked to its profile.

Higher education is offered by universities, colleges and higher schools. It has three stages, namely Bachelor, Master and Doctor's degrees. The Bachelor stage lasts for four years, the Master stage lasts for 1–3 years, while the Doctoral degree takes three years.

Theoretical Background

CHAT establishes that the development occurs within key, meaningful experiences (Bozhovich 2007). We can compare the experiencing of meaningful events that help the child to make sense of his/her surrounding and to find a position in this context, which is adequate to his/her development. The child 'overcomes and conquers a crisis, restores lost spiritual equilibrium and resurrects the lost meaning of existence' (Vasilyuk 1991, 10). Kozulin (1991) calls this process a psychological crisis. Indeed, the key experience is an emotional subject positioning. The ability to move from one position within the activity network to another is recognised because of 'contradictions and struggles' (Daniels and Warmington 2007, 377).

According to Lompscher, learning is a complex activity where cognitive, emotional, motivational, and other components and their interrelations take place. However, learning activity '... is performed and may be brought about according to social and individual prerequisites, goals, and opportunities' (Lompscher 1999, 266). Vygotsky (1934) claimed that the developmental role of the environment may be understood only through analysis of the particular relationship the child establishes with that environment. In his most explicit statement on the subject, he claimed that there is a dialectical relation between two sides. The first is the environment, understood as the event that causes experiencing, along with the characteristics of the personality of the subject, and the second are the characteristics of the experiencing itself. Vygotsky wrote that 'experiencing is a unit of analysis which combines into one entity the environment or objects of experiencing on one hand, and the way we experience it. In other words, the personal characteristic and characteristics of the environment are presented in lived-through experiencing' (1934, 97).

However, only those characteristics of the environment that are significant from the individual's point of view are objects of lived–through–experiencing and only they elicit emotional experiencing. Alternatively, as Van der Veen and Valsiner put it, it is important 'how I, myself, am experiencing this' (1998, 342). The distinctiveness of Vygotsky's conception of social reality is best understood in terms of the cluster of qualities he attributed to social relations. As Daniels (1993) rightly insists, Vygotsky's theory of experiencing 'suggests the need to move towards a broad analysis of behaviour and consciousness which articulates and clarifies the social, cultural and historical basis of development' (1993, 48). Hence, elaboration of the concept of experiencing may provide description of how specific historical, cultural and instructional settings in this analysis of the social processes underlying individual cognitive functioning (Wertsch 1991). Experiencing could be regarded as the unity where the individual and the surrounding are tied and could be any event, which has a crucial impact on child's development.

Nevertheless, in order to develop an interpretation of migrant children's learning experiences, the understanding of experiencing needs to be tailored to fit the social contextualisation of learning. Parental involvement may enrich the contextualisation of the environment. This contextualisation factor enables us to see how experiencing makes sense of people's learning process. This study will use the model of experiencing in learning, therefore, as a guiding structure from which to set up the variables and to make assumptions.

The study was designed to address developmental aspects of experiencing by utilising in-depth interviews with children and their parents. It sought to answer the following questions:

- What are the learning experiences of the Eastern European children during the transition from their home countries to the UK and how do they fit their prior learning experiences in their home countries?

- What are the parents' understandings of the philosophy of schooling in Britain in relation to the needs of their children and how do they seek to attain them?

Following the CHAT framework, and the research evidence accumulated in the literature about the migrant children's experiencing during the transition to a new educational context (Suarez-Orozco and Suarez-Orozco 2001), we can identify, as a first approximation, the following levels of making sense of learning experiences: consideration of prior planning for migration, motivation for education and parental involvement.

Research

This study used a qualitative research strategy to gather information about cultural, economic and affective aspects of children's experiencing of migration. In-depth interviews were applied and the products of data collection process included transcribed and coded interviews from children and parents.

Sampling

The precise number of Bulgarian children in the UK is unknown. The DCSF does not publish data about the school achievements of this particular group.[1] However, because the recent EU immigration into Britain has been of continuing interest and concern to policy makers for over four years now, we will consider the data from studies about other Eastern European migrants to identify occurring patterns. Several data sources suggest that among the registered workers, who came to the UK after EU enlargement in 2004, the number of dependants is relatively small. For instance, data from the Home Office on A8[2] migration shows that a small minority (7 per cent) of registered workers, who applied between May 2004 and June 2006, declared that they

1 This key list is the list of extended categories available to Local Authorities for the collection of ethnic data for the School Census. The EE children are listed in the Final Key List of extended Ethnic Groups as White/Other White Background, including Russian, Latvian, Ukrainian, Polish, Bulgarian, Czech, Slovak, Lithuanian, Montenegrin and Romanian.

2 The group of A8 countries is formed by the countries to which the 15 existing EU member countries had the right to regulate access to their labour market. This includes eight countries, namely Czech Republic, Estonia, Hungary, Latvia, Lithuania, Malta, Poland, Slovakia and Slovenia, who joined the European Union (EU) on 1 May 2004. From that date, nationals of Malta and Cyprus have had full free movement rights and rights to work throughout the EU. In order to restrict access to benefits, the UK Government regulates A8 nationals' access to the labour market via the Worker Registration Scheme.

had dependants living with them in the UK when they applied. Recent data, gathered in 2008 reveals that only 10 per cent of registered workers state that they have dependants living with them in the UK.

The sampling at this study reflected the age of the population of newly arrived migrants' children, and was divided equally between those at primary and secondary school and in higher education. The participants consisted of twelve children and their parents. Each group consisted of two girls and two boys. In the case of the primary and secondary school children they were either 5 or 10 years old, while those at college were either 16 or 19. There were 12 parents, 9 women and 3 men. Two parents were aged between 22 and 30, seven between 31 and 40, and three between 41 and 47. The participants were selected from those, who had already participated in a study exploring East European children schooling.

The perceptions of children's learning experiences were investigated by telephone and face to face interviews with the children and their parents. The longest interviews lasted 1 hour and 30 minutes and the shortest 15 minutes. The data collection was undertaken in English as well as Bulgarian during January 2007. The data analysis process consisted of two coding stages and the 24 interview transcriptions provided eight emerging themes.[3]

Results and Discussion

Theme 1: Motivation for Success

Parents and children drew on class narratives of shame and escape. For instance, a boy aged 16 stated: 'I don't want to be a labourer. I had to study hard.' This theme was also taken up by a girl aged 16: 'I was worried about my future. I wanted to go further and wanted to pass the GCSE.' Although the parents of both children came from middle class background, the narrative of escape was similar to that developed by white working-class students (Reay 2003). However, this theme was not emphasised during the interviews of the high achieving children. They showed more certainty regarding the choice of professions and were clearer about their educational goals.

Drive and determination to succeed are valued in many immigrant groups and have a profound implication on immigrant children's achievements (Booth et al. 1997). These findings may be explained with the immigrant parents' optimism about their children's future prospects in a new country (Kao and

---

3 The study was undertaken according to BERA's (British Educational Research Association) ethical praxis. Consent forms were sought for all participants in this study. There was an option in the consent forms which provided the participants and the guardians with the opportunity to refuse to participate, or to withdraw at any time without consequences. Anonymity and confidentiality were offered.

Tienda 1995; Suarez–Orozco and Suarez–Orozco 2001), as well as with the amount of time spent in homework by their children (Shields and Behrman 2004).

Theme 2: Parents' Lack of Confidence

Some parents spoke of having a limited input into the range of school activities, especially in Key Stage 3 (ages 11–14). They felt that there was a communication problem caused by their poor English knowledge. They were unable to ask teachers questions regarding their children's learning. As one parent commented: '... that's probably one of the major problems here [the lack of confidence]. It could be a lot better for the child if I could communicate with the teachers regularly' (Interviewee 7). This restricted children's opportunities to support their parents' involvement in the learning process as well.

The parent's lack of confidence impacts on their approach to the choice of a school and educational strategies for their children. Parents spoke about the less intense learning process in schools of Britain compared with those in Bulgaria. However, they did not provide their children with extracurricular activities, because they did not wish their child to become a *rara avis* (a rare person). An obvious explanation of the parents' lack of confidence would be that the majority of the parents interviewed were women. As Markova suggests earlier in this volume, Bulgarian women migrant workers report earning lower wages than men, even if their contribution to the family budget was essential (see Shutova 1999). East European women have difficulties in adapting to the new labour market since the collapse of communism. The transition to capitalism has increased the likelihood of women's unemployment and insecurity (Guobuzaite 1998; Purvaneckiene, 1998).

Theme 3: Parents' Mental Health

Research suggests that moving through an immigration experience, which involves finding somewhere to stay and earning a reliable income, places a great deal of psychological stress on the families (Bush et al. 2005). Parents during this study spoke about the effect which the transition had on their health. In particular, they spoke about anxiety and depression. One mother was coping with depression by using medication prescribed by a Bulgarian physician in London, whom she trusted. She stated that she was not able to cope with unemployment. Her son, aged 16, explained during the interview that his mother's anxiety was caused by homesickness. The boy noted that she had not being able to visit Bulgaria for more than a year.

Other studies also suggest that children are affected by their parents' mental health (Hammen et al. 1987; Radke-Yarrow et al. 1992). In particular, children whose mothers are depressed are found to be at risk of emotional problems (Hammen et al. 1987). However, the link between depression and poorly planned migration among the Irish in London was found to be stronger for younger than for older people. Research also indicates that older migrants may be the survivors, who have successfully adapted to life in mainland Britain (Ryan et al. 2006).

Theme 4: The Value of Parenting

Although the parents recognised that the decision to migrate to the UK was beneficial to the children's future, they also believed that the migration caused them a lot of stress, therefore. However, they felt that they had to make this sacrifice for the sake of their children's survival. This theme dominated the mothers' narratives and suggested that they followed a traditional style of parenting. This supports the findings of the study carried out by Robila and Krishnakumar (2004), who examined the attitudes toward gender roles, marriage and centrality of children among different cultural groups from Poland, Slovenia, Russia and Czech Republic, Germany, Bulgaria and Hungary. Their results suggested that among those Eastern European countries, Bulgaria and Hungary were the most traditional.

Theme 5: The SAT System

One strong topic to emerge was the parents' understanding of the British test system. The vast majority of the parents felt that they needed more information regarding the assessment tasks and procedures in the UK context. For example, four mothers reported that they were not familiar with the timing of SATs procedures at the point of transition. One mother, who arrived in the UK in August 2006 to join her husband, felt that her son would have achieved better results in the GCSE exams if she had migrated two years earlier, when he was younger. Her son also felt that the planning of their migration had a crucial impact on his educational experiences.

The parents also felt that as children got older they had less opportunity to achieve good GCSE and A-level results as evidenced by comments like 'definitely not enough time for older children's adjustment to the SATs system.' The parents thought that their limited language abilities, as well as their misunderstanding of the school system in general, did not help their children to succeed. They wanted more information in Bulgarian so that they could ensure effective assessment outcomes.

Theme 6: The Curriculum

The interviews with the children revealed that UK pedagogy was considered to be more child-centred than in Bulgaria. Several children felt that they enjoyed learning in UK classrooms, but they did not think that they learnt more than in their country of origin. They also believed that the curriculum in Bulgaria and the training they had received there was more intense.

Theme 7: English as a Second Language

Parents thought that school practices helping the transition between Bulgaria and the UK were important. They wanted language training available in school to help pupils integrate. Some parents felt that the provision of extra curricular classes and alternative language sessions by external agencies encouraged children, who would not normally be active to take part in school-based activity. Parents also felt that with a little improvement, schools could better encourage language learning. Several parents thought public policy and availability of funding played an important part in contributing to an environment, which promoted young people's English language training.

Further influences on language learning emerged under the theme of self-confidence. For example, parents felt that the children's language proficiency would affect their confidence: 'I really do think it's how she learns the language. If she [had] attended a language school in Bulgaria she would have developed the skills she needed.' Seven parents reported that their children had attended private language schools in Bulgaria, although two recognised that their children's prior language training had been inadequate for the requirements of the British educational system. The parents also suggested that the child's social and home environment would have a direct influence on language level, namely their friends, peers and family environment. Certainly, in this set of interviews all parents and children felt language was a major issue in children's educational and social adjustment and mentioned this frequently. Typical comments were: 'Language, I think, has a huge, huge impact. The educational level of the parent, their support in encouraging children's English learning is highly important.'

Theme 8: Meaningful Experiencing

The results of this study demonstrate that the Bulgarian children consider their transition to schools in London as a very important experience. They realise that their success in coping with the adjustment could have a very positive effect on their family. Migration helped the children make sense of their surroundings and act as agents in a new learning context. The crisis of identity, illustrated by the phenomenon of *rara avis* self-making, calls for a better understanding of the psychological crisis experienced by school children. The children positioned themselves in relation to family expectations and promises, struggling to come to terms with their parents' new 'worker' status and with a life in low income households.

Nevertheless, this recapitulation of the experience provoked children to discover a personal reason for reconstructing their identity as learners. Their narratives showed that experiencing is situated within a wider communicative situation, where individuals not only re-examine their judgements about themselves but also present this re-examination to members of their close family. As a 19-year-old student explained with regard to choosing a college: 'One of the big things I have noticed now is that you need to establish yourself well. There is such a big gap between the losers and the rich people. You must find your place.'

Conclusion

The study presented in this chapter has examined the learning experiences of Bulgarian children. The results highlighted the positive consequences of social factors on children's learning. Looking at the narratives of those interviewed, we can uncover the process of experiencing among the migrant children. These narratives showed how the children understood critical learning events and the social situations in which they occurred. Their experiences were shaped by their parents' strategies. Their parents' lack of confidence, increased anxiety and misunderstandings about British schooling appear to be key influences on children's successful adjustments to the new learning environment. As for the school environment, both children and parents found that practices designed to support children's adjustment to the life in the new country do not consider the families' particular needs in terms of their parents' language fluency and their ability to access information which was necessary for the children's education.

The findings of this study provide general pointers for further consideration of European labour mobility policies and show how the movement of people involves understanding the role played by parents in the education of migrant children. This study of Bulgarian children and their parents reveals the impact of national differences in parenting but it has also shown that we need more precise conceptualisation of those differences and a deeper understanding of the part they play in helping people to cope with migration.

Chapter 10
Settling or Surviving in London? The Experience of Poles and Other 'A8' Migrants in a Global City Borough

John Eade and Michal P. Garapich

The Resurgence of the Multicultural Global City and 'A8' Newcomers

As the long economic boom, which began in the mid-1990s, comes to an end, the cracks in the shiny edifice of the global city are appearing once more. London's prosperity has always concealed a sharp division between rich and poor, which has been shaped by the global flows of people, capital and goods (see Sassen 1991; Fainstein et al. 1992; Fainstein 1994; Eade 1997, 2000; Buck et al. 2002; Hamnett 2003; Kaplanis 2007). The most striking feature of the city's socio-economic hierarchy is the cleavage between the global elite and professionals within the new service class, on the one hand, and those at the lower levels of the economic hierarchy, who were competing for poorly paid and insecure jobs or facing long-term unemployment.

This polarisation may have been overemphasised, since London also possesses a large and long established middle and skilled working class. Furthermore, while the lower levels are disproportionately occupied by racial and ethnic minorities, significant numbers from the more established black and Asian communities are moving away from the poor, inner London ethnic enclaves into the leafier, more prosperous suburbs (see Samers 2002). However, the intensity of competition at the lower levels of the economic hierarchy has been strengthened by the arrival of Central and Eastern European migrants, particularly after the states which entered the European Union in May 2004 (A8 states). The willingness of these migrants to take up routine low wage jobs has worsened the plight of young black and Asian workers and those arriving more recently from war-torn regions in Africa and the Balkans, for example (see May et al. 2007; Gordon et al. 2007).

In other words, amid the general celebration of global movement it is crucial to examine the dark side shaped by political antagonism, racial prejudice, exploitation and even destitution. Research has pointed to indigenous resistance to newcomers across Europe and the ways in which different governments have sought to control the influx of poor, low-skilled migrant workers (see, for example, Wrench and Solomos 1993; Cesarani and Fulbrook

1996; Castles and Miller 2003). As we have seen in the chapter by Laurence Cooley and Dhanajayan Sriskandarajah, despite Britain's commitment to the free movement of labour in 2004 when the 'A8' countries joined the EU, it changed its stance when Bulgaria and Romania joined three years later. As criticisms of the British government's approach towards immigration strengthened, doubts about the benefits of the latest influx spread, particularly in localities where the newcomers' presence caught the public eye.

In this chapter we are going to focus on a particular London borough, which has a long association with European migrants and where Poles and other A8 migrants now work and/or live in substantial numbers. We will examine the part played by social networks in their move to this area of London and in helping them survive there. We will also look at those who were less successful in coping with the global city and the attempts by voluntary agencies to provide support. This dark side of the migration story also involves the local state, since NGOs and community organisations cannot cope on their own and sometimes community organisations exclude those who, they believe, may give their group a bad reputation. Yet, as Deema Keneff points out in her chapter, the cutbacks in welfare services play a key role in contemporary migration flows. The reduction in state welfare support, which encouraged British migrants to settle in Bulgaria, are impacting on those who have moved from the 'new Europe' to the 'old Europe'.

The Hammersmith and Fulham context

Traditionally, the borough of Hammersmith and Fulham has always drawn considerable numbers of migrants from a variety of countries. Its convenient location and transport links have made it a valuable connection point for newcomers. The borough's continuing attractiveness for migrants became evident when the A8 nations joined the European Union. However, 1 May 2004 was not the starting point for recent migration from Eastern Europe, especially from Poland. Hammersmith and Fulham contains a long established Polish community, created by Second World War refugees and displaced persons as well as by subsequent waves of immigrants and their descendants. The construction of the Polish Social and Cultural Centre on King Street in 1974 was a visible sign of this community's presence, not just locally but across London and further afield (Sword 1996; Habielski 1999). In many respects the social foundations of current dynamic migratory flows were laid down at least two decades ago.

It can be argued that this leaves other language groups from the A8 countries on the margins and excluded. Indeed, the area has been dominated by presence of Polish nationals and their institutional, financial and social base. Yet although the community organisations, bars and Eastern European food shops are frequented by Poles, they also attract Slovakian and Lithuanian migrants, for instance. The best example is the Eastern European Advice Centre, which has noted an increase since May 2004 in the numbers of Lithuanian nationals visiting and has also provided help for Roma migrants, who for various social and cultural reasons have limited connections with the established Polish institutions. In fact, as others have pointed out, the status of the Roma poses particular challenges, since they are often rejected and stigmatised by both the British majority and migrants from their countries of origin.

Hammersmith and Fulham clearly acts as a magnet for people seeking jobs, opportunities or simply contacts with their friends or family. This is visibly demonstrated in the many recent additions to shops and businesses across the borough. Since EU enlargement at least five major Polish commercial advice and information offices have opened in the area and one of the main Polish magazines and media group (a radio and television station) is based on King Street just opposite the Town Hall. In 2004 three Polish delicatessens had been established in the borough but by 2008 the number has grown to at least seven with most of small corner-shops and newsagents advertising Polish and other Eastern European food and newspapers. In addition, a number of businesses from bars and restaurants to hairdressers and even an estate agent specialising in property in Poland have opened. From an analysis of a Polish Directory,[1] and the local Polish press, some 91 Polish businesses and organisations can be identified within the borough. The council estimates that these enterprises employ some 660 people but this is undoubtedly an underestimate, since there will be other businesses which are not so visible.

The Town Hall itself is known to Polish nationals in the area, as there is a special employment fair held regularly on its premises. This event is widely advertised across London and is organised by media outlets. It brings together employers, job-seekers, the ethnic media, community organisations, trade unions and financial institutions.[2] The symbolic place, which Hammersmith holds among Poles was also highlighted and reinforced in October 2007 when the current Prime Minister of Poland, Donald Tusk, visited Polish workers at Tesco's on King Street during his campaign visit to the UK. This event received a lot of publicity in Britain and in Poland and confirmed that the borough, especially its central and northern end, is the place where Eastern Europeans, and especially Polish migrants congregate, work, shop and socialise. It may be said that while Victoria Station or Luton Airport serve as the physical entry points for migrants arriving in London, Hammersmith and Fulham is the social entry point, where people can get information, meet friends, eat ethnic food, establish networks and find employment opportunities.

As the social and economic hub for Polish nationals in London, the borough unsurprisingly attracts people from different class backgrounds, educational

1 *Informator Polski: Polish Directory 2007/8.*

2 This is a yearly event with the last one organised on 5 April 2008.

levels, skills and regions. As noted earlier, social networks influence individual migrants' success on the labour market – they enable people to rely on others in terms of information on jobs, housing, social services and so on. Their diverse backgrounds and networks show the limitation of viewing them as simply 'ethnics', 'communities' or 'migrants'. This complexity also adds another dimension to the ways in which national and local authorities, as well as wider civil society institutions, respond to these flows.

The Survey

These general comments are based on a survey conducted in January and February 2008 for Hammersmith and Fulham borough council on the needs of A8 migrants in the borough. Face-to-face interviews with 295 people were conducted in work places, streets, public places (bars, parks) and at the homes of the respondents. Of these, 180 were borough residents and the rest (115) work in the borough but live elsewhere. Altogether, 254 respondents work in the borough (86 per cent). All interviews, except the ones conducted with Lithuanian migrants, were conducted in their native languages – Polish, Slovak and Hungarian.

The survey sample was predominantly composed of people with strong links to the borough. Sixty-one per cent live here, with the remaining living outside (but working in the borough) and 86 per cent of our respondents work within the borough boundaries (the rest are people who just live within the borough). Sixteen per cent arrived between 1995 and 2001, 31 per cent between 2002 and 2004, 23 per cent in 2005, 14 per cent in 2006 and 18 per cent in 2007.

Arrival, Adaptation and Migration

Almost all participants came to the UK using their pre-existing social networks and very often found employment through them, commonly arranged by members of their family. Maria, for instance, came here because her husband already worked in London and together, they relocated to Hammersmith and Fulham.

> I found myself here by accident really; my husband came here, to London so I came after him. We lived for a while in a better area but we had to move here because the company moved us here [her husband is a pub manager].

Barbara also came because already her brother had been living in the borough:

> I also work here but I came here to my brother who lives here …

Stefan, however, looked for employment by himself and simply walked in to one of the IT shops and got a job:

> … it was also a bit of an accident for me, because I found employment in the area; it wasn't really my own choice, but it is a good area for this type of shop because clients are more affluent ….

Others have also mainly looked for employment on their own, sending CVs, browsing the web. Only one participant used the Job Centre and was pleased with their help:

> I used the Job Centre. When I arrived here I began on a building site, worked in a pizza place, then I was referred to another one and through contacts, friends and networks got it …

It is important to note here that two of respondents had worked in another country before coming to Britain. Consequently, while the migrants may identify with a particular nationality (i.e. Polish, Slovak or Czech), they may have developed a wider perspective concerning the labour market and local culture. For Gabriel, for instance, comparison with Germany convinces him that life and work in London is far more easy and relaxed:

> Well, I have this comparison with Germany and I found that over there it is so hard, all these problems, visas, permissions, papers … and here the fact that you have agencies, where you can come in and browse for jobs on the computer – this is incredible … in Germany, for example, when you rent a flat you need a bank account, references, letter from employer etc. … no way as easy as it is here. It is much easier here… I mean when I came here a friend helped me to stay for a few days, so I could find a place to live … it's simple.

In the case of Jacek and Pawel, however, it was their particular occupation – working in the Polish media – that influenced their decision. Hammersmith and Fulham is seen as a social and cultural centre of Polish migrants with major institutions, media, shops and general social and cultural infrastructure offers employment opportunities otherwise not available. Jacek, for instance, is aware that he could not really find the same job in the English language media as he enjoyed in a Polish newspaper:

> I sent some CVs by email, wrote things went to few places and got a chance … I came here before and worked in a restaurant, then came back but with bit more funds to afford to look for something I wanted to do.

The future plans and migration strategies of the group reflected the general attitudes highlighted in the survey. Two participants said that they actually look forward to staying in UK or at least not going back to Poland. Others did not exclude any possibility or declared that they are definitely going back to Poland soon. Gabriel is a typical case – he combines two positions in catering and plans to earn enough money to open up a business in his native Krakow:

> I have lived almost two years in London, but do not want to stay here forever … I am from Krakow and I like it there so much that I want to go back; my idea was to come for a while to earn a bit and then go back; I was living for a while in Germany so I have a kind of comparison … I graduated in Krakow and to be honest I came here to earn some cash; I want to save it for opening some business […] … as for my plans here I want to be here no more than two years and then I will go back.

Not surprisingly, the experience of working below their qualifications and not developing professionally encourages people to return. Both Barbara and Maria are clearly uncomfortable with what they do for living and despite being already here for some time, still see their stay as temporary:

> … my plans aren't precise also … I thought about staying here another year and then going back; I also do not feel very well, I do something not remotely connected with my studies; I came here mainly to earn a bit of money and improve my English. I've been here now for three years but I just do not see myself staying here [in UK] … I mean, I did graduate in Poland and I just feel bad working behind the bar all this time; at the moment, for instance, I'm looking for work, but I am tied up with my daughter's school so I would prefer to stay in the area … I look on the web, in the papers, I seek to do something related to estate agency and the property market … but if I had an offer from Poland, who knows … and if I knew that I could find a good job in Poland – I wouldn't think twice and would go back.

Kinga also seems undecided and refuses to state how long she aims to live in the UK:

> I don't have a clue … I may stay another three years … The thing is that it was a bit of an accident that I stayed, I came to visit my aunt and simply stayed. At the beginning I didn't work but found this place in this shop and here I am in the same spot four years later … I mean I don't complain – I like it there, but cannot really say how long I'll stay.

Interestingly, a few participants did not link leaving UK with returning to Poland but rather looked to migrate further to destinations, such as the USA,

Canada and Australia, which were also preferred by those from the British majority:[3]

> I thought about moving on to Australia, I'm going there to visit my friend just to see how is it there ... but if I don't like it, I'd probably come back to London rather than Poland; so I don't have precise plans but Poland doesn't feature anywhere.

This particular group tried to take full advantage of the opportunities arising from global mobility and seemed very comfortable with the idea of moving between places. Yet they very often expressed a willingness to move back 'not now but one day' and this represents an 'exit strategy' in the case of economic downturn, personal problems or an inability to work according to one's qualifications. As we have seen, participants are concerned about the fact that working below their qualifications in low paid sectors is a dead end and, psychologically, it may be more acceptable if someone treats it only as a temporary option. This also explains the strong desire to upgrade qualifications and the interest in adult education. Some focus group participants mentioned their plans to upgrade their qualifications and they saw that the main barrier to do this was their language skills:

> ...yes, but I still need the language skills to upgrade. I would like to ... and our company sends us for training ... they come forward with some offers, so here it is ok. ...the language is the problem because you are always behind those that speak fluently. I'm looking now for a course in management.

However, working in an ethnic firm has its own obstacles and limitations. The issue of a responsive employer, who seeks to upgrade his/her employee's qualifications, was seen differently by those employed in Polish businesses, mainly the media. Asking the question about whether they were willing to press their employers to upgrade their qualifications, one of the respondents employed in the Polish media remarked:

> Well, not in our trade [Polish media]; our employer would not come forward with such an initiative.

This issue shows the limits of the ethnic economy in the labour market. It is clear that with an oversupply of qualified individuals, Polish owners of media outlets are reluctant to invest in their employers. As employees see the opportunity to work in their occupation and not having to work in low-paid and low-status jobs as an advantage, they are less inclined to demand from their employers better conditions, additional training and so on. Nevertheless,

3 See the IPPR study on the British abroad.

it is clear that employees in the ethnic economy accept this, as it offers an opportunity to work according to qualifications even without appropriate English language skills or work experience in the UK.

The Darker Side of A8 Migration

The role of Hammersmith and Fulham as the social entry point for A8 migrants stems from its ability to provide people with the crucial social and cultural capital migrants need in a global city – networks, friends, information and gossip. Yet what happens when individuals lack these resources? How are these established when individuals do not have family or friends who can offer a helping hand?

The 'Wailing Wall' Phenomenon

Being a social entry point does not mean an institutionalised presence that could provide newcomers with services in the form of an official organisation. On the contrary, it may be an informal meeting place, which becomes well known among migrants and their friends back in Poland. It may come as a surprise that by far the most famous place among many Polish migrants for the last two decades has not been the Polish Centre – one of the biggest centres of the Polish diaspora in the world, with a largest Polish library outside the country – but rather the premises next door, a Gujarati family-owned corner newsagent where, since the late 1980s, there has been a window display full of job, accommodation and other adverts (mainly in Polish). As one of the most important informal casual labour markets for West London, this place with its surrounding streets has gained an infamous reputation. However, its tremendous longevity meant that for at least two decades this spot has fulfilled an important social role in the establishment and sustainability of migration flows and shaping migrants lives in the area.

This area – between Ravenscourt Park Underground station and King Street – in the words of police officers familiar with it – was much better known in Poland than Big Ben. As an informal labour market throughout the 1990s and until recently, it attracted casual labourers and also anyone looking for a flat, a nanny, transport to Poland or advice. Due to the secrecy guaranteed by using the Polish language in the advertisements, it also provided an opportunity for criminal activity. It was quite common to find there explicit adverts for the sale of counterfeit cigarettes, forged documents, passports, drugs or offers for the services of 'freelance bailiffs'. However, the place had been left relatively unnoticed by the public authorities and the media for over 15 years. It was the accession by Poland and other states, which encouraged public attention to focus on this area and with the increased numbers of people frequenting the 'wailing wall', the phenomenon gained a notoriously bad press. At the same time, due to the change in the law, migrants no longer felt the need to hide as they had done before under the fear of possible deportation.

A combination of these factors escalated into creating a real public order issue. Day labourers who failed to secure employment formed distinct groups of men, often drinking alcohol and threatening members of the local community, using private property for sanitary purposes and sleeping rough in nearby parks or gardens. What struck local government officials, who were trying to deal with the issue, was the reluctance of established Polish institutions to engage with the issue. Due to the fear of being associated with people of lower educational levels and class, the ethnic elites have strengthened the class boundary between them and those in need. The problem escalated and eventually – due to residents protests – led to the issuing of a dispersal order by the police. Nevertheless, the area still attracts numbers of individuals, who want to meet, seek employment opportunities, sell things, send or receive parcels from or to Poland, or simply hang around. The police force has recognised that this spot will remain an area where people will congregate, and the only feasible way to prevent it from becoming a problem, as it as it has been previously, is to have a permanent police presence there.

> The 'wailing wall' is here to stay; it is the informality of the place that makes it attractive and the fact that it is a known spot to seek casual labour – both for the employers and those seeking work. It caters to quite a large part of West London, as it is a known area where migrant workers congregate. The only way of preventing it becoming a criminalised place is to have a police presence there. (Police officer)

These details are important as they show that the phenomenon of migrant workers flowing into the borough is an old one and should not be treated as a sudden development. It shows also that the area has always been a place where Polish migrants could establish networks of support or seek opportunities. What has changed is the perception of numbers, but also the ability of many of these migrants to obtain legitimate employment; hence their reliance on informal labour markets such the one mentioned above is slowly decreasing. These negative aspects aside, it must be stressed that for years the 'wailing wall' offered to newcomers an important source of information, opportunities and networks for those who lacked them. Today, this information and range of opportunities can be obtained from a variety of sources and migrants readily use them.

For the local police force there is a clear link between the informal labour market around the area in question, presence of groups of men seeking casual work and drinking on the one hand and the rise in petty crime, begging and general perception of insecurity on the other. However, the persistence of the place as a meeting point means that it needs to be controlled, rather than totally eradicated, since this would simply transfer the problem elsewhere.

Despite a perception that Polish nationals dominate the influx of migrants to the borough, the Shepherds Bush Advice Centre maintains, for instance, that their main client base is still composed of non-EU migrants. They have experienced a considerable increase in enquiries from A8 nationals, mainly related to employment law, debt, and social benefits resulting in additional pressures from that part of population but, overall, this has not been overwhelming.

Those Who Lose Out

Asked if they have come across any particular problem in the last 12 months, the majority of migrants interviewed did not come across any and it seems clear that due to their skills, proficiency in English, or social networks they can tap into, are adapting quite well. Their sense of self-determination, individualism and ambition, noted in our previous study (Eade et al. 2007) leads them to see their migration as a move upwards on the social mobility ladder. Although this perception is relative, since individuals understand mobility in highly subjective ways, migration is clearly more than just about material factors. Migrants are interested in the higher status at home, which living in a global city might bring, and how to provide their relatives with information and assistance, and the greater freedom from social and cultural constraints they enjoy (especially important for women, see Coyle 2007).

However, migration movements have always had their losers and winners and the picture that emerges from interviews with service providers is that the charity/voluntary sector within the borough bears the burden of the ones that are not doing so well. As one person involved in legal assistance for Polish nationals said:

> We don't see or hear from those that are doing well and work. They are simply at work during the day; we receive those that have problems.

The reality is that, along with the successful majority, a distinct minority fall victims of either ill preparation in their migratory plans, pre-existing conditions (mainly related to alcohol abuse), structural restrictions imposed by the British state on A8 access to certain social assistance, unscrupulous employers, gross exploitation and general lack of awareness about local conditions on the labour market.

In general, all service providers agreed that the influx of A8 migrants after the EU enlargement exceeded expectations and that the government grossly underestimated the figures. A specific group of service providers run by the charitable, voluntary or social assistance sector has been particularly under pressure. All institutions that cater for vulnerable individuals with substance misuse problems, homelessness or unemployment recorded a dramatic rise in the presence of A8 migrants. For some institutions like The Broadway, The Upper Room and UR4Jobs, they were predominantly from Poland (according to the service providers they account for between 80 and 90 per cent) with very few Slovakian, Lithuanian, Romanian or Hungarian nationals.

The institutions, engaged in social assistance, emphasised the negative consequence of stripping A8 migrants from some of the welfare entitlements. This has clearly left a number of people in a state of legal limbo as they cannot claim Job Seekers Allowance or Housing Benefits, and have turned to rough sleeping, substance misuse and mental and physical decay. The restriction in policy has been designed to prevent unfounded claiming of benefits, but its human cost according to service providers is substantial. In their view, the overall economy and labour market benefits from these inflows, but it is the voluntary and charity sector that is left with the task to cater for less successful migrants. 'They rip up the benefits, we clean up the mess' – as one service provider bluntly put it.

The Shepherds Bush Advice Centre points to the fact that there is a general policy trend in the restricting of access to social benefits, so it is becoming increasingly difficult for larger groups of people to apply for them. This puts additional pressures on institutions, which help people to obtain them, but this relates to everyone, not only A8 nationals. The pressure on their service, then, is more a reflection of general policy trends rather than an increase of number of cases.

Practically, the restriction on social benefits means that if someone has lost work and accommodation and lacks the funds (or what's equally crucial as we saw – social networks) to rent, is left on the streets or has to return to their home country. Many choose the latter. Because A8 migrants are eligible for welfare provisions only after 12 months of documented employment, this leaves individuals working in a grey economy – a particularly difficult situation since they could never actually access some provisions from the welfare assistance and their exclusion can continue for years.

A number of people also rely on casual employment. The insecurity of the labour market and over-dependency on social networks led to a specific 'scenario of downfall', with individuals having very little resources and whose loss of a job means immediate eviction from their accommodation. This can then lead to sleeping rough and loss of documents, which further diminishes their chances of re-entering legitimate employment or finding suitable accommodation. The lack of access to homeless shelters further entrenches people in a spiral of decay, since they are left to their own devices in finding new accommodation or employment. This scenario has been described in several instances during the fieldwork. As one charity sector provider summarised:

> Well, it's like nineteenth-century capitalism, it's all very well when someone has a job, but once someone loses it, there is no safety net for them. (Charity worker)

In some cases the scenario of downfall has led to serious mental health issues or even death.[4]

> It is fair to say there is wide range of people; but I would say that there are many people who have been left behind by the new economic migrations, people who have come here for jobs but who have found that they are nor able to get onto the ladder. They may have been promised employment but these jobs turned out to be casual, that is without a fixed salary or with the first salary not being paid on time, and while they wait for it they cannot pay for their accommodation and so get into difficulties. (Social services street worker)

The 'scenario of downfall' means that it is very easy for individuals to fall from being relatively secure in their job/accommodation into a position of desperation with the very real prospect of having to live on the street. The following examples from our fieldwork reflect the very precarious position people found themselves in:

> A. In her 30s, lived with her friend; she went once for holidays to Poland, and on her return she found out that the flat had been rented to someone else; her friend disappeared with the deposit and her landlord was unwilling to help her, and the police couldn't do anything. She had to sleep on the street for several days, growing desperate, and finally found a charity that helped her to find a job outside London.

> B. In his 40s, has lived in London for six years now. He used to work in the building industry but at one stage began to drink, lost his job and place to stay. For a long period of time he lived on the street, or amongst other migrants in a similar position, and he is also a frequent squat dweller. His ID was stolen and he was seriously beaten up and had to be taken to hospital. His health began to deteriorate. At the moment he lives in a squat and hasn't got any ID since he cannot afford to have his passport renewed. Recently he learned about a charity where he could get meals and so became a frequent visitor. There, he volunteered as a kitchen help and has now has been offered training to become a chef which he considers is ideal for him as his health doesn't allow him to go back to construction work.

---

4 Reports about death from freezing, substance overdose or violence among this group are quite numerous. Detailed account of very similar A8 migrant circumstances can be found in already existing publications: *Routes into London's Homelessness Services: The Experiences of A8 Nationals. Key Findings and Recommendations*, October 2007, The Broadway.

> C. and D are Hungarian teachers who came to London from their home country through an employment agency. This agency turned out to be a bogus one; they had promised the women a teaching assistant's job which turned out to be false. They were left on the street without a placc to stay and were desperate. The local Hungarian priest offered them a place to stay and helped them to find other employment.

These cases match well with a general perception from the social assistance providers of A8 migrants using their services. In general, according to many providers, the possible scenarios fall into four categories:

a. The first one is composed of people, who are in need of help in relatively minor matters – registering for National Insurance, finding English courses, writing up a CV, advice on where to seek employment, connection with an employer, or translations.
b. The second group are people whose situation has suddenly deteriorated and are in immediate need of financial assistance or legal help – usually people, who (as in the first case.) have lost their jobs and are in danger of finding themselves on the street. Falling into this category are also people, who have been duped by various scams operating between EU states and Britain. Scams usually involve false advertisements in the press in the country of origin and naïve individuals, who pay up to £200 upfront for work and accommodation. They are often left penniless on the outskirts of London. Stressed and often ashamed by their naivety, they often turn to drink.
c. The third category are those who, like B, had work but are also suffering from substance misuse and have a long history of unemployment and homelessness.
d. Finally, there is a group of individuals, who had pre-existing substance misuse problems or mental health issues and are often long-term users of homeless charitable institutions. These individuals have sometimes already been living in London for years and often act as 'guides' for newcomers to the underworld of the London street population.

What is crucial is that the main users of voluntary agencies for vulnerable people (institutions like The Broadway, the Upper Room and Barka Foundation) are predominantly single men in their late 30s or 40s, with poor language skills. Language has been identified by all service providers in this sector as the main obstacle in overcoming difficulties. This demographic point is important, since the group using the social assistance sector differs markedly from the general demographic picture both from the available council statistics as well as the data emerging from the survey.

It is also difficult to assess the degree to which that group are resident in the borough. According to some providers, it is far too expensive for them to rent in the area, but the number of squats where people live proves that some are determined to stay within proximity of the places they frequent – the 'wailing wall', Polish shops or various social assistance providers. Others, after using these services for short periods, have disappeared and have never come back. The perception of this being a transitory group is very strong, as some providers stress that they do not see the same faces again after a while. However, it is clear that there is a small group of hardcore substance users, who have been known to all service providers for many years.

A lack of adequate information and language skills remain one of the major problems for these migrants, and institutions like The Broadway and Upper Room have Polish-speaking staff that work on a daily basis to address them. According to service providers that cater for these groups, their main task is to avoid the first two scenarios (a and b) becoming last two (c and d) as often happens in reality. As the organiser of the UR4Jobs project, that facilitates employment for people living on the streets, says:

> A lot of the support we do is bridging support, bridging that gap between destitution and getting going. This is crucial when someone just starts here and is vulnerable.

As seen in the case of P, whether someone ends up on the street and becomes a rough sleeper, is often a matter of sheer luck. For all institutions, which provide help and legal assistance, it was absolutely vital to stress that the costs of helping migrants to avoid slipping into homelessness, alcohol abuse and destitution are small compared to the costs of having to deal with someone who has experienced living on the street for months.

Transnational Response to the Problem

Despite the efforts of various voluntary organisations, it became clear that the overall rise in the street population from A8 states, especially Poland, was getting out of hand, and due to the legal framework seemed hard to address. The legal limbo, in which vulnerable individuals found themselves, has created a visible culture of street drinking and anti-social behaviour from a group of people, especially in Hammersmith area. This presented local authorities with a big problem of having to create social policies for people, who were denied access to welfare funds, but at the same time, as EU citizens, could not be deported to their home state.

After considerable research carried out by those Council workers in charge of dealing with the homelessness and substance misuse problems, the Barka Foundation – a Polish-based charity – was commissioned by Hammersmith and Fulham Council with CLG (Communities and Local Government) funds, to design a specific policy of 'reconnection' for these individuals who wish to return to Poland. Barka is an organisation with a Christian ethos and a belief that work and active participation in the community are the keys to success to the successful reintegration of excluded individuals back into society. It has a large network of community based farms with sustainable social enterprises and caters mainly for those, who back in Poland are excluded by the uneasy transition to a market economy.[5] In the words of its chairwoman, Ewa Sadowska, Barka takes care of those 'who are migrants in their own country' and who are willing to start a new life. It seemed logical that such an institution takes care of migrants, who are also victims of a sudden move to a mature market economy but lack the social safety net or personal social networks that are so vital for migrants when they are vulnerable.

The policy of 'reconnection' was based on giving certain individuals an avenue whereby they could lift themselves up from current lifestyles which most often involved heavy alcohol abuse and rough sleeping. This policy has not been termed 'repatriation', since that would simply mean a return, while 'reconnection' involves a commitment on the part of individuals to abstain from alcohol and to work and contribute to the economy of the community they are joining, which is a type of social enterprise.

Individuals were approached by 'leaders' (Barka street workers) at The Broadway and Upper Room and through long conversations, casual talk and listening, who gradually and patiently introduced potential returnees into what Barka's communities would have to offer them and what they would have contribute themselves. People involved in this work are often former alcoholics and rough sleepers themselves and have a lot of understanding of the delicate nature of persuading someone to give up their previous lifestyle.

> It is a long process … you need to get to the bottom of people's problem and understand them … it is difficult and takes time. (Barka street worker)

Initially, Barka was commissioned to persuade three people per month to return to Poland. After six months of working in London and carrying out street work and assistance with Polish migrants, using The Broadway and Upper Room premises, around 90 people who were approached had decided to go back. It needs to be stressed that people are free to choose where they want to live upon their arrival in Poland, and that a vast majority of them stay within Barka's communities.

Both the council and voluntary sector service providers agree that Barka's work has been very successful and beneficial. There is a shared view that Barka has achieved what other institutions could not have done, not only removing people from the streets and their substance misuse habits, but also giving individuals a coherent prospect of development, improvement and integration

---

5 More information about Barka can be found in internal Hammersmith and Fulham council reports and also on www.barka.org.pl.

back into society – whether Polish or British. It is also perceived as very cost effective:

> I don't know any other service that has done 400percent more than they have been paid to do, I can't point to one. It's irrefutable that it is working …. (British charity street worker)

The general profile of people approached and helped by Barka, reflects the type of individuals, who are most prone to finding themselves in this vulnerable situation and does not differ much from the picture given by other service providers in this area. The average age of Barka's clients is 35, 90 per cent are males; 89 per cent have secondary or vocational education but with poor English skills. Two thirds have alcohol misuse problems and three per cent mental health issues. Almost all, at the moment of initial enquiry, have lived in on the streets, in squats, convents, with casual friends or hostels. An average length of stay in the UK was around two and a half years. However there are cases of individuals living in UK for 22 years, or for just one week.[6]

Apart from the reconnection policy, Barka runs daily surgeries in cooperation with The Broadway where more immediate enquiries are addressed – related to employment, National Insurance registrations, CVs, mail and translations. This extra assistance stems from the realisation – shared by all service providers and Barka itself – that what Barka has to offer in terms of its social enterprise in Poland and its ethos, is not for every Polish national, who needs assistance in London. As all providers agree, there are a number of people that are unwilling to return, for personal, financial and legal reasons and so a more integrated approach, adapted to British circumstances, should be designed.

The problem that arises when social assistance for vulnerable people is successful is that, potentially, it creates a 'magnet effect', drawing in people otherwise unconnected to the borough just to use the service. Most providers that were interviewed were aware of that issue but saw the problem as being in the structure of government funding rather than the service itself. As Barka has seemed to attract attention from a number of London local authorities, as well as those in Dublin, Berlin and Rome (which have their own issues of Polish migrants losing out), the view of all respondents was that a London-wide or centrally funded scheme would be the most logical and practical answer to the 'magnet' dilemma. In addition, most providers saw the idea of services for migrants being selected according to their local residency as inaccurate and unrealistic as these are very mobile and transient individuals changing addresses very often throughout the year. This especially applies to the group

6 A detailed account of Barka Foundation activities can be found in their report: *Centra integracji migrantów zarobkowych w Londynie i Dublinie. Sprawozdanie merytoryczne*, Program Fundacji Pomocy Wzajemnej Barka 2007.

that uses the social assistance provision through The Broadway or the Upper Room and UR4Jobs service.

> It doesn't make sense to think that these people are resident here and will be here in the longer term… one day they are here, the next over there … (Charity worker)

However, in case of Barka, providers disagree that it has created a magnet effect:

> There is no evidence that the work we do with Barka acts as a magnet for Poles from other areas of London. It's a bit of red herring and I don't think this is an issue. (Charity worker)

Service providers believe that the main lesson arising from the successful partnership between Barka and Hammersmith and Fulham council is the realisation that there is a pressing need to create a London-wide or even European-wide response network, independent from local funding:

> The first thing I would suggest is a pan-London response, not an individual, borough by borough response. (Charity worker)

This perception of the need for a coordinated approach was widely shared by other service providers. Barka's workers stress that one of major obstacles in their work is the lack of places in homeless shelters where individuals from Accession states willing to return could prepare psychologically and physically for the journey. The fact that people who want to return are still living on the streets and come into frequent contact with the street drinking culture means that many attempts at reconnection fail. Special places in hostels would allow the workers to increase their successful reconnection rate. It would also deter individuals who often act as 'leaders' of the Polish homeless group.

From the interviews with British voluntary sector workers it is clear that Barka's experience has brought an additional asset in the form of a different approach to the problem of alcohol misuse and the role of social economy in reintegration of vulnerable individuals back to society. In the eyes of some workers from the British charity sector, Barka's culture of service provision was free of many of the barriers and burdens the British system suffers from. It also exposed the fact that the British benefit system may make individuals dependent and simply entrenched in their position. As one service provider working for homeless charity notes:

> There is a huge amount of learning we should do. We have a culture of form filling, bureaucracy riven with protocols and procedures, and Barka is free from that. This is great in Poland, but it makes it difficult to work here. As

> an established charity you have all these hoops to jump through; this has a tendency to increase the protocols, the health and safety issues – all these that get between you and the client. So we have that bridge to cross ... We are stuck in here with the system – it is based on harm minimization. We will work with people even if they continue to use substances. The Barka ethos is based on the fact that we will work with you to get you through, but in order to complete this process you need to take part in the community life. You don't have to stay, you can leave, it is not cultish ... but the other side is that over here we have hostels with people drinking themselves to death. There is no way we can say yes to this. We can evict them for breaking the rules but they end up dying on the streets and it's me that needs to pick them up. And then we offer the same avenue again and again ... and Barka just says – you have to change, you have to stop drinking, you have to contribute. (British charity worker)

The difference and resulting tensions between the institutionalised, bureaucratic, target driven and professional work style of the British voluntary sector and the model of informal, quasi-family and community centred ethos of Bark, has been also highlighted by Polish service providers. These difficulties aside, for both parties this has been an important learning curve and an opportunity to shape common responses to a common problem. It highlighted one of the consequences of European integration and the fact that as borders disappear and people become more mobile so civil society institutions and charities need to increase their scope. It can be argued that as the current migration of EU citizens is a pan-European issue, so choosing a pan-European response would be the most logical thing to do.

Response of Community Organisations

An organisation with the most experience in offering legal help to that particular sector of the population, is the East European Advice Centre, which has been in place since the early 1980s and has been catering to various groups of migrants, refugees and newcomers. Throughout these years its client base changed dramatically, from being 98 per cent based on Roma asylum seekers in the years 2002/2003, to the end of 2004 when that group constituted only 16 per cent, with the remainder coming mainly from the A8 states, but also from the Balkans. As the EEAC notes, the nature of enquiries has changed with more now being related to employment, debt and translation/interpreting enquiries. The total number of enquiries from clients increased from 2,146 in 2003–2004 to 3,034 in 2004–2005, and seems still on the increase.[7]

7 For more information, the report by EEAC to the council is available on request.

One interesting difference comparing EEAC (Eastern European Advice Centre) client base with institutions that deal with issues of homelessness is that its male/female ratio reflects more accurately the overall demographic profile of the flows. This confirms the already mentioned fact that the problems with street drinking and anti-social behaviour are due to specific combination of factors where casual employment, male companionship, lack of access to welfare provision and market insecurity has made a particular group of men in their late 30 and 40s very vulnerable.

After May 2004, the Federation of Poles in Great Britain emerged as one of important links between British institutions and migrant workers. Initially underfunded and understaffed and basically an umbrella organisation, in the immediate aftermath of the May 2004 Accession it was overwhelmed by the volume of cases of people with problems and requests that were coming to their premises at the Polish Centre in King Street. As its president, Jan Mokrzycki says, it was not only the fact that no-one expected the numbers that came but also no-one expected 'the general level of unawareness of migrants about the local conditions they are going to encounter in London'.

Relying on funding from the established Polish community institutions, it had limited abilities to respond to the pressures. Since then, the Federation has received specific funding from the Polish Senate and at the moment runs an information centre. It has issued a popular booklet in Polish about life and work in Great Britain.[8] It also maintains links with the trade unions and Polish authorities at central and local levels and has also become the voice of the Polish community in the UK, frequently appearing in the national press. Along with an organisation established by newcomers – Polish Professionals in London – it has recently launched a social campaign to encourage Polish migrants to register on the Electoral Register prior to the London Mayoral elections. The PPL emerged recently as quite an active organisation, which runs weekly legal surgeries at the Polish Centre, where a professional lawyer sees clients. The scheme is relatively new and is staffed by volunteers. It needs to be noted, however, that from the perspective of the Shepherds Bush Advice Centre, the issue is not so much the information, but rather quality of legal help that a lot of voluntary community organisations cannot afford. In their opinion, the real need is in guaranteeing that this professional legal help is there, rather than producing another information access point. Our fieldwork showed that the number of different community organisations do not not provide a quality service. Many different institutions often compete for the same resources and instances of internal animosity are not uncommon. Although clearly valuable, the role of an information point has its clear limits when it comes to offering professional advice.

---

8 The booklet can be found at: http://www.zpwb.org.uk/pl/Jak_zyc_i_pracowac_w_Wielkiej_Brytanii.pdf,

The Federation's role focuses on basic information dissemination and translations and acts as a contact point, although it cannot provide professional legal help. The most common set of problems relate to issues of employment rights. In the year 2007, 462 people addressed the Federation of Poles with problems of unpaid wages, breaches of the National Minimum Wage, breaches of employment law etc.; 164 people contacted the organisation asking for help in the area of social benefits, Home Office registrations, immigration matters, pension issues and domestic violence. Another 67 people were helped in filling in applications to schools and universities, and over 100 found English courses through Federation referral. For many people, the organisation offers the use of its postal address, which for transient individuals provides some level of security so that their employment documentation does not get lost.[9]

In many respects the response from community organisations has been specifically targeted and selective. For instance, the Association of Polish Engineers attempts to address an issue highlighted in the survey, which is that of the brain-waste of migrants with engineering degrees. The POSK (Polish Cultural Centre) has been focusing on cultural events and its newly opened Jazz Café targets particular Polish and non-Polish audiences with high profile concerts. Others, like the Catholic Church, concentrate on issues of access to religious education, rituals and maintaining cultural values of the ethnic group. The number of different institutions and organisations means that it is difficult to talk about a coherent response to issues that arise, especially when they concern unemployed, the homeless or street drinkers.

Our research suggests that there are clear limits in the ability of an ethnic network of organisations to tackle particularly difficult problems involving members of the same ethnic group, as these people may be perceived negatively due to their low status, working class background or poor behaviour. Ethnic institutions are particularly concerned about issues related to reputation, public image and association with specific social class (Garapich 2008b). The reported reluctance of some institutions to engage fully with the negative consequences of migration (which is in overall terms beneficial for the ethnic community in terms of businesses generated, membership etc.) stems from that fear of loss of reputation and condemnation from British society. This makes the role of organisations like Barka excellently suited for work with Polish migrants, because it is not concerned with the public image of the Polish community in Britain, but with direct action towards socially excluded migrants. Barka is removed from the local power relationships and internal politics of ethnic institutions, which may be reluctant to engage with certain issues due either to a lack of funding and the pressure to project a positive image of the community.

9 Data from The Federation of Poles report to the Polish Senate, December 2007.

Nevertheless, the Federation with its experience and vast links across London and Britain, as well as with the Polish government, has been a valuable resource facilitating some service provision for migrants. It has recently engaged with local schools to assist children who have not been given a place in school, via the appeals process. It has also assisted in diffusing some racial tensions arising between Polish and ethnic minorities teenagers (not within the borough) and has recently voiced strong concerns over the coverage of migration from Poland in some sections of the British press. The strong view of the officials at the Federation is that there needs be more work in developing links between the Polish community and the local authorities.

Although there are links between the Polish Centre management and the council, the Federation stresses that the average man on the street may know very little about what the council actually does.

> I think the time is ripe for organizing some sort of a surgery for Poles and other Eastern European migrants who contribute strongly to the area. It would mean that the Poles would become more aware what their responsibilities are and what they could expect from the council; it would strengthen communication and links between the community and the council and would raise the profile of the councillors. (Federation spokesman)

What is crucial in this context is that there was a feeling that compared to the traditions and mutual partnerships between the community and authorities in Ealing, Hammersmith and Fulham council could do much more to engage and interact. The perception is that this borough is becoming a major focus where Polish social and cultural life occurs, hence there is a need for its recognition. This point was also made by the media and local businessmen.

One important issue the Federation raised was the fact that the public scrutiny of newcomers has the consequence of making people forget about the needs of older émigrés who have been living in the area for decades. Although very different in terms of needs, it should be stressed that according to the Federation spokesmen, these Poles, sometimes in their 80s and 90s may feel more comfortable in communicating in their native language, hence there should be some language provision for them.

The Catholic Church is an important institution for Polish nationals, but its engagement with wider community also has its limits, as the parish priest recognises, in that there are other more specialised institutions that deal with issues of employment, legal advice, homelessness or substance misuse. Interestingly, this is contrasted with the experience of the Hungarian priest, who just after the enlargement of the EU acted as a go-between for many Hungarian migrants, hosting them in his house, offering translation work and assistance. Because of the lack of any specific resources available for Hungarians, he was the only point of information where someone from Hungary without command of English could ask for help.

Nevertheless, Polish priests are an important source of information about any potential problems or issues that may arise within the community. However, it needs to be stressed that the Polish Church in question – the St. Andrzej Bobola Parish Church– is perceived by the established community as the religious and spiritual centre of the veterans, with symbolic iconography detailing their tragic fate during WWII. As the priest explained, 'the Ealing Church has been taken over by the newcomers, so the old *emigracja*[10] sees our Church as their place, their holy spot'. Yet this does not mean that newcomers are excluded – they have also come up with some special initiatives and the church encourages some activities. At the same church, young migrants have organised a Mothers and Toddlers group, and there are also regular AA meetings. The Church offers assistance with proofs of baptism and church attendance as required by certain Catholic schools as an entry condition, and these schools seem to be strongly preferred by Polish nationals.

The overall perception of the priest was that the minority who suffer from unemployment and homelessness have brought their problems on to London streets from Poland, since it is 'easier to live here'. He recognises that there are people who may have had bad luck, but emphasised – as mentioned earlier already from other service providers – that there is a clear need for a more coherent, London-wide and organised response to this problem and his Church is not equipped with dealing with that particular issue.

As mentioned above, the Hungarian Church (which has a base in Hammersmith) is in a different position. The priest that was interviewed recalled that after May 2004 he suddenly experienced a huge influx of migrants asking for help and advice. This is a church that catered for the Hungarian émigrés that left their country in the aftermath of the 1956 revolution, and 50 per cent of its congregation is composed of these people. The other half are mainly young people whom the respondent perceives as short term, transient migrants,who work in low-wage jobs. In 2004, he was receiving and assisting ten people a day with the usual problems linked to employment, translations and lack of awareness, while at present it has dropped to around two per week.

It is striking how news about the very existence of the Church spread, because – unlike Polish institutions – the Church is not listed in any media, websites and has not had much publicity. The perception of this respondent differs from those of the Polish priest, as he notes that the majority of migrants asking for assistance or help are women (around 60 per cent) and prior to accession this was the overwhelming majority. He has not had much contact with the local authorities on the issues he was confronted with. What he would like to see, ideally, is better information distribution, preferably in Hungarian, as most of the problems he encounters are due to inadequate English.

10 A term used to denote the established Polish community.

Conclusion

The picture emerging from this study is a complex one but migration is a complex phenomenon affecting social and economic life in many different ways. As migration flows affect different localities in different ways, it is vital to emphasise that detailed findings of this research should not all be extrapolated to a national level. However, the role of short term migration, its fluidity and its impacts on public services may well have similar features in common with other areas. The Hammersmith and Fulham context is very specific and this research shows that without the existing migrants' networks, institutions and a history of migration in the area, the pressures on local services would be much more intense.

It is crucial to recognise the historical continuity of the flows we have tried to analyse. Social networks and historical links between this borough and hundreds of localities in Poland have been woven for many years and today we are seeing the consequences of a long process that began some time ago. This research shows that, in general, this has mainly brought significant benefits to the local economy and society – as the migrants, who are predominantly economically active, perform crucial jobs for the local area and contribute to it, rather than stretching public services to the extent it is portrayed by some. We conclude that the impact on public services is relatively small, bearing in mind the numbers, the dynamic of change and the central position of the borough when it comes to migration between Poland and the UK. There are certainly some pressures, but we believe that the overall social and economic benefits outweigh the costs. In addition, this study showed that ethnic, community institutions, contrary to general assumptions, are not always suited, equipped or even willing to engage with particular sensible issues. Therefore, the social policy implication of this study is that a transnational problem needed a transnational response, which helped to ease the problem.

The picture from the survey and the focus group is a very positive one, with young, aspiring people, who are ambitious about their futures but also worried about issues concerning all other Hammersmith and Fulham residents – crime, education, housing and employment. However, the interviews with service providers offer us a more sober reminder that in a modern free market democracy, a basic structure of security and safety is vital to prevent people paying the costs of bad luck with their health, well being, mental state and ultimately life. The voluntary and charitable sector cannot be the sole pillar of this supporting structure – there is a clear need for the local and central authority to take responsibility.

References

Ágh, A. and Ferencz, A. (eds) (2006), *Deepening and Widening in an Enlarged Europe: The Impact of the Eastern Enlargement* (Budapest: Corvinus Kiado).

Albrow, M. (1996), *The Global Age* (Cambridge: Polity).

Almond, G. and Verba, S. (1963), *The Civic Cultures. Political Attitudes and Democracy in Five Nations* (Princeton, NJ: Princeton University Press).

Amin A. (2002) ‘Ethnicity and the Multicultural City: Living with Diversity’, *Environment and Planning A* 34: 6, 959–80.

Anderson, B., Ruhs, M., Rogaly, B. and Spencer, S. (2006), *Fair Enough? Central and East European Migrants in Low-wage Employment in the UK* (Oxford: Centre on Migration Policy and Society), <www.compas.ox.ac.uk/changingstatus/Downloads/Fair%20enough%20paper%20-%201%20May%202006.pdf>, accessed 1 July 2008.

Angelov, G. (2006), ‘Demographic Data: an Occasion for Reflection’, Institute of Market Economy, ‘IME. Review of the Economic Policy’, No. 268, March 2006, <http://www.ime.bg/pr_bg/268-3.htm>, accessed 28 March 2007.

Angelov, G. et al. (2004), ‘Anatomy of Transition: The Economic Policy of Bulgaria from 1989 to 2004’, Ciela Publishers, 2004, <http://georgiangelov.com/wp-content/uploads/anatomia_na_prehoda.pdf>, accessed 11 March 2007.

Anthias, F. (1998), ‘“Evaluating “Diaspora”: Beyond Ethnicity?’, *Sociology* 32: 557–80.

Arestis, P., and Sawyer, M. (2005), ‘The Neoliberal Experience of the United Kingdom’ in A. Saad-Filho and D. Johnston (eds) (2005), *Neoliberalism: A Critical Reader* (London: Pluto Press).

Aspden, D.N. (2005), ‘Methodological Improvements to UK Foreign Property Investment Statistics’, *Economic Trends*, No. 619 (June): 54–60. [This paper can be found at www.statistics.gov.uk/cci/article.asp?ID=1176.]

Audit Commission (2007), *Crossing Borders: Responding to the Local Challenges of Migrant Workers* (London: Audit Commission), <www.audit-commission.gov.uk/Products/NATIONAL-REPORT/05CA5CAD-C551-4b66-825E-ABFA8C8E4717/CrossingBorders.pdf>, accessed 1 July 2008.

Baldwin-Edwards, M. (2006), ‘Patterns of Migration in the Balkans’, UEHR Working Papers No. 9.

Bank of England (2006), *Inflation Report*, August (London: Bank of England), <www.bankofengland.co.uk/publications/inflationreport/ir06aug.pdf>, accessed 1 July 2008.

Bauer, T. and Gang, I. (1998), *Temporary Migrants from Egypt: How Long Do They Stay Abroad?*, Centre for Economic Policy Research.

Bauer, M. and Gaskell, G. (1999), 'Towards a Paradigm for Research on Social Representations', *Journal for the Theory of Social Behaviour* 29, 163–86.

BBC News (2006a), '"Nearly 600,000" New EU Migrants', BBC News Online, 22 August, <news.bbc.co.uk/1/hi/uk_politics/5273356.stm>, accessed 1 July 2008.

BBC News (2006b), 'Council Tax "Rises for Migrants"', BBC News Online, 8 August, <news.bbc.co.uk/1/hi/uk_politics/5255038.stm>, accessed 1 July 2008.

BBC News (2006c), 'Warning Over New EU Immigration', BBC News Online, 31 July, <news.bbc.co.uk/1/hi/uk_politics/5231768.stm>, accessed 1 July 2008.

BBC News (2006d), 'Immigrant Worker Restriction Call', BBC News Online, 20 August, <news.bbc.co.uk/1/hi/uk_politics/5267880.stm>, accessed 1 July 2008.

BBC News (2007c), 'EU Worker Restrictions to Remain', BBC News Online, 30 October, <news.bbc.co.uk/1/hi/uk_politics/7069129.stm>, accessed 1 July 2008.

BBC News (2007b), 'EU Free Movement of Labour Map', BBC News Online, 4 January, <news.bbc.co.uk/1/hi/world/europe/3513889.stm>, accessed 1 July 2008.

BBC News (2007c), 'Roma Children Flood into Slough', BBC News Online, 12 May, <news.bbc.co.uk/1/hi/england/berkshire/6649049.stm>, accessed 1 July 2008.

Bekyarova, N. (2004), 'Demography and Security', Sofia: Voenno Izdatelstvo Publishers [Military Publishing House]. Posted 19 December 2004, <http://www.vi-books.com/lib/d_s/cont.htm>, accessed 22 June 2008.

Benda-Beckmann, F. von and Benda-Beckmann, K. von (2000), 'Coping with Insecurity' in F. von Benda-Beckmann and K. von Benda-Beckmann (eds), *Coping with Insecurity: An 'Underall' Perspective on Social Security in the Third World*, (Indonesia and the Netherlands: Pustaka Pelajar and Focaal Foundation).

Benda-Beckmann, F. von, Benda-Beckmann, K. von and Wiber, M.G. (2006), 'The Properties of Property' in F. von Benda-Beckmann, K. von Benda-Beckmann and M.G. Wiber (eds), *Changing Properties of Property.* (New York: Berghahn).

Bennett, M. (1993), 'Towards Ethnorelativism: A Developmental Model of Intercultural Sensitivity' in R.M. Paige (ed.), *Education for the Intercultural Experience*, 2nd edn (Yarmouth, ME: Intercultural Press).

Bernhardt, P., Hadj-Abdou, L., Liebhart, K. and Pribersky, A. (2009), *Europäische Bildpolitiken. Politische Bildanalyse am Beispiel der EU-Politik* (UTB wuv).

Beyme, K. von (1994), *Systemwechsel in Osteuropa* (Frankfurt am Main: Suhrkamp).

Blanchflower, D., Saleheen, J. and Shadforth, C. (2007), *The Impact of the Recent Migration from Eastern Europe on the UK Economy* (London: Bank of England), <www.bankofengland.co.uk/publications/speeches/2007/speech 297.pdf>, accessed 1 July 2008.

Boeri, T. and Brücker, H. (2000), *The Impact of Eastern Enlargement on Employment and Labour Markets in the EU Member States* (Berlin and Milan: European Commission DG Employment and Social Affairs), <ec. europa.eu/employment_social/employment_analysis/impact_en.htm>, accessed 1 July 2008.

Boomgaarden, H.G. and Vliegenthart, R. (2007), 'Explaining the Rise of Anti-Immigrant Parties: The Role of News Media Content', *Electoral Studies* 26, 404–17.

Bozhovich, L. (2007), *Lichnost and ejo formirovanie v detskom vozraste* [Developing personality in childhood] (Sankt Peterburg: Piter).

Brits Abroad Forum <http://ippr.typepad.com/brits_abroad/> 'As emigration increases, learning foreign languages decreases'. Posted by Catherine Drew at 01:51 PM, 29 August 2006, accessed 18 August 2008.

Brits in Bulgaria [forum posting] (2007), 'I Have Something to Say', 14 December 2007, <http://www.novinite.com/view_news.php?id=88530>, accessed 25 June 2008.

Brücker, H., Alvarez-Plata, P. and Siliverstovs, B. (2003), *Potential Migration from Central and Eastern Europe into the EU-15 – An Update* (Berlin: DIW for the European Commission DG Employment and Social Affairs), <www.diw.de/deutsch/produkte/publikationen/gutachten/docs/report_ european_commission_20040218.pdf>, accessed 1 July 2008.

Buck, N., Gordon, I., Hall, P., Harloe, M. and Kleinman, M. (2002), *Working Capital: Life and Labour in Contemporary London* (London: Routledge).

Bulgarian Homes 4 Sale (2007), 'Young British Home Buyers Head For Bulgaria'. Posted 25 September 2007, <http://www.bulgarianhomes4sale. com/news/young-british-home-buyers-head-for-bulgaria-I504/>, accessed 29 May 2008.

Burrell, K. (2008), 'Time Matters: Temporal Contexts of Polish Transnationalism' in M.P. Smith and J. Eade (eds), *Transnational Ties: Cities, Migrations, and Identities* (New Brunswick, NJ and London: Transaction Publishers).

Bush, K.R., Bohon, S.A. and Kim, H.K. (1994), 'Adaptation among Immigrant Families' in P.C. McKenry and S. Price (eds), *Families and Change: Coping with Stressful Events* (Thousand Oaks, CA: Sage).

Casado-Diaz, M.A., Kaiser, C. and Warnes, A. (2004), 'Northern European Retired Residents in Nine Southern European Areas: Characteristics, Motivations and Adjustment', *Ageing and Society* 24: 3, 353–81.

Casciani, D. (2005), 'Morecambe Bay: One Year On', BBC News Online, 5 February, <news.bbc.co.uk/1/hi/uk/4238209.stm>, accessed 1 July 2008.

Castles, S. and Miller, M. (2003), *The Age of Migration* (Basingstoke: Palgrave Macmillan).

Cecil, N. (2005), 'Million Migrants Flood In', *The Sun*, 9 February, <http://www.thesun.co.uk/sol/homepage/news/article102557.ece>, accessed 1 July 2008.

Cesarani, D. and Fulbrook. M. (eds), *Citizenship, Nationality and Migration in Europe* (London and New York: Routledge).

Cheshire, J. (2002), 'Who We Are and Where We're Going: Language and Identities in the New Europe', in P. Gubbins et al. (eds), *Beyond Boundaries: Language and Identity in Contemporary Europe* (Clevedon: Multilingual Matters).

Cholakov, N. (2003), 'The Statistics on Outbound Migration and the Demographics of Bulgarian Population', *Economic Thought* 5, 53–64.

Chongarova, I. and Katsarska, M. (2007), 'British in Bulgaria: Representation in Bulgarian Press'. http://www.surrey.ac.uk/Arts/CRONEM/cronem-conference-february2007/slides.htm, accessed 16 August 2008.

Chun, A. (ed.) (2004), *Globalization: Critical Issues* (London: Berghahn Books).

Cohen, R. (1997), *Global Diasporas: An Introduction* (Seattle: University of Washington Press).

Cooley, L., Farrant, M. and Sriskandarajah, D. (2005), *Selecting Wisely: Making Managed Migration Work for Britain* (London: Institute for Public Policy Research), <www.ippr.org/members/download.asp?f=%2Fecomm%2Ffiles%2Fselecting%5Fwisely%2Epdf>, accessed 1 July 2008.

Cracknell, D. (2006), 'Migrant Fear over 45,000 "Undesirables"', *Sunday Times*, 23 July, 1.

CRONEM (2006), 'Polish Migrants Survey Results', poll commissioned by BBC Newsnight, July, <www.surrey.ac.uk/Arts/CRONEM/CRONEM_BBC_Polish_survey%20_results.pdf>, accessed 1 July 2008.

Daily Express (2005), '1M Migrants Flood Britain', *Daily Express*, 9 February, 2.

Daily Mail (2007), 'Pickpocketing on the Increase as Eastern European Gangs Trawl London's West End', *Daily Mail*, 16 February, <http://www.dailymail.co.uk/news/article-436687/Pickpocketing-increase-Eastern-European-gangs-trawl-Londons-West-End.html>, accessed 1 July 2008.

Daily Star (2004), 'Stop the Invaders', *Daily Star*, 12 February, 6.

Dainov, E. (2007), 'Input Some Thought into this City. On the Difference Between Sofia and Gorna Oryakhovitsa and on the Hearing of the Capital City Chiefs,' 14 May 2007, http://www.zagrada.bg/show.php?storyid=339481, accessed 23 June 2008.

Daniels, H. (1993), 'The Individual and the Organization', in H. Daniels (ed.), *Charting the Agenda: Educational Activity after Vygotsky* (London, Routledge).

Daniels, H. (1996/2005), *An Introduction to Vygotsky* (London: Routledge)

Daniels, H. (2003), *Vygotsky and Pedagogy* (London: Falmer Press).

Daniels, H. (2004a), 'Activity Theory, Discourse and Bernstein', *Educational Review* 56: 2, 121–32.

Daniels, H. (2004b), 'Cultural Historical Activity Theory and Professional Learning', *International Journal of Disability Development and Education* 51: 2, 185–200.

Daniels, H. and Warmington, P. (2007), 'Analysing Third Generation Activity Systems: Labour-Power, Subject Position and Personal Transformation', *Journal of Workplace Learning,* 19: 6, 377–91.

Datta, K. et al. (2006), *Work and Survival Strategies Among Low Paid Migrants in London*, Department of Geography, Queen Mary, University of London, London, available at <http://www. geog. qmul. ac. uk/globalcities/wpaper3. pdf>.

Datta, A. (2009), 'Places of Everyday Cosmopolitanisms: East-European Construction Workers in London', *Environment and Planning A* 41 forthcoming.

Davydov, V.V. (1981), 'The Category of Activity and Mental Reflection in the Theory of A.N. Leontiev', *Soviet Psychology* 19: 4, 3–29.

Davydov, V.V. (1983), 'Uchenie A.N.Leontieva o vzaimosviazyi deiatelnosti I psihicheskova Otrazhenia', in A.B. Zaporozhec, V.P. Zinchenko, O.B. Ovchinnikova, O.K. Tihomirov (eds), *A.N.Leontiev and savremennay psihologiya* (Moscow: Izdatelstvo Moskovskogo Universiteta).

DeFrain, J., Cook, R. and Gonzales-Kruger, G. (2004), 'Family Health and Dysfunction', *Family Therapy Review: Preparing for Comprehensive and Licensing Examinations.*

Demmers, J. (2002), 'Diaspora and Conflict: Locality, Long-Distance Nationalism, and Delocalisation of Conflict Dynamics', *The Public* 9: 1, 85–96.

Dench, S., Hurstfield, J., Hill, D. and Akroyd, K. (2006), 'Employers' Use of Migrant Labour: Main Report', Home Office Online Report 04/06 (London: Home Office), <www.homeoffice.gov.uk/rds/pdfs06/rdsolr0406. pdf>, accessed 1 July 2008.

Department for Children, Schools and Families (DCSF) (2008), *New Arrivals Excellence Programme: Primary and Secondary National Strategies*, Multiverse, http://www.multiverse.ac.uk/ViewArticle2.aspx?ContentId=13909, accessed 20 December 2008.

Department for Work and Pensions (2007), *National Insurance Number Allocations to Overseas Nationals Entering the UK, 2006/07* (London: Department for Work and Pensions), <www.dwp.gov.uk/asd/asd1/niall/niall_report.pdf>, accessed 1 July 2008.

Downing, J. and Husbands, C. (2005), *Representing Race: Racisms, Ethnicity and the Media* (London: Sage).

Dragomir, M. (2004), 'Media as Scare-mongering', Open Society Institute EU Monitoring and Advocacy Program, <www.eumap.org/journal/features/2004/migration/pt2/mediascare>, accessed 1 July 2008.

Drew, C. and Sriskandarajah, D. (2006), *EU Enlargement: Bulgaria and Romania – Migration Implications for the UK: An IPPR FactFile* (London: Institute for Public Policy Research), <www.ippr.org/members/download.asp?f=%2Fecomm%2Ffiles%2Feu%5Fenlargement%5Ffactfile%2Epdf>, accessed 1 July 2008.

Drinkwater, S., Eade, J. and Garapich, M. (2006), *Poles Apart? EU Enlargement and the Labour Market Outcomes of Immigrants in the UK*, IZA Discussion Paper 2410 (Bonn: Institute for the Study of Labor), <ftp.iza.org/dp2410.pdf>, accessed 1 July 2008.

Dumenil, G., and Levy, D. (2005), 'The Neoliberal (Counter-) Revolution' in A. Saad-Filho and D. Johnston (eds), *Neoliberalism: A Critical Reader* (London: Pluto).

Dustmann, C., Casanova, I., Fertig, M., Preston, M. and Schmidt, C. (2003), *The Impact of EU Enlargement on Migration Flows*, Home Office Online Report 25/03 (London: Home Office), <www.homeoffice.gov.uk/rds/pdfs2/rdsolr2503.pdf >, accessed 1 July 2008.

Dustmann, C., Fabbri, F. and Preston, I. (2005), 'The Impact of Immigration on the British Labour Market', *The Economic Journal* 115 (507), F324–F341.

Dwyer, P. (2000), 'Movements to Some Purpose? An Exploration of International Retirement Migration in the European Union', *Education and Ageing* 15, 3: 353–77.

Eade, J. (ed.) (1997), *Living the Global City: Globalisation as Local Process* (London and New York: Routledge).

Eade, J. (2000), *Placing London: From Imperial Capital to Global City* (Oxford and New York: Berghahn Books).

Eade, J., Drinkwater, S. and Garapich, M. (2006), 'Class and Ethnicity: Polish Migrants in London', ESRC final report at www.surrey.ac.uk/Arts/CRONEM.

EB 273: Special Eurobarometer 273 'European Social Reality', Report.

Fieldwork November-December 2006 (2007), <http://ec.europa.eu/public_opinion/archives/ebs/ebs_273_en.pdf > access 15 August 2008.

Elliot, L. (2006), 'Migrants Threaten Social Fabric, Says CBI Chief', *The Guardian*, 6 September, 21.

Ernst & Young ITEM Club (2006), *Economic Outlook for Business* 35, <www.ey.com/global/download.nsf/UK/Economic_Outlook_for_Business_04-06/$file/EY_ITEM_Economic_Outlook_Spring_Apr_06.pdf >, accessed 1 July 2008.

Ernst & Young Item Club (2006), *EU Enlargement – Benefits Outweigh Downsides for UK*, at http://www.ey.com/global/Content.nsf/UK/Media-04_03_03_DC-ITEM_Club_update_03_04).

European Commission (2006a), *Report on the Functioning of the Transitional Arrangements Set Out in the 2003 Accession Treaty (period 1 May 2004–30 April 2006)* COM (2006) 48 Final (Brussels: European Commission), <europa.eu.int/eur-lex/lex/LexUriServ/site/en/com/2006/com2006_0048 en01.pdf>, accessed 1 July 2008.

European Commission (2006b), *Monitoring Report on the State of Preparedness for EU Membership of Bulgaria and Romania.* COM (2006) 214 Final (Brussels: European Commission), <eur-lex.europa.eu/LexUriServ/site/en/com/2006/com2006_0214en01.pdf>, accessed 1 July 2008.

Eurostat (2007), 'Euro area labour cost up by 2.4%', *Euro-indicators News Release* 38/2007, <epp.eurostat.ec.europa.eu/pls/portal/docs/PAGE/PGP_PRD_CAT_PREREL/PGE_CAT_PREREL_YEAR_2007/PGE_CAT_PREREL_YEAR_2007_MONTH_03/3-15032007-EN-AP.PDF>, accessed 1 July 2008.

Evans, Y., Herbert, J., Datta, K., May, J., Mcllwaine, C. and Willis, J. (2005), *Making the City Work: Low Paid Employment in London* (London: Queen Mary College, University of London).

Fainstein, S. et al. (eds) (1992), *Divided Cities: New York and London in the Contemporary World* (Oxford and Cambridge, MA: Blackwell).

Fainstein, S. (1994), *The City Builders: Property, Politics and Planning in London and New York* (Oxford and Cambridge, MA: Blackwell).

Farrant, M., Grieve, C. and Sriskandarajah, D. (2006), *Irregular Migration in the UK: An IPPR FactFile.* (London: Institute for Public Policy Research), <www.ippr.org/members/download.asp?f=%2Fecomm%2Ffiles%2Firregular%5Fmigration%2Epdf>, accessed 1 July 2008.

FÁS (2006), *The Irish Labour Market Review 2006: A FÁS Review of Irish Labour Market Trends and Policies* (Dublin: FÁS), <www.fas.ie/NR/rdonlyres/F63B6DCE-61FA-49B5-A4CC-E34522B16944/0/LABOUR_MARKET_REVIEW_2006.pdf>, accessed 1 July 2008.

Favell, A. (2004), 'Eurostars and Eurocities: Free Moving Professionals and the Promise of European Integration', *European Studies Newsletter* (Council for European Studies), VI: 3–4.

Favell, A. (2008), 'The New Face of East–West Migration in Europe', *Journal of Ethnic and Migration Studies* 34: 5, 701–16.

Favell, A. and Hansen, R. (2002), 'Markets against Politics: Migration, EU Enlargement and the Idea of Europe', *Journal of Ethnic and Migration Studies* 28: 4, 581–601.

Finch, J. (1997), 'Individuality and Adaptability in English Kinship' in M. Gullestad and M. Segalen (eds), *Family and Kinship in Europe* (London: Pinter).

Findlay, A.M. and Stam, A. (2006), 'International Student Migration to the UK: Training for the Global Economy or Simply Another Form of Global Talent Recruitment?', paper presented at the conference *International Competition for S&E Students and Workers*, Washington.

Friedman, J. (2004), 'Champagne Liberals and the New "Dangerous Classes": Reconfigurations of Class, Identity and Cultural Production in the Contemporary Global System' in Chun (ed.).

Garapich, M. (2008a), 'The Migration Industry and Civil Society: Polish Immigrants in the United Kingdom Before and After EU Enlargement', *Journal of Ethnic and Migration Studies* 34:5, 735–52.

Garapich, M. (2008b), 'Odyssean Refugees, Migrants and Power: Construction of the "Other" within the Polish community in the United Kingdom' in D. Reed-Danahay and C. Brettell (eds), *Citizenship, Political Engagement and Belonging* (Chapel Hill, NC: Rutgers University Press).

Garcheva, V. (2007), 'The British Who Are Going to Vote as Bulgarians', Sega Newspaper, No. 102, 7 May 2007, <http://www.segabg.com/online/article.asp?issueid=2637&sectionid=5&id=000140>, accessed 2 May 2008.

Geertz, C. (1973), 'Thick Description: Toward an Interpretive Theory of Culture', in C. Geertz, *The Interpretation of Cultures: Selected Essays* (New York: Basic Books).

Geertz, C. (1996), *Welt in Stücken. Kultur und Politik am Ende des 20. Jahrhundert.* (Wien: Passagen).

Gilpin, N., Henty, M., Lemos, S., Portes, J. and Bullen, C. (2006), *The Impact of Free Movement of Workers from Central and Eastern Europe on the UK Labour Market*, Department for Work and Pensions Working Paper 29 (London: Department for Work and Pensions), <www.dwp.gov.uk/asd/asd5/wp29.pdf>, accessed 1 July 2008.

Glick Schiller, N. et al. (1994), *Nations Unbound* (London and New York: Routledge).

Glick Schiller, N. (2005), 'Transnational Social Fields and Imperialism: Bringing a Theory of Power to Transnational Studies', *Anthropological Theory* 5: 4, 439–61.

Goffin, R. (1994), 'L'eurolecte: Oui, Jargon Communautaire: Non', *Meta* 36: 4, 636–42.

Goodridge, P. (2006), 'November 2006 Assessment', *Labour Market Trends* 114(12): 397–440, <www.statistics.gov.uk/downloads/theme_labour/LMT_Dec06.pdf>, accessed 1 July 2008.

Gordon, I. et al. (2007), *The Impact of Recent Immigration on the London Economy*, City of London and LSE.

Green, A. (2007), 'Local Action on Labour Market Integration of New Arrivals: Issues and Dilemmas for Policy', *Local Economy* 22: 4, 349–61.

Guobuzaite, R. (1998), 'Modern Women in Lithuania' in S. LaFont (ed.), *Women in Transition: Voices from Lithuania* (Albany, NY: State University of New York Press).

Gupta, S. and Omoniyi, T. (eds) (2007), *The Cultures of Economic Migration: International Perspectives* (Aldershot: Ashgate).

Gustafson, P. (2007), 'Transnationalism in Retirement Migration: The Case of North European Retirees in Spain', *Ethnic and Racial Studies* 31:3, 451–75.

Gyáni, Gábor (2005), 'Felejthetö-e a Kádár-éra?', *Élet és Irodalom* 18: 46.

Habielski, R. (1999), *Życie społeczne i kulturalne emigracji*, Węź.

Halbwachs M. (1992), *On Collective Memory* (Chicago and London: Chicago University Press).

Hall, S. (ed.) (1997), *Cultural Representations and Signifying Practices* (London: Sage).

Hall, S. and du Gay, P. (eds) (1996), *Questions of Cultural Identity* (London: Sage).

Hammen, C., Gordon, P.D. and Burge, D. (1987), 'Maternal Affective Disorders, Illness, and Stress: Risk for Children's Psychopathology', *American Journal of Psychiatry* 144: 6, 736–41.

Hamnett, C. (2003), *Unequal City: London in the Global Arena* (London and New York: Routledge).

Hartmann, P. (1974), *Racism and the Mass Media: A Study of the Role of the Mass Media in the Formation of White Beliefs and Attitudes in Britain* (Lanham MD: Rowman and Littlefield).

Hardy, J. and Clark, N. (2005), 'EU enlargement, workers and migration: Implications for trade unions in the UK and Poland', paper presented to the Global Unions Research Network Workshop on Trade Unions, *Globalisation and Development: Strengthening Rights and Capabilities of Workers*, Novo Hamborgo, Brazil, January, <www.tuc.org.uk/international/tuc-9472-f0.pdf >, accessed 1 July 2008.

Harvey, D. (2005), *A Brief History of Neoliberalism* (Oxford: Oxford University Press).

Harvey, O. (2004), 'See You in May: Thousands of Travellers Are on Their Way', *The Sun*, 19 January, 4–5.

Hickley, M. (2006), 'Eastern European Immigrants Carry Out Tenth of Crime', *Mail on Sunday*, 2 November, <http://www.dailymail.co.uk/news/article-413985/Eastern-European-immigrants-carry-tenth-crime.html>, accessed 1 July 2008.

Home Office (2004a), *Control of Immigration: Statistics United Kingdom 2004* (London: Home Office), <www.homeoffice.gov.uk/rds/pdfs05/hosb1405.pdf >, accessed 1 July 2008.

Home Office (2004b), 'No UK benefits for EU accession countries', press release, 23 February, <press.homeoffice.gov.uk/press-releases/No_Uk_Benefits_For_Eu_Accession_>, accessed 1 July 2008.

Home Office (2006a), 'Controlled Access for Accession States', press release, 24 October, <www.homeoffice.gov.uk/about-us/news/accession-states-limits>, accessed 1 July 2008.

Home Office (2006b), *A Points-based System: Making Migration Work for Britain* (London: Home Office).

Home Office (2007), 'Forum to Advise on the Social Impacts of Migration Launched', press release, 21 June, <press.homeoffice.gov.uk/press-releases/forum-migration-impacts>, accessed 1 July 2008.

Home Office and Department for Work and Pensions (2007a), *Bulgarian and Romanian Accession Statistics: January–March 2007* (London: Home Office), <www.ukba.homeoffice.gov.uk/sitecontent/documents/aboutus/Reports/bulgarianromanian/report1/report1.pdf?view=Binary>, accessed 1 July 2008.

Home Office and Department for Work and Pensions (2007b), *Bulgarian and Romanian Accession Statistics: April–June 2007* (London: Home Office), <www.ukba.homeoffice.gov.uk/sitecontent/documents/aboutus/Reports/bulgarianromanian/report2/report2.pdf?view=Binary>, accessed 1 July 2008.

Home Office and Department for Work and Pensions (2007c), *Bulgarian and Romanian Accession Statistics: July–September 2007* (London: Home Office), <www.ukba.homeoffice.gov.uk/sitecontent/documents/aboutus/Reports/bulgarianromanian/report3/report3.pdf?view=Binary>, accessed 1 July 2008.

Home Office and Department for Work and Pensions (2008), *Bulgarian and Romanian Accession Statistics: October–December 2007* (London: Home Office), <www.ukba.homeoffice.gov.uk/sitecontent/documents/aboutus/Reports/bulgarianromanian/report4/report4.pdf?view=Binary>, accessed 1 July 2008.

Home Office, Department for Work and Pensions, HM Revenue and Customs and Department for Communities and Local Government (2006), *Accession Monitoring Report: May 2004–June 2006* (London: Home Office), <www.ukba.homeoffice.gov.uk/sitecontent/documents/aboutus/Reports/accession_monitoring_report/report8/may04jun06.pdf?view=Binary>, accessed 1 July 2008.

Home Office, Department for Work and Pensions, HM Revenue and Customs and Communities and Local Government (2008), *Accession Monitoring Report: May 2004–December 2007* (London: Home Office), <www.ukba.homeoffice.gov.uk/sitecontent/documents/aboutus/Reports/accession_monitoring_report/report14/may04dec07.pdf?view=Binary>, accessed 1 July 2008.

Homeless Link (2006), *A8 Nationals in London Homelessness Services* (London: Homeless Link), <www.homeless.org.uk/policyandinfo/research/archive/A8%20nationals%20Executive%20Summary%20low%20res.pdf>, accessed 1 July 2008.

House of Lords Select Committee on Economic Affairs (2008), *The Economic Impact of Immigration, Volume 1: Report* (London: The Stationery Office), <www.publications.parliament.uk/pa/ld200708/ldselect/ldeconaf/82/82.pdf>, accessed 1 July 2008.

IPPR (2006), *EU Enlargement: Bulgaria and Romanian Migration Implications for the UK: an IPPR FactFile*, April.

Ivanov, S. (2007), 'The Changes in the Volume on the Real Property Market in Republic of Bulgaria During the Last Five Years/Strakhil Ivanov, Mladen Mitov/Construction Contracting and Real Property: Proceedings of the Scientific Conference with International Participation, November 2007, *Varna* 2007, 137–43.

Johnston, P. (2004), 'Eastern European Migration "Far Exceeds Estimate"', *Daily Telegraph*, 11 November, 10.

Kaneff, D. (2002), 'Work, Identity and Rural-Urban Relations', in P. Leonard and D. Kaneff (eds), *Post-Socialist Peasant?* (Basingstoke: Palgrave).

Kaneff, D. (2006), 'Holiday Location or Agricultural Village? British Property Owners in Rural Bulgaria', *Eastern European Countryside* 12, 79–92.

Kaneff, D. (2006), 'Holiday Location or Agricultural Village? British Property Owners in Rural Bulgaria', *Eastern European Countryside* 12, 79–92.

Kaneff, D. (forthcoming), 'Informal Paths of Economic Integration into Europe: British Involvement in the Bulgarian Property Market', *Sociologia – Slovak Sociological Review* 6.

Kanev, M. (2000), 'The Transition to Market Economy – Determination, Referent Models and Policy', *Economic Studies* 2: 3–31.

Kao, G. and Tienda, M. (2001), 'Optimism and Achievement: The Educational Performance of Immigrant Youth', *Social Science Quarterly* 76: 1, 1–19.

Kaplanis, I. (2007), 'The Geography of Employment Polarisation in Britain'. IPPR Working Paper, London: Institute of Public Policy Research.

Kaplan, R. (1990), 'Concluding Essay: On Applied Linguistics and Discourse Analysis', in R. Kaplan (ed.), *Annual Review of Applied Linguistics* II, 202–3.

King, R., Warnes, A. and Williams, A. (2000), *Sunset Lives: British Retirement Migration to the Mediterranean* (Oxford: Berg).

Kozulin, A. (1991), 'Life as Authoring: The Humanistic Tradition in Russian Psychology', *New Ideas in Psychology* 9: 3, 335–51.

Krasteva, A (ed.) (2005), *Immigration in Bulgaria* (Sofia: IMIR).

Krasteva, A. (2006), 'Post-Communist Discovery of Immigration: The Case of Bulgaria, *South East Europe Review for Labour and Social Affairs* 2, 25–34, <http://www.ceeol.com>, accessed 7 January 2009.

Kress, G. (1990), 'Critical Discourse Analysis', in R. Kaplan (ed.), *Annual Review of Applied Linguistics* II, 84–5.

Krippendorff, K. (2004), *Content Analysis: An Introduction to Its Methodology* (Thousand Oaks, CA: Sage).

Lafan, G. (2007), 'British Invasion Brings Boom for Bulgaria', *The Daily Telegraph, News*, <http://www.telegraph.co.uk/news/worldnews/1543627/British-invasion-brings-boom-for-Bulgaria.html>, accessed 18 June 2008.

Lawrence, F. (2007), 'Misery at Bottom of Supermarket Supply Chain', *The Guardian*, 15 August, 13.

Lazaroiu, S. (2003), *The Risks of Irregular Migration to the European Union: Perceptions and Trends* (Bucharest: International Organization for Migration Mission in Romania).

Learning and Skills Council (2004), *National Employers Skills Survey 2003: Main Report* (Coventry: Learning and Skills Council).

Leontiev, A.N. (1983), *Izbrannie psihologicheskie trudy*, Vol. 2 (Moscow: Pedagogika).

Levitt, P. (2001), *Transnational Villagers*. (Berkeley, CA: University of California Press).

Lewis, J. (2007), 'Exposed by TV in Romania … How Easy it is to get a British Job', *Daily Mail*, 17 February, <http://www.dailymail.co.uk/news/article-436829/Exposed-TV-Romania--easy-British-job.html>, accessed 1 July 2008.

Lompscher, J. (1999), 'Activity Formation as an Alternative Strategy of Instruction', in Y. *Engestrom,* R. *Miettinen and R.-L. Punamaki* (eds), *Perspectives on Activity Theory* (Cambridge: Cambridge University Press).

Longhi, S., Nijkamp, P. and Poot, J. (2005), 'A Meta-analytic Assessment of the Effect of Immigration on Wages', *Journal of Economic Surveys* 19: 3, 451–77.

MacGregor, S. (2005), 'The Welfare State and Neoliberalism' in Saad-Filho and Johnston (eds).

Manacorda, M., Manning, A. and Wadsworth, J. (2006), *The Impact of Immigration on the Structure of Male Wages: Theory and Evidence from Britain*, IZA Discussion Paper 2352 (Bonn: Institute for the Study of Labor), <ftp.iza.org/dp2352.pdf>, accessed 1 July 2008.

Markova, E. and Black, R. (2007), *East European Immigration and Community Cohesion*, Joseph Rowntree Foundation Report: York Publishing Services Ltd.

May, J., Wills, J. Datta, K., Evans, Y., Herbert, J. and McIlwaine, C. (2007), 'Keeping London Working: Global Cities, the British State and London's New Migrant Division of Labour', *Transactions of the Institute of British Geographers* 32: 2, 151–67.

Mazzoleni, G., Stewart, J. and Horsfield, B. (eds) (2003), *Media and Neopopulism: A Contemporary Comparative Analysis* (Westport, CT: Praeger).

MigrationWatch UK (2006), *Potential Immigration from Romania and Bulgaria*, MigrationWatch UK Briefing Paper 4.7 (Guildford: MigrationWatch UK), <www.migrationwatchuk.org/pdfs/EuropeanUnion/4_7_Potential_immigratio_%20from_Romania_and_Bulgaria.pdf>, accessed 1 July 2008.

MORI (2001), 'Citizenship 21: Briefing Notes on Profiles of Prejudice', MORI poll for Stonewall, 19 June, <www.ipsos-mori.com/polls/2001/stonewall-b2.shtml>, accessed 1 July 2008.

MORI (2003), 'British Views on Immigration', MORI poll for MigrationWatch UK, 10 February, <www.mori.com/polls/2003/migration.shtml >, accessed 1 July 2008.

MORI (2006), 'The Most Important Issues Facing Britain Today', *Political Trends Monitor*, <www.ipsos-mori.com/polls/trends/issues.shtml#2006>, accessed 1 July 2008.

Moscovici, S. (1972), 'Society and Theory in Social Psychology', in J. Israel and H. Tajfel (eds), *The Context of Social Psychology: A Critical Assessment* (London: Academic Press), 17–68.

National Statistics Institute (1994), *Ikonomicheskatat sigurnost v zhivota na domakinstvatat* (*Economic Security in Daily Household Activities*), Sofia.

National Statistics Institute (1995), *Rezultati ot prebroiavaneto na zhilishtniya fond*, tom: 2 (*Results of the Housing Census*, vol: 2). Sofia.

Natzionalen Statisticheski Institute (1994), *Republica Bulgaria*, Vol. III: 90, Sofia.

Nelson, N. (2004), 'Blair's Bid to Save UK jobs from EU Gipsies', *The People*, 1 February, 2.

Nijman, J. (2002), 'The Effects of Economic Globalisation: Land Use and Land Values in Mumbai, India' in R. Grant and J.R. Short (eds), *Globalization and the Margins* (Basingstoke: Palgrave Macmillan).

Offe, C. (1994), 'Der Tunnel am Ende des Lichts. Erkundungen der politischen', *Transformation im Neuen Osten* (Frankfurt am Main: Suhrkamp).

Office for National Statistics (2006a), 'Over 500 a Day Gained through Migration to the UK', News Release, 2 November, <www.statistics.gov.uk/pdfdir/intmigrat1106.pdf >, accessed 1 July 2008.

Office for National Statistics (2006b), 'Visits to the UK from the Enlarged EU', August, <www.statistics.gov.uk/downloads/theme_transport/Visits_to_UK_Aug06.pdf >, accessed 1 July 2008.

Office for National Statistics (2007), 'Emigration from UK Reaches 400,000 in 2006', 15 November, <www.statistics.gov.uk/pdfdir/emig1107.pdf>, accessed 1 July 2008.

Office for National Statistics (2008a), 'Employment: Rate Increases to 74.8%', 19 March, <www.statistics.gov.uk/CCI/nugget.asp?ID=12>, accessed 1 July 2008.

Office for National Statistics (2008b), 'Average Earnings: Pay Growth Steady in Year to January 2008', 19 March, <www.statistics.gov.uk/CCI/nugget.asp?ID=10>, accessed 1 July 2008.

Open Europe (2006), 'Migration from Bulgaria and Romania: Lessons from the Most Recent Enlargement', Open Europe Briefing Note (London: Open Europe), <www.openeurope.org.uk/research/bulgariaromania.pdf>, accessed 1 July 2008.

O'Reilly, K. (2000), *The British on the Costa del Sol: Transnational Identities and Local Communities* (London and New York; Routledge).

O'Reilly, K. (2002), 'Britain in Europe/the British in Spain: Exploring Britain's Changing Relationship to the Other through the Attitudes of its Emigrants', *Nations and Nationalism* 8: 2, 179–93.

O'Shea, G. (2006), '£4 Flights to Bring EU Invasion', *The Sun*, 30 December, <http://www.thesun.co.uk/sol/homepage/news/article77438.ece>, accessed 1 July 2008.

Parutis, V. (2006), 'Construction of Home by Polish and Lithuanian Migrants in the UK', UCL School of Slavonic and East European Studies Economics Working Paper No. 64 <http://www.ssees.ac.uk/publications/working_papers/wp64.pdf> accessed 20 September 2008.

Pillai, R. (2007), 'The Reception and Integration of New Migrant Communities', IPPR report for the Commission for Racial Equality (London: Commission for Racial Equality), <www.cre.gov.uk/downloads/newmigrancommunities research.pdf>, accessed 1 July 2008.

Plasser, F. et al. (1998), *Democratic Consolidation in East-Central Europe* (London: Avebury).

Pollard, N., Latorre, M. and Sriskandarajah, D. (2008), *Floodgates or Turnstiles? Post-EU Enlargement Flows to (and from) the UK.* (London: Institute for Public Policy Research), <www.ippr.org/members/download.asp?f=%2Fecomm%2Ffiles%2Ffloodgates%5For%5Fturnstiles%2Epdf>, accessed 1 July 2008.

Portal Europa, Regional Policy (2008), 'National Strategy for the regional Development of Republic Bulgaria During the period 2005–2015. Population and Demographic Situation. Regional Policy 2007–2013' [Portal Europe Website], (Ministry of Regional Development and Public Works) http://www.europe.bg/htmls/page.php?category=264&id=2231&page=3 Accessed 19 June 2008.

Porter, A. (2006), 'Migrant Work Quotas "a Sham"', *The Sun*, 25 October, <http://www.thesun.co.uk/sol/homepage/news/article68470.ece>, accessed 1 July 2008.

Portes, A., Guarnizo, E. and Landolt, P. (1999), 'Transnational Communities', special issue of *Ethnic and Racial Studies* 22: 2.

Portes, A. and DeWind, J. (2007), *Rethinking Migration: New Theoretical and Empirical Perspectives* (Oxford: Berghahn Books).

Portes, J. and French, S. (2005), *The Impact of Free Movement of Workers from Central and Eastern Europe on the UK Labour Market: Early Evidence*, Department for Work and Pensions Working Paper 18 (London: Department for Work and Pensions), <www.dwp.gov.uk/asd/asd5/WP18.pdf>, accessed 1 July 2008.

Pribersky, A., Liebhart, K. and Kurtán, S. (2002), 'A Temple for the Nation: Redesigning a Common Symbolic Space of Central European Conservatism', in C. Lutter and L. Musner (eds), *Cultural Studies, Theorizing Politics, Politicizing Theory* 16: 6, Special Issue *Austrian Cultural Studies*, 797–808.

Purvaneckiene, G. (1998), 'Women in the Domestic Domain', in S. LaFont (ed.), *Women in Transition: Voices from Lithuania* (Albany, NY: SUNY Press).

Radke-Yarrow, M. et al. (1992), 'Young Children of Affectively Ill Parents: A Longitudinal Study of Psychosocial Development', *Journal of the American Academy of Child and Adolescent Psychiatry* 31: 1, 68.

Reay, D. (2003), 'A Risky Business? Mature Working-class Women Students and Access to Higher Education', *Gender and Education* 15: 3, 301–17.

Robertson, R. (1992), *Globalization: Social Theory and Global Culture* (London: Sage).

Robila, M. and Krishnakumar, A. (2004), 'The Role of Children in Eastern European Families', *Children and Society* 18: 1, 30–41.

Robinson, D. and Reeve, K. (2006), *Neighbourhood Experiences of New Immigration: Reflections from the Evidence Base* (Sheffield: Sheffield Hallam University).

Rose, R. (2008), 'Evaluating Democratic Governance: A Bottom Up Approach to European Union Enlargement', Aberdeen (Centre for the Study of Public Policy, University of Aberdeen) <www.abdn.ac.uk>, accessed on 10 October 2008.

Ruhs, M. (2006), 'Greasing the Wheels of the Flexible Labour Market: East European Labour Immigration in the UK', COMPAS Working Paper 38 (Oxford: Centre on Migration Policy and Society), <www.compas.ox.ac.uk/publications/Working%20papers/WP0638-Ruhs.pdf>, accessed 1 July 2008.

Ruhs, M. and Anderson, B. (2006), *Semi-Compliance in the Migrant Labour Market*, COMPAS Working Paper 30 (Oxford: Centre on Migration Policy and Society), <www.compas.ox.ac.uk/publications/papers/Ruhs%20Anderson%20WP0630.pdf>, accessed 1 July 2008.

Rumbaut, R and Portes, A. (2001), *Ethnicities: Children of Immigrants in America* (Berkeley, CA: University of California Press).

Ryan, L. Sales, R., Tilki, M. and Siara, B. (2008), 'Social Networks, Social Support and Social Capital: The Experiences of Recent Polish Migrants in London', *Sociology* 42: 4, 672–90.

Ryan, L. et al. (2006), 'Depression in Irish Migrants Living in London: Case-Control Study', *British Journal of Psychiatry* 188: 6, 560–66.

Saad-Filho, A., and Johnston, D. (eds) (2005), *Neoliberalism: A Critical Reader* (London: Pluto Press).

Saad-Filho, A. and Johnston, D. (2005), 'Introduction', in Saad-Filho and Johnston (eds).

Salt, J. (2005), *International Migration and the United Kingdom: Report of the United Kingdom SOPEMI Correspondent to the OECD* (London: UCL), available at <http://www.geog.ucl.ac.uk/mru/docs/Sop05fin_20060627.pdf>.

Samers, M. (2002), 'Immigration and the Global City Hypothesis: Towards an Alternative Research Agenda', *International Journal of Urban and Regional Research* 22: 2, 389–402.

Sanna I. (2006), *What Does it Mean to be an EU Citizen? How News Media Construct Civic and Cultural Concepts of Europe*, Westminster Papers in Communication and Culture (University of Westminster: London), 3: 3, 71–90.

Sassen, S. (1991), *The Global City: New York, London, Tokyo* (Princeton, NJ: Princeton University Press).

Schwelling, B. (ed.) (2004), *Politikwissenschaft als Kulturwissenschaft* (Wiesbaden: Nomos).

Sharpley, R. (2004), 'Islands in the Sun: Cyprus', in M. Sheller and J. Urry (eds), *Tourism Mobilities: Places to Play, Places in Play* (London: Routledge).

Sheller, M. and Urry, J. (eds) (2004), *Tourism Mobilities: Places to Play, Places in Play* (London: Routledge).

Shields, M.K. and Behrman, R.E. (2004), 'Children of Immigrant Families: Analysis and Recommendations', *The Future of Children*, 14: 2, 4–16.

Shutova, O. (1999), 'Post-Soviet Belarus: Childhood, Family and Identity', *Journal of Psychohistory* 27, 8–17.

Slough Borough Council (2006), 'Local Government Seminar Calls for Adequate Funding for Councils Facing Migration', press release, 28 July, <www.slough.gov.uk/news/articles/archive/11434.asp>, accessed 1 July 2008.

Smith, M.P. and Guarnizo, L. (eds) (1998), *Transnationalism from Below* (New Brunswick, NJ: Transaction Publishers).

Smith, M.P. and Favell, A. (2006), *The Human Face of Global Mobility* (New Brunswick, NJ: Transaction Publishers).

Smith, M.P. and Eade, J. (eds) (2008), *Transnational Ties: Cities, Migrations, and Identities* (New Brunwick, NJ: Transaction Publishers).

Somerville, W. (2007), *Immigration under New Labour* (Bristol: Policy Press).

Spencer, S., Ruhs, M., Anderson, B. and Rogaly, B. (2007), *Migrants' Lives Beyond the Workplace: The Experiences of Central and East Europeans in the UK* (York: Joseph Rowntree Foundation), <www.jrf.org.uk/bookshop/eBooks/2045-migrants-experiences-UK.pdf>, accessed 1 July 2008.

Sriskandarajah, D. (2004), *EU Enlargement and Labour Migration: An IPPR FactFile* (London: Institute for Public Policy Research), <www.ippr.org/members/download.asp?f=%2Fecomm%2Ffiles%2FipprFFEUenlarge1%2Epdf>, accessed 1 July 2008.

Sriskandarajah, D. (2006), 'Measuring the Impact of Intra-EU Labour Mobility: Migration Statistics in Public Discourse in the UK – The Case of EU Enlargement in 2004', paper presented to 28th CEIES seminar on *Migration Statistics: Social and Economic Impacts with Respect to the Labour Market*, Riga, 9–10 June: 74–82, <epp.eurostat.ec.europa.eu/cache/ITY_OFFPUB/KS-PB-05-001/EN/KS-PB-05-001-EN.PDF>, accessed 1 July 2008.

Sriskandarajah, D. and Drew, C. (2006), 'Brits Abroad: Mapping The Scale and Nature of British Emigration', IPPR, <http://ippr.typepad.com/brits_abroad/files/brits_abroad_final_exec_summary_pdf.pdf >, accessed 7 February 2008

Sriskandarajah, D. and Drew, C. (2006), *Brits Abroad: Mapping the Scale and Nature of British Emigration* (London: Institute for Public Policy Research).

Standart, home page <http://www.standartnews.com>.

State Gazette (1982), No. 42, 28.55.1982, 545–51.

Stevens, P.A.J. (2007), 'Researching Race/Ethnicity and Educational Inequality in English Secondary Schools: A Critical Review of the Research Literature between 1980 and 2005', *Review of Educational Research* 77: 2, 147.

Suárez-Orozco, C. and Suárez-Orozco, M.M. (2001), *Children of Immigration* (Cambridge, MA: Harvard University Press).

Swinford, S. (2006), 'How Many Others Can We Squeeze In?', *Sunday Times*, 27 August, 12.

Sword, K. (1996), *Identity in Flux; The Polish Community in Britain*, SSEES, University of London.

Tahir, T. (2004), 'We've Had Enough: Thousands of EU Migrants who Arrived on 1 May Leave after Failing to Find London Homes and Jobs', *Evening Standard*, 3 June, 17.

Tamas, K. and Münz, R. (2006), *Labour Migrants Unbound? EU Enlargement, Transitional Measures and Labour Market Effects* (Stockholm: Institute for Futures Studies).

Thornton, W.H. (2004), 'Civil Antiglobalism and the Question of Class' in Chun (ed.).

Tomova, N. (2007), 'Brits in Mindya (Singing in the Choir and Being Treated to Chocolates by Annie Thomas)'. Posted in Bulgarian 28 July 2007, from *Daily Telegraph*, http://e-vestnik.bg/1820, accessed 25 June 2008.

Travis, A. (2006), 'Home Secretary Wants to set "Optimum" Level of Immigration', *The Guardian*, 7 August, 8.

Tsenova, K. (2006), 'Whole Villages are Now Populated by British', *Dnevnik Newspaper* (reprinted), posted 12 September 2006, http://money.ibox.bg/interview/id_1487142307, accessed 11 June 2008.

Turner, T. (2004), 'Shifting the Frame from Nation-State to Global Market: Class and Social Consciousness in the Advanced Capitalist Countries' in Chun (ed.).

United Nations World Population Prospects (2005), data for 2005, <http://en.wikipedia.org/wiki/List_of_countries_by_population_density>, accessed 25 June 2005.

Valsiner, J. and Veer, R. van der (1991), *Understanding Vygotsky: A Quest for Synthesis* (Oxford: Basil Blackwell).

Vasilyuk, F. (1991), *The Psychology of Experiencing* (London and New York: Harvester Wheatsheaf).

Velinova, S. (2005), 'Bulgarian Land for Foreigners but not before 2010', *Capital Newspaper* 7, 19 February.

Verdery, K. (2003), *The Vanishing Hectare: Property and Value in Postsocialist Transylvania* (Ithaca, NY and London: Cornell University Press).

Vertovec, S. (2002), 'Transnational Networks and Skilled Labour Migration', available at <http://www.transcomm.ox.ac.uk/working%20papers/WPTC-02-02%20Vertovec.pdf>.

Vertovec, S. (2007), 'New Complexities of Cohesion in Britain: Super-Diversity, Transnationalism and Civil Integration', Commission on Integration and Cohesion.

Vertovec, S. and Cohen, R. (1999), *Migrations, Diasporas and Transnationalism* (Aldershot: Edward Elgar).

Vygotsky, L.S. (1934), *Osnovy pedologii* (Moscow: Izdatelstvo Vtorogo Med. Instituta).

Vygotsky, L.S. (1982), *Sobranie sochinenii [The Collected Works]* (Moscow: Izd-vo Pedagogica), Vol. 2.

Vygotsky, L.S. (2005), *Problema kulturnova razvytia cheloveka, in Problema razvytiy cheloveka* (Moscow: Izd-vo Smysl, Eskimo).

Waldren, J. (1997), 'We are not Tourists – We Live Here' in S. Abram et al. (eds), *Tourists and Tourism: Identifying with People and Places* (Oxford: Berg).

Walling, A. (2007), *Labour Market Summary for the UK Household Population by Country of Birth* (London: Office for National Statistics), <www.statistics.gov.uk/articles/nojournal/Birthcountry.pdf>, accessed 1 July 2008.

Watt, N. and Travis, A. (2006), 'Romania and Bulgaria to Enter – with a Warning', *The Guardian*, 27 September, 14.

Weiss G. and Wodak, R. (ed.) (2007), *Critical Discourse Analysis: Theory and Interdisciplinarity* (Basingstoke: PalgraveMacmillan).

Wertsch, J.V. (1991), *Voices of the Mind: A Sociocultural Approach to Mediated Action*(Cambridge, MA: Harvard University Press).

Wimmer, A. (2003), 'Methodological Nationalism, the Social Sciences and the Study of Migration', *International Migration Review* 37: 3, 576–610.

Wimmer, R. and Joseph, D. (2005), *Mass Media Research: An Introduction*, 8th edn (Belmont, CA: Wadsworth).

Wimmer, A. and Glick Schiller, N. (2002), 'Methodological Nationalism and Beyond', *Global Networks* 2: 4, 301–34.

Wintour, P. (2006), 'Inaccurate Migrant Numbers May Lead to Rise in Council Tax', *The Guardian*, 8 August, 9.

Wrench, J. and J. Solomos (eds) (1993), *Racism and Migration in Western Europe* (Oxford and Providence, RI: Berg).

World Association of Newspapers (WAN 2007), http://www.warc.com/LandingPages/Data/NewspaperTrends/PDF/Bulgaria.pdf.

The World Factbook. 'People. Bulgaria. Population' (2008), last updated 19 June 2008, <https://www.cia.gov/library/publications/the-world-factbook/geos/bu.html#People>, accessed 26 June 2008.

World Population Prospects (2005), Population Division of the Department of Economic and Social Affairs of the United Nations Secretariat, 'World Population Prospects: The 2006 Revision and World Urbanization Prospects: The 2005 Revision', <http://esa.un.org/unpp>, 25 June 2008, accessed 26 June 2006.

Yahoo Groups directory (2008), 'Alternative Brits in Bulgaria', <http://uk.groups.yahoo.com/group/alternative_britsinbulgaria/?v=1&t=directory&ch=web&pub=groups&sec=dir&slk=9>, accessed 21 June 2008.

Index